Memories:

The Life
and
Two-Pronged Ministry
Of
Les Niemi

*To Elizabeth
With All Good
Wishes and
Blessings,
Les*

Leslie E. Niemi

Scott Falls in Au Train, MI, M-28

Cover photo of Wagner Falls, Munising MI, by Norma J. Bogetto
Prints and other images can be purchased through the website at
www. normabogetto.com

Most of the scriptural quotes contained in this narrative are the translations of the author from a Finnish language source.

First published by Dog Ear Publishing
4010 W. 86th Street, Ste H
Indianapolis, IN 46268
www.dogearpublishing.net

ISBN: 978-1-4575-0390-0

This book is printed on acid-free paper.

Printed in the United States of America

CONTENTS

PREFACE

The initial idea of writing memoirs came to me back in 1986 when I obtained my first personal computer, a now-ancient Korean *Leading Edge*. Word processing seemed so easy as I went on to set in writing an account which by 2008 surpassed a thousand pages and was continually in process. Since, to the later generations, reading seemed like a fading art, I ventured an abbreviated version of memoirs in easy large print with a couple hundred pages.

So I will describe what it was like to be born and grow up during The Great Depression and the Second World War in the harsh climate of an otherwise beautiful Upper Peninsula of Michigan. This was not Main Street USA, nor did we want it to be. It was the perfect place to be born, grow up, and to serve the common good.

Recalling stories from life was a pleasurable experience. Oldsters find great comfort in it, especially if they had done the right things. Youth today have more difficulty in today's pop culture due to narcissism, mass media, our inherited human condition and propensity to evil.

Time-wise, the fourteen chapters can be grouped into five periods of my life:

Chapters 1-4, Childhood, the Great Depression and the Big War
Chapters 5-7, Education and Calling
Chapters 8-10, Ministry to Christian Congregations
Chapter 11, Ministry to Accumulated Resources
Chapters 12-14, Retirement Years

May these stories enrich your appreciation for how life was lived in the hard times leading up to mid-twentieth century, and how God can use even one so untimely born to carry out the his ageless mission: "Thy Kingdom come." "To be sure, the kingdom of God comes of itself, without our prayer, but we pray in this petition that it may come also to us."[1] I have entitled this short story "The Two-Pronged Ministry of Les Niemi."

My life story is a simple statement of my faith and apologetics, a defense of a Christian worldview. It can be compared to eating fish. If you get a fishbone lodged in the throat, simply remove it to the edge of your plate and keep eating.

CHAPTER ONE

The Big Inning, 1930-1931

My life began in 1931 in the Munising hospital two blocks south of the southern-most tip of Lake Superior. Was I merely the result of the survival of the fittest as in godless Charles Darwin's theory? Or, was I *"knitted together in my mother's womb . . . and fearfully and wonderfully made"*2 by a loving God?

I was born <u>in</u> wedlock, but not very far into wedlock. I wish I could report that I began under normal circumstances into a God-fearing happy home. But that would be a lie. I was born "an instrument baby" in the dead of winter only two months after my parents were married. I was an accident, except, except not for God (where it matters the most). I was not illegitimate, but my parents were. My mother, at age ninety, hinted to me that I may have been conceived in the back seat of a car, behind a Finnish lumber camp. When she said this I merely smiled understandingly. My parents "had to get married," because of me, and per-haps under duress, with a less than an adequate courtship. My dad wanted an abortion. This marriage ended nineteen years later in divorce, as is often typical for such circumstances.

My conception and birth brought true meaning to David's great confessional prayer *"I was brought forth in iniquity, and in sin did my mother conceive me."*3. I can't remember how old I was before I realized these circumstances. But I believed I was a product of God's wild and wonderful imagination and design. Unlike most of my peers I was born in a hospital, and good thing, as special tools were needed to help me along. Dr. T. W. Scholtes charged twenty-five dollars for this piece of work, and I have the original billing statement as proof. My first automobile ride was the eighteen curvy miles on a gravel road from Munising to Cold Springs south of Chatham. It was **February 25, 1931** and it was a Tuesday. I came to the Niemi Farm as we had no home of our own. My mother felt very ill at ease under these circumstances. Gosh, this is so long ago that our national anthem, *The Stars Spangled Banner*, was adopted the following week, and frozen foods hit the market the previous year.

My grandfather was **Emanuel Niemi**, and people called him "Manu." He had emigrated from Juupajoki, Finland, in 1903. On Midsummer's Eve, June 23, 1906, Manu and Alma Sjö-gren (Järviö) were married in Ironwood, Michigan, by Lutheran pastor Peter Hirvi. She was from Halli, Finland, but the roots were in Längelmäki, not far from Juupajoki. Alma immi-grated in August of 1905 to her uncle's lumber camp near Hurley, Wisconsin. They pro-ceeded to have a daughter and three sons, my dad, Edward, born in 1907, Helmi in 1908, Harvey (Arvo) in 1912 and John born in 1913.

My mother, **Ilmi (Pearl) Sipilä**, was born on January 10, 1910 in Loudspur, a Buckeye Co. lumber camp located between Eben Junction and Traunik. Her father, **Henry Sipilä**,

Sipila Farm, Tiistenjoki, Finland.

immigrated in 1900. He had married mom's mother, **Maria Saari**, in Lapua, Finland, and she followed him to Cooks Mills Camps two years later. Mother's siblings were: Oiva, Jalo, Verne, Onni, Eino, Lauri, Elmer, Helen, Impi and Tyyne. (All survived childhood except Oiva and Impi; the latter accidentally fell into a tub of very hot water.) The Sipiläs were from Lapua (Tiistenjoki), Finland, the center of Finland's agriculture in Ostrobothnia.

Alma Sjögren-Järviö was the only grandparent to come to the USA by way of Ellis Island in New York, along with twelve million others. The Finns called Ellis "surun saari," the island of sorrow. There heroic William Williams in 1902 established "the hospital of all nations," where "the germs of the world converged." It was the "house of Babel." In May 1921 quotas were imposed on countries, and in 1954, the year I was ordained, Ellis Island closed. The nation's first aircraft carrier, *USS Ranger*, was launched on my second birthday in Virginia in 1933.

My three other grandparents, Manu, Heikki and Maria, all took the shortcut by coming into the USA through Canada via *The Soo*, where perhaps all of them waited for the next train west in the lobby of Sam Kokko's Hotel on Portage Avenue.

After Buckeye Camp closed the Sipiläs farmed a Guernsey herd on two forties a mile north of the Buckeye Camp, and where Henry also continued as the community blacksmith. The township of fourteen hundred people was ninety percent Finnish in 1940 and Finnish was spoken throughout. I knew all of my immigrant grandparents being their first grandchild of the new generation.

The two farms were exactly two miles apart and were almost exactly east and west of the other. Due to the curse of alcohol the Sipiläs were poor, while the Niemis had one of the finest farms in Rock River Township. But in Finland the two families were rich and poor in reverse. Our new house built in 1932 for $175.00 was on the 160-acre Niemi Farm, on the future M-67, on the site of what was from 1912-20 the **Cold Springs** cordwood camp. When the wood ended, grandpa built a fifteen-building Holstein dairy farm, almost all buildings constructed by my dad. The two families appeared like oil and water, which cannot mix, yet there were pros and cons. Alma-Manu family furnished marvelous stability family-wise and materially. The four grandparents were peasants in Finland, forced to leave home because the eldest child always inherited the farm, which they were not.

My father, **Edward Niemi,** was born on April 9, 1907 at a lumber camp in Dunham, Michigan, between Wakefield and Marinesco, and near the new Chicago & Northwestern Railroad. Within the year they moved to Deimling in the Rumely Valley in Alger County, and within a mile of the lovely Laughing Whitefish Falls.

Dad began public school at the **Cold Springs** School. It had two rooms. He completed his eight grades of formal education at the four-room school in Chatham. Dare I suggest that an eighth grade graduate was vastly more mature than an eighth grader in 2010. Somehow farm kids are naturally smart. Very few completed high school in those years because they were needed on the farm or in the woods. Dad was destined to become the premier carpenter/builder of Alger County, and beyond, for forty years, ca 1930 to 1970.

Mom completed only six grades at the **Loudspur** School. When she quit Mike Seppi came to hire her as a cook's helper at a Finnish lumber camp. When Ilmi was in school, the teacher, Anna Kehoe, thought she should change her weird Finnish name; *Ilmi* sounded like Helmi, and Helmi means Pearl. So Pearl it was. "Toiskieliset" (other-tongued) were so flippant and careless with our priceless Finnish names. This is how Pearl became Pearl. Pearl was destined to be an entrepreneur famous for *Pearl's Pasties* during the last third of the twentieth century.

The college barrier was broken in my family by Aunt **Helmi** Niemi-Kaiser, my dad's younger sister. Helmi not only completed high school in 1927, but enrolled at Ferris State University (Ferris Institute), receiving an associate degree in commercial courses. She went on to teach business at **Paradise** High School for a decade. Previously she served as the secretary for the superintendent at the *Upper Peninsula Experiment Station* ("State Farm") just two miles away. In Newberry she had been the secretary at the Eastern Upper Peninsula Health Department office.

Uncle **John** Niemi worked a lifetime for the Department of the Interior, namely for the *Hiawatha National Forest,* which was established in 1931. For years he was a one-eyed tower man at the Forest Lake Tower. He lost his left eye as a teenager bringing the cows home as he threw a stone that struck a moonshine bottle, the flying glass flying back destroying his eye. They raced to Marquette but it was too late. He also lost a mail carrier job because of tuberculosis. He married **Beatrice** Chartier of Munising in 1951. He was a philanthropist in later life.

Uncle **Harvey** (Arvo) Niemi was the farmer, and heir to the Farm Niemi, until it was sold with the onset of severe arthritis. Harvey married **Joyce** Hase, while Helmi married **Earl** Kaiser (their second marriages). I kept Harvey company at the farm, tagging along like his shadow.

Mom's brothers basically were woodsworkers. **Elmer** Sipilä was a prisoner-of-war in 1944-45 in Limberg, north of Berlin, after driving his thirty-ton M-4 Sherman tank into 88 m.m. anti-tank fire near Epernay in France. Patton's tanks had a top speed of 30 m.p.h.

Elmer's Note of Capture in France

Lauri was wounded in the Apennines (mountains) of Italy, which changed his job from a machine gunner to a medic. **Jalo** came home from the military and committed suicide a year later. None of the Niemis served in the World War 2 military. **Helen** married **Carl** Anderson, **Werner** married **Lydia** Wiitanen, and **Tyyne** married **Vern** Erickson, all of Eben.

My grandfather, Manu, learned in 1911 in Deimling that Cleveland Cliff Iron Company was about to establish a new cordwood camp a mile and a half south of Chatham on the old Whitefish Trail. He was the first to move to the new location in 1912, followed by a couple dozen families two-thirds of whom were Finnish and one-third Slovenian. Additionally, a number of bachelors of both ethnicities lived in boarding houses. This camp functioned from 1912 to 1920, complete with a six grade school, Matt and Alexandra Pantti's general store, and a CCI office. Horse barns and a blacksmith shop were needed. The location was adjacent to a remarkable spring which bubbled up from the limestone below, and which supplied water for the entire operation. Hardwoods and cedar were harvested. Lutheran services were intermittently held in the Niemi living room by Pastor J. H. Heimonen of Marquette, who arrived by train to Chatham.

* * *

The village of **Chatham**, named after Chatham Lumber Company of Chatham Ontario, began in 1896, when the Munising Railway Company (later Lake Superior and Ishpeming) arrived. Chatham became a shipping point of timber and quarried sandstone for building purposes. The quarries were located in Chatham and Eben Junction.

Eben Junction is the meeting point of the aforementioned railroad with the Soo Line which ran up from Rapid River in 1902. Eben was named after **Ebenezer** Young, a railway official. Finns arrived in Chatham and Eben around 1902-03, which accounted for the starting of several Lutheran congregations. Eben is a Jewish name which means *my stone of help*,4 (which took on new meaning to me in 1941 when I was age ten.)

True to its name, the Eben Quarry was an early industry, along with timber. It was begun in 1902 and ceased in the early 1920s. Its 'stone of help' built Eben high school in 1915, the Munising Paper Mill, and was crushed for local roads. It later became a popular swimming hole and skating pond. Eli Lampi built a sawmill next to it, and I nearly drowned in it at age ten. Hobos would camp next to it during the Great Depression. I can remember as a child going with grandpa Manu, and a crew, to harvest ice in the winter from it and storing it in the icehouse covered with sawdust. Indeed, the stone of help, Ebenezer . . . **Eben** for short.

Small schools sprang up in Chatham, Cold Springs, Loudspur, Slapneck, Rumely, Dorsey, Limestone, Traunik and Forest Lake. Eventually the entire area, including Mathias and Onota Townships, consolidated in one school system in Eben, later named "Superior Central."

Chatham incorporated in 1964, and in 2000 the village population was two hundred twenty-six. On April 25, 1925, nearly ninety percent of the village burned to the ground. But the Pacific Hotel was still standing. Of the original landowners numbering three hundred thirty-five all were Finnish except thirty-five. The neighbors, when I was born, had surnames like Laitinen, Luoma, Frigard, Seppi, Kauppila, Heino, Hill, Tunteri, Woimanen, Männistö, Kallinen, Hämäläinen, Ranta, Takkinen, Lahti, Koskela, Mäki, and Hänninen. Only four of these went to church. The Finnish language was heard every day.

Baby Les at just under One

In 1899 it was Chatham's good fortune that Michigan State College built a large experimental farm on the north and east sides of the village, called "The State Farm." It was at their Camp Shaw at which I later responded to the call into the Lutheran ministry on August 27, 1949 at a church youth event, which defined the course of my life forever.

Isn't it interesting that the first "land-grant college" in America wanted to put its Upper Peninsula experimental station smack in the middle of the U.P.? If you do the "string test," running a string from the equivalent latitude of the eastern tip of Drummond Island to that of Little Girl's Point near Ironwood, and then the longitude string from Copper Harbor to the outlet of the Menominee River, the string will cross dab over my house in Cold Springs of Alger County. Doesn't that tell you something?

Why, it's almost biblical. *"The star . . . came were over the place where the child was . . . they were overwhelmed with great joy."⁵* Just kidding! We can't get too "messianic" but a bit interesting nonetheless. So Chatham is the geographic center of a beautiful peninsula, a peninsula which has a total of 1,100 miles of shoreline, and with one hundred forty waterfalls. *Si quaeris peninsulam amoerium* is written on our state of Michigan flag, which means *if you seek a beautiful peninsula, look about you.* We have trees, the deepest mine shafts in the world, the third oldest community in the USA (*The Soo*), uncrowded with only 300,000 people. and Chatham is the bull's-eye!

In 1907 Theodore Roosevelt said:

"In the first place, we should insist that if the immigrant who comes here in good faith becomes an American and assimilates himself to us, he shall be treated on an exact equality with everyone else, for it is an outrage to discriminate against any such man because of creed, or birthplace, or origin. But this is predicated upon the person's becoming in every facet an American, and nothing but an American . . . We have room for but one flag, the American flag . . . and we have room for but one loyalty and that is a loyalty to the American people."

The 1936 "Push-snow"

CHAPTER TWO

The Cold Spring's Kid, To Age 5, 1931-35

So I was born as a two week "preemie" in Munising, where I would one day serve as a Lutheran pastor for eighteen years. I was the only Niemi grandchild for the next twelve years because the one who followed me was aborted.9 But I was the prince for four grandparents as I was the first grandchild. Dad was twenty-four, mom was twenty-one years of age at the depths of the Great Depression in the world at my birth.

I have sometimes joked about being able to remember my birth. Freud and Jung would have relished my reoccurring childhood nightmare in which I identified with moving toward a closing space with anxiety as to whether I would in fact be able to successfully do it. This same dream came repeatedly until my early teens. It was always troubling and stressful.

I was **baptized** on April 26 (1931) when I was two months of age following a Finnish language church service in the afternoon, at the Ed Luoma Farm in downtown Eben Junction. The Rev. Dr. Antti Könönen of Gwinn officiated in Finnish; my baptismal certificate is in Finnish. My mother was present, but not my father. Herman and Hilma Seppi were present as my primary godparents. John Niemi and Elsie Ranta were sponsors by proxy.

The more important internal content was that my baptism was likely prompted by my grandmother, Maria Saari-Sipilä, steeped in "awakened-movement" piety from Lapua, Finland. Let's say that she went to bat for me. The Word of God says:

"Know that all of us who were baptized into Christ Jesus were baptized into His death . . . we were buried with Him so that, as Christ was raised from the dead with the same glory as the Father's, we too will live a new life. If we were united with Him in this likeness of His death, than we will be united with Him also in the likeness of His resurrection."6 And,

"You were buried with Him in baptism and raised with Him through faith produced by God, who raised Him from the dead." (St. Paul)

Baptism is an unreasonable thing, but we are bold to believe I was adopted into God's family. I was born spiritually, hence it was an important event in my life. When dad saw me at home later he did not see that I was the new kid on the block. Perhaps he would find out later, maybe when eighteen years later he asked: *Why do you want to become a pastor?* The world has ears but it does not hear.

Martin Luther said in 1522 in a sermon: *"Christ has a holy and pure birth. Our birth is sinful and accursed, and we can only be helped through the holy birth of Christ. It was Christ's will and pleasure to be born as a man so that in him we might be born again. In this way Christ takes our birth away from us and immerses it in his own birth, giving us his birth that we may be made new and clean, as if it were our own birth. The one who does not believe that, or doubts, is no Christian. Make this birth your own, exchanging with him, so that you might be rid of your birth, and might take on his, which happens when you believe."*[7]

I was born and baptized not only into a hostile economic climate, but also a hostile spiritual one. To symbolize this I quote from *El Socialista*, an atheistic newspaper in Spain, four months following my baptism in 1931: *We must destroy the Church and eliminate from all consciences its infamous influence.* Thus the battlelines were unmistakably drawn.

* * *

Work was scarce in the **Depression** for my dad, and he went to work for the Chatham Telephone Company in 1931, which included doing the main line to Chatham from Rock River. It also allowed us to live in the company house in downtown Chatham. The only other project he had in 1931 was an addition to the Abel Hänninen barn with concrete floors, at the end of Frenchtown Road. On my birth certificate dad's occupation was recorded as "woodsman." Also, I got more nervous when my mother's full name was recorded as a "Femi Seppälä." I never met her.

It was while living in Chatham that my mother, while watching for my safety, got her left breast caught in the ringer of an electric washing machine in the basement. It seriously discolored. Even Julius Peterson who lived next door was amazed how black and blue the breast became, as the story goes.

* * *

Within the year in addition to building three **cedar block barns** for the Isaac Pitkämäkis, Victor Mickelsons and Oscar Nelsons, and remodeling the Unity Co-op Store in Eben, dad built a new small home across the road from the Niemi Farm. We moved to it as soon as we were able in 1933.

The house was located behind a previous row of tarpaper houses and I can remember the square and rectangle outlines of these houses on the roadside as the soil was pushed up against the walls. Our little house had only a kitchen and living room on the first floor, two bedrooms upstairs, and a basement. Entering from the west into a small entry and into the kitchen, the porcelain stove[8] was to the left, a running water sink and cabinets on the right, next the kitchen table and chairs adjacent to a window, and finally a real refrigerator. The living room had a Zenith floor radio on the right, a maroon sofa and chair set, a box stove with isinglass windows on the left which heated the entire house, and the stairs to the second floor. The basement had the water pump and covered dug well, shelves for canned food, and fruit/vegetables, and storage.

There was an outhouse straight to the west, and a garage with a shop. Soon we had a new sauna-woodshed building with a new outhouse attached. Within five years a bedroom wing was added to the living room. It was a modest place with space outside for apple trees and a vegetable garden. The apples were suited only for pies. A fence with gates surrounded it. There was a slight slope from east to west and drainage was good. It was set in a field which ran the length of the forty but over half of the forty on the west was a thick cedar swamp so dense it was hard to penetrate.

*　*　*

This was the physical environment of my childhood. Hay, oats and even sunflowers took turns dominating the adjacent field. The north edge of the field offered a steep hill to the swamp where I did my childhood downhill skiing. All the neighbors were immigrant Finns. One neighbor, **Arvo Heino**, became a millionaire, and I served as his trustee later for his family Trust. He had a college degree. Dad, age 20, had built his original house back in 1927. It was not imperative to know English in our community to survive. Many immigrants never learned English.

A little child had absolutely nothing to fear in this environment. After the trees were felled, the land was cleared with hard work. The topography might be termed gently undulating with a mix of deciduous and evergreen trees. The soil was light brown and darker near the low areas. **Black Creek** flowed through two forties of grandfather's land, where I caught all the brook trout I needed all through my childhood. Finnish bachelor lumberjacks helped Manu clear the land during the summers, some of whom lived at the farm during summers when lumber camps shut down. The area received around 36 inches of precipitation a year, which included an average **snowfall** of one hundred forty-six inches. But a record three hundred fifteen inches fell in 1995-96. We were in the *snowbelt* about ten miles inland from Lake Superior. The climate in summer was warmer in Cold Springs, than at the shore if the big lake. The farm was a daily experience in my childhood.

Grandpa from the outset operated a **Holstein dairy farm** of fifty head, growing hay and oats on four forties, half of which was forested. There were fields on all the forties. The farm sold milk to the Marquette dairies. Good water was never a problem. But the economy was hard in the Great Depression of the 1930s. It was no less difficult during the war years of the 1940s. Serious economic depression and war marked my childhood and adolescence.

1931 Ford Coupe.

The Great Depression gradually eased, and our small family enjoyed conveniences that were above the average. At first we owned a car and soon dad went to work with his pickup. By 1936 he invented the snow scoop with which our driveway was cleared and which task I inherited as soon as I was able. I grew up with a calico cat named **Smokey** who lived into my high school era. But we were not serious dog owners, though we had one or two. One was named **Blackie**.

*   *   *

I grew up, however, in a spiritual environment which did not include faith. I never went to Sunday school, or church worship, as a child. My evening prayer was limited to: *Now I lay me down to sleep, I pray the Lord my soul to keep . . .* Nor was religion present with either set of grandparents. Godless socialism dominated the Niemis while alcohol cursed the Sipiläs. **Maria** Sipilä tried quietly to hold down the fort spiritually all by herself with her pietism from Finland. Albeit all were baptized and were confirmed at age fifteen, as a cultural thing.

Why is this important? Pop **culture** seduces us to believe that life consists only of externals, cerebral enlightenment, and materialism. The truth of the matter is that true intellect and wisdom sees the internal, the invisible, not merely the appearance of things, but the thing itself. It is using the whole brain, not merely the left brain. It is soul and spirit that makes life meaningfully worth living. Spiritual as well as physical makes the man. My life until age sixteen was incomplete. I was a ship without a rudder and trying to function with no compass. I needed to return to the true meaning of my holy baptism, and to a right brain experience.

*   *   *

Otherwise my early years to age five were normal. Infantile amnesia prevents many memories from that period. I can remember a spring evening, before five, with mom and dad, raking the lawn and the big moon rising over the hill across the road. Every kid remembers discovering fireflies for the first time. As far as I knew both mom and dad were caring and loving parents, feeding their young eaglet still lacking his white feathers. Pearl was a stay-at-home housewife, while Ed built a house in 1933, for Hilda Trelford who was dad's teacher (as well as later my teacher in grades two and three). In the Depression dad received $125 wages for this entire house.

In the next three years he built houses for Eli and Sophie Lampi, Julius Peterson, and Jack Salminen; three cedar block barns for Otto Maienknecht, Charles Johnson and his dad (horse barn). He worked on two Civilian Conservation Corps camps at Au Train and Evelyn. He built a trench silo, remodeled for Carl Christofferson and worked on the Wetmore Hill and Federal Forest Highway 13 road jobs. The Great Depression was mismanaged by Washington. Carpentry was a seasonal activity and dad worried about the winter lull, compelling him to work overtime in summers.

*   *   *

Outside my home, I was fawned over by the Niemi grandparents, aunt Helmi, and tagged behind Harvey on the farm. **The farm** was only several hundred yards away. They were all exceptionally good to me. I learned Finnish. I told grandpa once that: *Puuseppää aina tarvitaan* (A carpenter is always in demand.) And, *Minä söin leipää ja maitoa ja makkaraa*, to the question from Manu as to what I ate. (I ate bread and milk and baloney.) Alma told Helmi: *Mene leikkimään Leslien kanssa.* (Go play with Leslie.) Mom would say to me about crossing the road to the farm: *Ole varovainen.* (Be careful.) I answered: *Minä olen aina varovainen.* So it was. I recall the home birth of Marvin Anderson, my cousin, at the end of Sipilä Road in Loudspur. Mom and I were assisting. I was four.

*   *   *

We visited friends: Sipilä Farm, Vern and Lydia Sipilä, Heinos for sauna, Lauri and Saimi Ollila, Bill and Jennie Haapala, Urho and Hilma Ranta, Bill and Lizzie Laitinen, Matt and Jennie Hendrickson, Joels, Palonens, Al Pasanen's Tavern, some of dad's clients, etc. Only Joels of these were church people.

Dad was a good provider, but it leaned to dialectic materialism. The right side of my brain was starving. Martin Luther preached in 1535; *"Christ thinks much more highly of what comes to pass within the soul than what happens to the body . . . the soul is so much more precious than the body . . ."* My soul was on hold.

Turku Cathredal, Finland

11

CHAPTER THREE

School and Play, Ages 6-11, 1936-42

I can't remember my first day of school. It happened in September, 1936, and the school was a four-room elementary school in Chatham. It was not enough of an event to be worth remembering for seventy-five years. Only a portion of my Class of 1949 was present as there were elementary schools also in Eben, Rumely, Traunik, and Deerton who merged during 1941-1945.

A cool yellow and black pug-nosed bus picked me up in front of my house. I loved that bus and loved getting on it each day. A generation earlier my aunt Helmi had to walk the four miles to and from Eben high school. The Chatham school yard was surrounded by an iron pipe fence. I, like others, learned our lesson of keeping our tongues in our mouths in winter. On the sidewalk was a pump-house, from which the neighborhood came to fetch water. There was a nice playground behind the school which included swings, teeter-totters, a chin-up pole and a basketball court. We played softball on the side street just south of the school, and next to the John Gatiss home; I don't ever recall a broken window.

My teacher in kindergarten and first grade, which were in the same room, was **Louise Flack**. It was here that I met my first wife, **Betty Sjostrand**, a cute yellow-blonde. Maybe we became friends at the sandbox. We took naps on our own rag rugs each day.

The whitewashed basement held the hot lunch program, and the huge furnace, from which large asbestos-covered white pipes distributed the heat throughout the school. As my mother disfavored vaccination shots, I can remember hiding behind the furnace in the first grade. I never had childhood shots. The dentist also came to our school, but I had Dr. Leonard Ruggles in Munising, being a privileged kid. Many could not afford such a dentist. I saw myself as just a normal, average kid.

*   *   *

I started school following one of the hottest Upper Peninsula July heat waves on record to date in the nation. This was connected to the Great Dust Bowl disaster, and it broke the state record of 112 degrees in Mio in Lower Michigan. Air conditioning wasn't a decade old yet, having appeared in 1928 in a San Antonio office building. I don't remember it at age five. This heat was preceded by a record wind and cold wave of January and February, 1936. I remember when dad was pouring cement on the new bridge at the West Whitefish River on U.S-41 south of Trenary, how his work clothes were frozen solid and how he had to stand next to our box stove to thaw so that he could remove them.

This was also the winter that dad remodeled the Chatham post office for Roy Heldmann, and in that connection, as the story goes, built two "**snow-scoops**," one for Heldmann and one for us.

Even with school I continued to spend a lot of time at the **Niemi Farm** with grandparents Manu and Alma, and Harvey and Helmi. John was employed by the postal department and later the federal Hiawatha Forest, living on the farm.

The first Niemi house burned to the ground in 1916, and the second house was built by Gust Lintula and Jack Koivisto in 1920, when my dad was age 12. There were sixteen farm buildings, all built by my dad, except the house, barn, and machine warehouse. Unique were the chicken coop and the root cellar.

The Manu and Alma Niemi Cold Springs Farm.

The house, with a basement and second floor, is worthy of description. The east entry led into an entry area where boots and barn clothes were shed before stepping into the large kitchen, which was the main room. The hand pump/sink was on the left but soon replaced with running water. A pantry was off to the right; the north wall had a standard cabinet and fair size kitchen table for meals and coffee. The wood box and black kitchen stove on the west wall. Just beyond the sink was entry to Alma and Manu's small bedroom. A dining room with the heirloom china-cabinet, rocking chair and radio took up the NW corner of floor one, and the SW area was the living room which was never used except by guests who seldom came, and me and Helmi.

The second floor housed three bedrooms, all with dormers. On the west side overlooking the highway was a sun porch and seldom-used entry with steps. The apple orchard which contained the root cellar buffered the view of the Laitinen Farm to the south. The transparent apple tree was my favorite. There was a plum tree. Under a huge beech tree, downhill, was a hanging swing. The machine warehouse was "left over" from the Cleveland Cliff Iron Co. horse barn. There was a combination woodshed and **sauna**. A cedar block chicken coop. The 1934 horse barn, the 3-car garage with attached two-compartment outhouse (containing a Sears catalog). Behind the garage was the ice house. The huge dairy barn had a connected milk house. Down the hill close to the road was a "winter garage," and across the road was the blacksmith shop. Every building overflowed with great memories of secure, happy, fun times. It was a handsome modern farm for the times.

Cows were milked around six a.m. and 5 p.m. and evening work was unusual, except for exciting haying and threshing times. Those forty-five head of cattle also had to be fed twice

IN ADDITION TO EXTRACTING THE MILK FROM THE COW, WE HAD TO LEARN HOW TO DEFEND OURSELVES FROM THAT PESKY TAIL!

SOMETIMES, IT WAS TIED TO THE COW'S LEG OR CLAMPED BETWEEN THE MILK PAIL AND THE KNEE.

IF WE DIDN'T SECURE IT IN SOME WAY...

SWISH
DRY AND CUTTING
OR
SPLAT
SOFT AND WET
OR
BONG!
HARD AND HEAVY

Milking Cows in 1930s.

a day. Each cow had automatic drinking cups. By pressing down with her nose, the cow could release fresh water and the valve would close by itself. My earliest recollection of producing milk was that it was done by hand. First one had to clean the udder and teats. Some grease was applied to hands as the milker sat on a small stool. Beware of that cow's tail which was sure to come and get you in the face. The cats were usually sitting nearby waiting for a squirt of warm milk.

The small eight by ten milk house was attached to the barn where the almost full milk pail was emptied into a high cooling tank. The cold water ran through a radiator kind of contraption. The raw milk ran down the outside and into a ten gallon can. These cans were stored in a well full of cold water, and shipped in the morning. Initially these five or six heavy cans were rolled with a big-wheeled rig down the driveway to a platform by the road, where the Bancroft (or Northern) Dairy truck from Marquette would pick them up daily.

Soon, maybe around 1938, a big change happened as the farm went to those miraculous **milking machines.** (Perchance Art Mattson of Sundell sold Manu the new Surge machine; Art, later a good friend, also sold Maytag washers house to house; he became a 'millionaire.') There were two milking units which operated from a vacuum pump. These units were moved from cow to cow, and suspended under the cow's udder by a belt over the cow's back. Each unit had four teat cups. When the valve was opened to begin the pulsating action, squeeze hard and release, just like milking by hand. Later, pipeline milking further improved sanitation. Government regulations kept demanding greater expenditures causing the majority of Finnish farmers in Rock River Township to go out of business. No wonder we react to government regulation and interference!

The cream was not separated at the Niemi Farm as it was at the Sipilä Farm, which sold only cream to the Rapid River Creamery, the last operating creamery in the Upper Peninsula. Only Harvey and Manu did the milking, followed by grandma Alma coming to carefully wash all the equipment in the milk house each time. Interestingly, and initially, the water pump pulled the cold water from the original 'Cold Springs' beneath Michigan State Highway-67 directly to the milkhouse. Initially, Manu sold milk to many of the neighbors during the Depression and before shipping milk started to Marquette. Dad said he quit drinking milk during meals in the Depression when all the milk was needed to be sold. I believed him. He drank water.

The threshing fervor which began the end of August might have been a part of the Loudspur Milling Company, which existed to 1960. Membership allowed access and scheduling of the thresher owned by grandpa.

I had certain chores at home which demanded more ability as I got older. One of them was to fetch the unpasteurized milk from the farm every day around 5:30. I was in charge of hauling wood, including kindling. This accounts for my lifelong scars on my hands and feet from the axe. I did grass control with a push lawnmower. I maintained a vegetable garden, including joining the local 4-H Club already in elementary school. In 1945 I raised a pig, the pen being at the wood's edge, west of our house. It was a big chore to bring her the "slop" (food) each day and the water. Fall came and the pig had to die, and we ate it. Each fall we made our own wood, and it was my job to take the wood from the circular saw and throw it in a large pile. Next I hauled it to the basement and/or woodshed to pile it.

On the farm I did various things including weeding the garden, getting the cows, killing flies in the house, woodchuck control in the fields, field work with the Farmall tractor, etc. The farm afforded me a chance to learn how to drive, how to use the .22 gun, and so forth. Once, leaving the farm on a threshing trip, the fogged windows in the pick-up diverted my attention from the road causing me to narrowly missing driving into the concrete abutment at a culvert in the ditch at Luoma's corner.

Once, using a single-shot .22 caliber rifle I missed the woodchuck, but having him cornered from his hole, he ran right for me, at which point I took the gun by the barrel and swung, breaking off the gun handle. This mishap advanced me to the use of a new semi-automatic .22 rifle. I had no bad accidents until I was ten. So much for the adventure of the farm, where, when the work got too long and hard I had a simple answer: go home. I worry that it taught me the art of evasion which was not good.

* * *

Although grandpa had hosted church services during the Cold Springs early days, soon he became enamored by a godless socialism during the Depression. He was a Democrat with F.D. Roosevelt as his hero starting in the early 1930s. He was a part of the Co-op Store breakaway and the first chairman of the Unity Co-op board in Eben in 1914. As a result all of our groceries were purchased at the Unity. Some foods had a red star symbol on them. This cooperative suffered a communist control takeover in the late 1920s and presumably sent funds to Moscow. My childhood store had gone communist.

* * *

While earlier I commented on the winter and heat wave of 1936 when I was age five, the *U.P. Storm of the Century*, when I was seven, deserves mention. A great low pressure system rose up from Illinois to the U.P. starting on Monday, January 25, 1938. The storm lasted only 36 hours, the wind blew across the area at 50 mph, and the roads were completely closed for a week. I was home with mom, but dad was stranded at Rock River where he had been building a store building for Chan Brown. During that time he waded through deep snow to visit the small cabin of Manu Eklund. Manu never planned ahead, and was heating his abode with a long tree which stuck out the door of the stove, and the place was filled with smoke. Three years later Manu was confined to an ice flow for three days and nights while on a fishing venture on Lake Superior with two companions (Lammi and Luoma). But he was a survivor.

After four days, Julius Peterson arrived from the Chatham with a plow via Forest Lake and Au Train. Dad asked him if he could make it home; Julius said, *Yes if you leave right now!* He did, and he made it. I can remember the strong wind blowing so hard it blew the main electrical lines together which came west from the Forest Lake power plant, causing bright flashing in the sky one half mile away. Only the tops of telephone poles could be seen above some drifting. Not many had telephones, much less cell phones. Drifts of almost twenty feet were not uncommon. A huge fire in downtown Marquette burned down four large buildings on Washington St., including the Opera House and the Masonic Temple. In retrospect it was the worst winter storm that I had seen in the U.P.

* * *

World War Two began in 1939 when the U.S.S.R. ruthlessly attacked Finland in the Winter War; I was age eight. It tended to unite the Finns, who had divided themselves as "reds" and "whites." A year earlier Helmi, age thirty-one, made her first trip to visit relatives in Finland on the *Queen Mary*. Subsequently both grandpa Manu and uncle Harvey would accompany her.

Helmi was my favorite aunt. She spent a lot of time with me; some activities were stamp collecting, and skiing. Once she hired me to kill all the flies in the farmhouse at a penny a fly; devious as I was by nature, I learned that I could make more money if I left the door open to allow more flies to enter the house. Later at her eighty-eighth year I would prepare her for death with devotions at a Newberry nursing home, with uncle John as my sidekick. Although Helmi had taught at socialist youth camps, she ended life at a Methodist Church and attended my Finnish worship services in Newberry for twenty-five years, along with grandpa Manu.

As an only child, I believe I was indulged upon almost too much in retrospect. Mother, Helmi, Harvey, grandparents all fawned over me. Although never gushy verbally nor physically, my dad seemed to respect me. I was never spanked. The worst I can recall is when I misbehaved mother once threatened: *"If you don't behave, we're going to send you to Newberry."*

Pearl Sipila-Niemi, ca 1995.

I sometimes wondered if being so adored in childhood resulted in what is known as "love avoidance." In other words, later in life, when individuals and congregations smothered me with praise and affection, too much "prince" rather than "frog," it affected the relationships. In other words when people love you excessively then you push them away. As soon as they get too close, you push them away. I may have done this to various degrees with some who entered my life. It is merely something I have pondered.

My childhood was also enriched by travel on weekends with my parents as we made trips around the Upper Peninsula: Copper Harbor, Ironwood, The Soo, and Green Bay. Considering the times these were luxuries. Once in 1941 we visited Hugo and Ellen Sjostrand in Detroit, and their daughter, **Betty,** with whom at age ten I was experiencing puppy love. Often my dad would take me along on evenings as we went to see clients and check on construction jobs. But dad could not play games. A son and his dad should be able to "play catch." Dad never touched a ball; only a hammer. No one in the Niemi family hunted or fished. Dad loved us by providing and I learned to understand that.

We sometimes attended the Escanaba State Fair as a family. Once dad gave me a five dollar bill as my allowance for the fair. I was so embarrassed to have suckered into blowing it all at once on throwing baseballs at some targets. I learned my lesson. Often we attended movies at the Chatham movie house on weekends. Sometimes as a child we would go at night to watch homes burn down, having been struck by lightning. Lightning rods were sometimes placed on roofs to be able to ground the lightning strike and keep the place from not burning. Once it struck a tree 150 yards from our house. Also we would go to see forest fires burn at night, of which there were many in the 1930s. These are some early childhood memories.

*   *   *

By this time our economic condition improved as a family. Our bank was Trenary State Bank, my dentist was Dr. Leonard Ruggles, my family doctor was Dr. Howe of Marquette, and our favorite store in Marquette was Montgomery Ward. As a child I had braces on my teeth to correct an overbite. Often they would come off while eating. I enjoyed a new red bicycle, my own little shop, a red wagon, two dozen weasel and a half dozen fox traps, balls and bats, erector sets, Lincoln logs, Red Rider BB gun, toys and puzzles, balsa airplane kits, skis, sleds, toboggan, Norway snowshoes, and even a guitar. We had a Zenith radio but yet no telephone. We received the *Mining Journal, Munising News*, and the *Grit*.

Bernie and Elmer Frigard lived a quarter mile north of me. We would visit back and forth. They were my immediate childhood playmates. We set up baseball diamonds in fields and practiced. We "batted rocks." With only a bat-like wooden stick, we would walk down the road, find stones and bat them into the fields and woods. We played "knife baseball," whereby we opened the jackknife blades and flipped the knife on a soft wooden board to see which blade would stick and how. The options were singles, doubles, home runs, etc. And we kept score. The Frigards were poor as Ed Frigard died young. They could not have my kind of toys. They ran barefoot all summer, while I peddled my new bike next to them. Result: they became track and baseball stars in Chatham. After the Albert Johnson family bought the Laitinen farm, we played ball quite a lot in their fields. Earlier we played "cowboys." I had a cowboy outfit around age seven. And I knew how to make an igloo.

My teachers at Chatham Elementary were Louise Flack (Kindergarten and first grade), Hilda Trelford (2 and 3), Melba Mills (5), and Russell Boogren (6). Boogren clearly warranted anger management rehab as he constantly physically and emotionally mistreated his sixth grade students. But we did pay attention and learned in his class. I first touched a basketball in grade five at the school playground. I recall biking to Chatham to play softball. Also all manner of games we played with nearest neighbor kids. The first books that I read were Jack London's *Call of the Wild, Kazan*, and, *Barrie Son of Kazan*. I subscribed to *Fur, Fish and Game*. I owned the *Book of Knowledge*, as a type of encyclopedia. It was apparent that I was drawn to history and geography in the social sciences.

The food from the **Unity Co-op** was often Wheaties, pancakes and eggs for breakfast. We always had milk from the farm. Mom made good hamburgers and potato salad. Campbell's vegetable soup from a can was a favorite. She made good pies. But it was a time of a long Depression and a long war.

Dad was critical of mom once because she had not put any meat in his lunch bucket. One butcher shop put it: *A meal without meat means nothing to eat.* There was often canned fruit from either the basement or the Unity. At a co-op you saved all your receipts and received a cash rebate at the end of the year. Co-op store managers were trained in Superior WI and frequently came and left at the whim of the boards of directors who came to meetings with manure on their boots.

The nearest thing to a picnic in the Niemi family was an all-day event to the Hovey Lake plains to pick blueberries in August, which then were canned, and stored in the root cellar or basement. As a young man dad once made a rowboat which was named *Helmi.* But I never remember it being in the water, until I inherited it later for Lake Au Train. It was very heavy and painted green.

We would also go to the "communist hall," as it was affectionately known, a hall just north of the Unity Store in Eben. Viola Turpeinen, America's number one Finnish secular entertainer (accordion and song), would occasionally appear in Eben for dances. While there it was typical for single lumberjacks to buy me a bottle of pop for a nickel from the cold water cooler. Devoid of their families, they were likely lonely for children they remembered from Finland. Raw socialist boys would often fight behind the hall usually resulting in bloody noses. Socialist lectures were sometimes held at said hall but I never attended those as a young child. Once they raised the Russian flag, resulting in three men going to jail.

As children, and with friends, we played games like: tag, knife baseball, pom-pom-pull-away, hide and seek, anti-I-over, jacks, pick-up-sticks, and cards. I began fishing brook trout, and trapped weasels, muskrats and fox. When I got a bit older I boiled my fox traps on the kitchen stove in a boiler of water and assorted bark mixed in. I always wore canvas gloves when handling them. One day I caught five fox in my six traps. Once I received a check for furs from Sears for $36.00, big money in the early 1940s. I had a stamp collection which I later sold to Gordon Christofferson for five dollars, obviously desperate for cash.

Since age one I have taken **Finnish saunas**, first at the farm, often visiting neighbors, and finally at our own sauna. I went to sauna with mother until junior high school. It was heated once or twice a week, as we had no indoor shower. I grew up with a sauna at home. Heck, it was not surprising then that the 1973 Eden Church in Munising would have a sauna in it, and was featured incidentally in the 2010 book *The Opposite of Cold: The Northwoods Finnish Sauna Tradition*, by Michael Nordskog and Aaron Hautala.

* * *

But arrived my so-called "**mid-childhood plateau.**" This plateau is seen as delightful time of achievement, curiosity, learning, even social graces, of a fifth or sixth grader. Here's what happened to me. For the first time all the area school fourth graders were together in one class. This class was on the first floor of our lovely limestone school in Eben. **Eleanor Stenstrom** of Ironwood was our teacher and she was wonderful. One day, after I had free-handed a map of the world, she brought Superintendent Bill MacNeil in to see my work, resulting in lots of good strokes.

In the spring that year, after the snow melted, we were enjoying our cinder track located south of the school. While I was scissor-stepping at the high jump stands, I let my right arm lag beneath the bar, and landing on the bar, resulted in a broken wrist. Two or three weeks later, Arnie Ikkala and I, thought it would be a great idea during noon hour to fish rock bass at the stone quarry, three hundred yards west of the school. Behold, the bell rang. Arnie inadvertently bumped me. I fell into the deep. I recall thinking I might climb the rock wall up, but after bobbing up and down twice (three is the limit), I happily decided to dog paddle. Mother had never let me near water previously, trying to protect me. I saw Arnie reaching for me, and he pulled me out. I coughed up a lot of water. We ran to the school. I dried in the furnace room. My suspenders had discolored my white shirt, later causing mother to become suspicious. I then confessed what had happened. The next day she came to the school to protest endangerment to her son. Wouldn't you know that just prior to this, Miss Stenstrom had us sing a church hymn in class, with the appropriate words:

"Guard us waking, guard us sleeping, And, when we die,
May we in your mighty keeping all peaceful lie.
When the last dread call shall wake us,
Then, O Lord, do not forsake us,
But to reign in glory take us with you on high."   (LBW 281)

The hymn has been hauntingly special ever since. As a ten year old, I somehow made the connection to grace. Later, I likened the experience to my baptism; to my rising from death to life. It was a lesson about undeserved grace.

I got pretty good grades in Melba Mills' fifth grade class, back in Chatham, the next year, but she was tough. I once dropped my pencil on the floor and out the door I went to sit in the hallway as my punishment. In this grade I discovered basketball at the outdoor court behind the school.

In grade six, also in Chatham, I experienced **Russell Boogren**, the one who literally terrorized his class. Sheer fear caused me, and others, to advance three years in our knowledge, according to tests. The learning-challenged had an awful time in his class. I had no formal religious training during my elementary years. Yet, there was a value system at home; it set the stage for what was to come later, and for which I am grateful. It included hard work, thrift, study hard in school, be courteous, don't lie, don't steal, behave, and don't swear even if the rest of us do. I was simply a good candidate for something better to arrive later. At that time my ears could be unstopped and the scales removed from my eyes. It is how God worked his alien righteousness in my life.

We were ready for junior high school in Eben and our class size would be thirty, ethnically twenty Finns, six Slovenians, one Swede, one French, one Dutch and one other (a mutt). The Upper Peninsula has always been very nationality-conscious. We are prone to be suspicious of outsiders and phony pretension.

Unbeknownst to me in 1942, in far-away Leningrad (St. Petersburg) in the Union of Soviet Socialist Republics (USSR), my third cousin, Waino Sjögren, was shot in the back of the head in Leningrad (St. Petersburg). Sjögren was grandma Alma's uncle's son, who was a **communist** during the Finnish Civil War, escaping to the Soviet Union for his life in 1918. He survived until Joseph Stalin's police found that he had published five books in Superior, Wisconsin, at *Työmies Society*, the first of which was *The Fugitive*. His wife Lempi and son Jimi, escaped to Finland, and lived out their lives in Old Pylkki, north of Korkeakoski. They are buried in Juupajoki. Grandpa Manu's roots were in Old Pylkki. *"Työmies"* had been the leftist-leaning tri-weekly Finnish-language newspaper published in Superior. Its *Finnish-*

American Reporter was donated to Finlandia University later and survives as our most successful ethnic publication in America. Reds and whites finally united and were working together on a monthly periodical.

Members of some Chatham-Eben families who chose to move to **Russia** in the early 1930s were: Arpiainens, Juntunens, Jusunens, Kerttulas, Haapalas, Hämäläinens, Laaksos, Marjaniemis, Jokinens, Mäkis, Ojalas, Niemis, Rukkilas, and Wälimäki. They were enticed by Soviet propaganda. Some families were terribly conflicted politically. Times were hard all around the world during The Great Depression. Most of the above did not survive but were victims of Stalin's purge in the late 1930s. It is the Ingrian Finns, not these Finns, who belong to the **Ingrian Lutheran Church** today in Russia. Some Ingrians had roots in St. Petersburg as early as when the city was first founded. Her great river, *Neva*, is a Finnish word.

So you see how difficult the times were, not only economically, but also politically and spiritually. But, as history will show today, is it any easier now? Same song, second verse. **Freedom and liberty** must be continuously on guard. The evil empires rise and fall and rise again. We need to be vigilant to preserve liberty and our freedoms.

Socialism's boast of equalizing the wealth has never succeeded very long in any country and usually fails when someone else's money has run out. European "soft socialism" is a case in point. America and the Constitution were based on capitalism and a Christian society by Christian leadership. I was converted out of a socialistic background so the old adage, been-there, done-that, can apply. I hope we don't go there. But if we don't study the past history we will made the same mistakes. I am mature and old enough to recall the lessons of hard communism and Nazism. The conflict in my childhood between *Reds* and *Whites* was fierce. Don't invest your future in socialism.

The Brownstone Inn, Au Train, 1946

CHAPTER FOUR

Junior High School, Age 12-14, 1943-45

Junior high school meant mingling with high school students at the same campus, starting in grade seven. It also meant changing classrooms for each course. My home room advisor was Mary Alleman.

The really big news of my junior high years was the surprise birth of **a sister and brother** to our small family on February 13, 1943 at Marquette's St. Luke's Hospital. Medical science was still in such infancy that none of us knew there were twins. The entire event was filled with adventure. First of all, we got hopelessly stuck in a drifted-closed M-94 highway at the "Sundell Pass" on the way to Marquette. Dad's super effort at shoveling was finally solved by the arrival (again) of Julius Peterson with the county plow. Until then we were getting concerned.

We dropped mother at Dr. Howe's office in the Old Bank Building on Front and Washington Streets. Dad and I went to *Doc's Delicatessen* for coffee. Shortly, we were all dispatched directly to the hospital. After the birth of **Betty** (Elizabeth Ann), who weighed in at five and a half pounds, **Bill** (William Allen) was discovered, and born twenty minutes later at four and a half pounds. I can still remember Dad's reaction to the twins. Perchance this was poetic justice to make up for the aborted one in between me and them. Dad was thirty-five and mom was thirty-three at the time, and I was twelve.9

Needless to say, it changed things at home. Dad and I got elevated up to the upstair's bedrooms, while mom and the twins slept in the lower level bedroom. She seemed stressed with all the work. I was given a voice in the picking of the names, Elizabeth Ann (Betty) and William Allen (Bill). Shortly, Pastor **Hugo Hillilä**, who preached at our local Eben Church on alternate Sunday afternoons, came to the house to perform two **baptisms**. Helmi and William (Bill) Mäki of West Loudspur Road were the primary sponsors. Our family never went to church. I was still in grade six in Chatham, but the following fall I changed school buildings and began the seventh grade.

* * *

My junior high school years, in addition to the birth of my brother and sister, were affected by the deprivation caused by **World War Two**. From the Great Depression we moved into all the sacrifices necessary to defeat Hitler, Stalin, Mussolini, and Hirohito. They symbolized the enemy. They represented the philosophies and notions of Charles Darwin, Karl Marx, Vladimir Lenin, Friedrich Nietzsche, and others of that ilk. I salute Elmer, Lauri and Jalo Sipilä, Eugene Belmas, Roy Morrison, Ken Mäki, and others of our families, who put their lives in great danger to preserve liberty at home and abroad.

At home in Chatham, many items were rationed by the government for the war effort. I scoured the countryside to look for iron, rubber, aluminum, and copper, to sell to junk dealers for money and because the factories needed them to produce tanks, planes and ships. With my dimes into savings stamps I collected enough to buy $ 25 war bonds. It taught us thrift. Franklin Roosevelt, my grandpa's hero, rallied America, but on April 13, 1945 my diary simply said: *President Roosevelt died yesterday.* Someone said that my grandpa wept openly. Harry Truman, a good man, succeeded him. Roosevelt had been our first president to travel by airplane in 1943. In 1942 Pan American Airlines was the first to commercially fly around the world.

We received letters from Elmer Sipilä in 1944 from a German prison camp in Limberg, north of Berlin. We had letters from Lauri, wounded in the Apennines in Italy, and whose job description had changed from light machine gunner to medic, which says something about the greatest need. Jalo came home and within a year committed suicide, but not before he lovingly made a pair of cross-country skis for me. High is the price of freedom. Did these sacrifices prompt me to volunteer to serve on the Selective Service Board during the Vietnam War? My dad, 37, although he went to Marquette for a pre-induction exam, was not called to go into military service as the war was almost over.

The war powerfully dominated life in the early forties in many ways. Starting at age ten I kept maps and read newspapers following military advances and retreats. Americans supported the war effort sacrificially, economically and with life and limb. It was a time of sorrow and sadness. After it was over the ghastly stories of atrocities reached home from both holocaust camps and the Pacific theater. Many returning soldiers chose not to talk about it.

*   *   *

I was now into organized sports, e.g., the junior high basketball team and track and field. Our practices were at the Chatham Hippodrome, which had been built in 1916 and remodeled in 1940. Superintendent **Bill MacNeil** was our coach in junior high. It was also our first outing at organized track and field. My fourth grade high jump injury (broken wrist) had healed. I soon found out I was neither a good sprinter, nor durable enough for the distances. But I was a fair jumper.

After my school year I had my first job away from home/farm. A Dutchman named Nagel from Kalamazoo came north to grow tulips. Our job at a dime an hour was to pick tulip bulbs for ten hours a day. There were six or eight of us. It was about this time, give or takes a year, that I began trapping weasels. It looked promising. A weasel pelt brought $2-3.00 from Sears in Chicago. Living through the Depression came with a powerful lesson on thrift, and so it had a positive effect, and which has endured for life.

Nestor Salminen and Don Hakanen were two of my good friends. They invited me to attend a *church summer school* (Vacation Church School) for two weeks in June, 1944. I accepted. We biked to and from school each day. The director was Seminarian Ahti Karjala of the **Suomi Theological Seminary** in Hancock. Included in the body of new information for me, having never attended a Sunday school, was to memorize the New Testament books in their order by the use of a song. I could sing it. There was a public program at the church at the conclusion.

A big surprise confronted me in grade seven as **Betty Joan Sjostrand**, my elementary grade girlfriend, returned from Detroit to live at their home in Slapneck. And she was in class, and now had changed into a marvelous-looking young woman. Furthermore, she captained our school cheerleader teams, definitely an "Alpha" position, to say nothing of being very street smart from Detroit. Her grandparents, Jack and Mary Oja, lived on a Slapneck farm, while her dad was a Trimountain native from the Copper Country. He began employment at the Munising Paper Mill. Betty's great grandfather had died in the Champion Mine in Painesdale. We were best of friends immediately. She had belonged to Detroit's St. John's Lutheran congregation, singing in a church choir.

I was on the track team, competing in the Alger County meet. **Basketball** eventually became "my game." Grade eight was a harbinger of things to come as my team not only won the Alger County junior high tourney, but we marched right into Marquette and beat their best, Howard School, in the tourney finals, 23-19. They had been undefeated and had beaten us during the year. I had ten points. I played center at a hair below six feet in height. I also continued my baseball. I took first in long jump and second in pole vault in the county junior high meet.

An interesting thing happened in 1992 when mother found my one-year **diary** that I had kept for 1945. It described my activities, e.g. fishing, trapping, basketball, track/field, threshing (430 bushels at Niemis), buzzing wood, hunting woodchucks, making hay, tending my garden, skinning weasels, muskrats and fox, (by December 27 I had ten weasels). My life was getting quite interesting. A bad thing happened on January 15, 1945. As my diary reported that our gymnasium (**The Hippodrome**) burned to the ground. I lost my gymnasium on the eve of beginning high school. On June 10, 1945 my diary said that I helped my dad build a pigpen at the edge of the woods. There was nothing about girls.

Confirmation Day.

* * *

An important entry was made for June 2, which said, *"I got confirmed today with twenty-two others . . . I joined Luther League with B. Frigard."* Pastor Hugo Hillilä was our confirmation pastor, who lived in Marquette. We attended classes all day for two weeks prior to confirmation. There was a closing program on the Friday before Sunday which included questioning? There was three inches of new snow on the ground on June 2, our **confirmation day**. Little did they know that I was the one that would become a Lutheran pastor. So I was confirmed at age 14. The altar painting of Jesus ascending into heaven was intriguing to me at the time. The new information fed not only the mind but also the heart. **Sally** and **George Lelvis,** who had recently moved to Chatham, became our Luther League advisors.

On October 19 I saw my very first football game. The school took a bus to bring us to a Negaunee game, "to give us some culture." Bill Jennings (later Dan's father-in-law) carried the ball to a 41-28 win over Marquette.

A month later on November 21 our new basketball coach, **Walfred Mickelson,** had me start as a freshman on the varsity team in Rapid River. My first shot from the top of the key swished through the net. We won by the low score of 24-22. Was my shot a harbinger of better things to come? It was the first game of eight years of organized ball, three of which were good enough for the collegiate all-conference dream teams.

It was while in junior high that we obtained our first **telephone**. We were on a party line, which meant people could listen on the sly to the conversations of others (don't sneeze!). Visiting seemed more meaningful in those days before TV. Radio was big. As a teenager I listened to the *Hit Parade* with its top songs across the country. I was beginning to attend the school dances.

Since I was still involved at the farm, a word needs to be said about this basic human activity. When I was a child (and the scene changes rapidly with progress), beginning at the end of June, **the hay** was first cut with a mower, which cut a eight foot swath, then it was allowed to dry for several days. It was hoped that it did not rain, which would fade out the green colors and the nutrients. There was a primitive ten-foot wide, two-wheeled rake with a man riding and operating it which put the hay in furrows. Three-tine pitch forks then loaded the dry hay on our tractor-pulled, rubber-tired hay rack.

The load was brought to the barn with the red Farmall tractor. Horses had been used until about 1938. The load was positioned in the loft drive-through. Harvey operated the hay scissors, Les pulled the load up with the pick-up and rope, on the steel tracks, while Manu wearing his dust mask distributed the hay to all corners in the loft. Often the word "Whoe!" was heard. It was hard work. (Later, the rake was exchanged for a "side deliverer," a totally different principle. And still later, after I left, the baler went right out into the field and baled the hay, the bales then loaded to the trailer. Hay was put into two barns, but the Niemis never left hay in the field as is done today. The farm was an exciting adventure to me.

* * *

Incidentally, for normal farm work, Harvey and Manu were not slobs. Each had blue denim matching outfits: shirt, trousers and jacket. This was a classy farm. Now, a word about **threshing** oats.

When those green oats (and sometimes barley) turned yellow and gold, harvest time had come in late August. The first step was the binder, complete with its sickle bar, belts and knotter. It cut a swath and dumped a bundle held by binder twine every six feet. Next, by manual labor, a crew went out to shock it, putting 4-5 shocks standing upright in a group to dry. It was done by hand, grain on top, and leaning against each other. These bundles were light.

I was at the farm in the era of the stationary threshing machine. The shocks had to be dry. Thresher-ready, men with two or three hayracks brought in the shocks from the field. They were fed into the feeder of the monster machine one by one. The thresher was thirty feet long, eight feet high and four feet wide. After passing the feeder, next came the beater and chewed up the bundles, then separated the grain, straw and chaff, a long blower pipe blew the straw and chaff into a big yellow pile.

I can remember as a sophomore when Betty appeared at Hakanen's farm. She was wearing those denim cut-offs, which Jane Russell once made famous in a movie in the hay, so I caught her and threw her into the straw pile. The color of her hair matched the straw. Lo, what was this strange attraction? It was normal.

Back to the thresher: the oats came out down a pipe into gunny sacks, and the machine also counted the sacks. It was my job to grease all the grease nipples. The meals were terrific. At threshing and haying times the sauna was heated every day. The machine was driven by a long thirty foot belt from the tractor pulley. It was important that all parts were level. It could also be dangerous. Each farmer paid Harvey for the machine. Later, our farm purchased a combine, where the entire operation happened on wheels in the field. The oats had to be especially dry with ideal conditions.

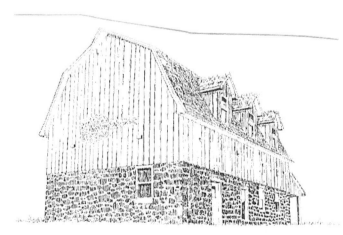

Dad started his career with barns.

Farming demanded a big investment. The Niemi Farm also had a trench silo into which sunflower and corn was put, and fed to the cattle over winter. It fermented and smelled bad. Beware of methane gas. Dad built the silo in 1935.

In 1945 dad built the following: home for Alle Höyhtyä , apartment house in Munising for Eli Lampi, remodeled Hayes Drug, the A & P Store and the offices at the Woodenware Company, built a warehouse for the Unity Co-op, and floors and stalls at the Aalto Farm, both in Eben, and re-roofed a sheep barn at the State Farm.

* * *

26

Having lived my first fourteen years of my life with Ed and Pearl, and the greater family, I need to acknowledge the abundant benefits of material things, of **the external** aspect of life. Present was materialism, the visible, the rationale, the cerebral, the apparent. But yet missing was **the internal**, the invisible, the profound, the gut issues, the sin problem, and the faith issues. But what you've never had you don't miss.

Our Christmas and birthday events were empty in meaning. We had no family rituals. Meaning and purpose were absent, as was Finnish mythology. Man lived by bread alone, and missing was the One who said: *Man shall not live by bread alone.* Perhaps it made sense only <u>after</u> one really had some bread, for example, bread following the Depression and the War. For fourteen years we had little bread, but a lot more than most folks that we knew. Yet there was an emptiness, a God-shaped emptiness, in my life of major proportions that needed to be filled. And if God didn't fill it, well, maybe evil might be most happy to do so.

Let's counter that serious thought with something lighter. The eighth grade class was discussing the qualifications for being President of the United States. After the teacher commented that a person must be a natural-born citizen, a student in class raised her hand and inquired: *"Does that mean that if you were born by Caesarean section that you can't be President?"*

If you look closely at the following map of the United States, you will observe that Eben is at the center of my universe at this point in time.

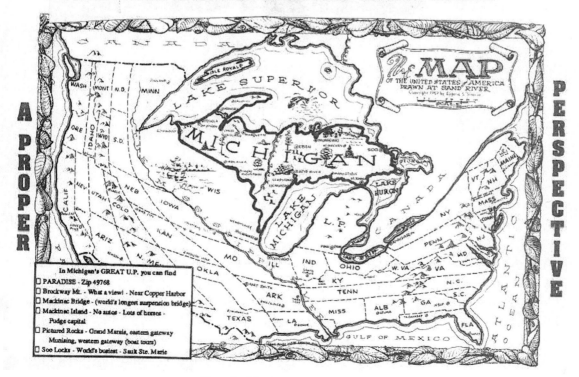

How the World Looked from Here.

27

CHAPTER FIVE

Rock River Twp. High School, Age 15-18, 1949

My high school days at Eben could not have been more exciting. What a wonderful place to grow up! Chatham-Eben: the "stone of help!" The war had come to an end, and we won. National socialism was defeated in Europe and imperialism in the Pacific. Some of those who left for the military returned to finish high school with us. My uncles and neighbors returned home. Finns who survived on subsistence farming during the Depression and the War, now slowly got back on their feet again. They were poor but most didn't know they were poor, for we were all in the same boat, as the expression went.

I began my high school career with **straight A's** in the classroom and as a part-time starter on the varsity basketball team. Frank Pelkonen replaced Hugo Hillilä as my pastor at Eben Lutheran. I worked summers at the State Farm, and, by and by, helped invent the hybrid *Chatham tomato* in the greenhouse.

My English teacher talked me into giving the **first speech** of my life. It was not long but it was famous. It was Abraham Lincoln's *Gettysburg Address* given originally sixty-four years earlier. I delivered it before the student assembly in the study hall. Donald Grenfell was our superintendent, a Gladstone native. Athletics went well as I was into track and field, basketball, baseball and softball. My outdoor hobbies also included fishing, trapping and hunting. I shot two deer while in high school. Our school did not offer art, or music (except tonettes). I had never seen a golf ball. In fact, Chatham could not offer a gymnasium, but we did have a cinder track. Exciting baseball and softball were played in Chatham.

We won the varsity district basketball titles in 1946 and 1947; I scored 21 in one of the tourney games as a sophomore center. But we were no match for Greenland-Mass in their three-year mastery of state titles. In the summer of 1947 I began planting evergreen seedlings for the Hiawatha National Forest out of the Munising office. But when they discovered I was only age sixteen, and uninsurable, I was laid off. This may sound like bad news, but it resulted in the best news, because that was just in time to be convinced by my girlfriend, Betty, to attend the church's **Bible Camp** at Lake Nesbitt in north Iron County. I was only sixteen, and August 7, 1947 was to become the defining moment of my entire life. I accepted Jesus Christ as the savior and lord of my life. I felt my conscience cleansed, which is the core of every personality. It was like being born again. And like real birth it was both painful unto death, but filled with great joy. My renewal led to becoming a child of God, like an adoption. I didn't know I was carrying a heavy load until the load was gone. Satan lost his charge over me, not by my own reason or effort, nor my decision, but solely by the Holy

Spirit's work and power, and because of what Jesus Christ had done for me on the cross. My personal great controversy was won or lost that night. *"In all these conflicts He who has loved us gives us a celebrated victory."10*

I was allowed to go through the "Door" of the sheepfold. *"I am the Door for the sheep . . . He who enters through Me will be saved. He may go in and out and find pasture . . . I have come to give life, the abundant life." 11* I had a "door" experience. I was introduced to the One who said: *I am the Good Shepherd*, and I responded in faith, *The Lord is my shepherd*. I believe in the forgiveness of sins, and the resurrection of the body. I had never known such happiness in my young life.

Fourteen of our **Eben Luther Leaguers** were there, and the prayers of Betty, Nestor, Bernice, Sally, Pat, Marge, Ray, and others, were answered. It was an inward spiritual experience of colossal proportions. There were also others. It was a moment of forgiveness, grace, hope, and love. Seminarian Norm Lund wrote about that particular Thursday night:

"How can I describe this night and find words to do justice to what took place around the bonfire . . . Inside, much greater things were taking place; they were things which can only happen when Jesus shouts into the hearts of men, 'You must be saved '. . . When the Spirit gives assurance that all is well with them, then is bound to be rejoicing. Now that is just what happened.12

St. Paul wrote: *"Now since God has made us, who believe, justified, we have peace with God earned by our Lord Jesus Christ."13*

In 1531 Luther preached on Christmas Day: *"Such joy is indeed offered everyone, but only those can receive it who are frightened in their consciences and troubled in their hearts . . . Is it now a wonderful thing that this joy is nearest to those whose consciences are the most restless?"*

Finally, Synod president **Ray Wargelin** wrote in 1945 about bible camping:

The 1947 Suomi Synod bible camp in Michigan; Les is seventh from the left, first row; Some campers are missing in picture.

"The effect of bible camping have been able to be channels of blessing because there we met for a period of time, apart for one week to hear God's Word. When this is allowed to happen in a spirit of prayer, and a blessing from the Lord is sincerely sought, God's Word has the possibility through this proclamation to soften and warm hearts."14 In the picture of the 1947 camp, ninety-seven were in the entire picture of which 27 became full-time church workers, pastors, missionaries, and their spouses.

"By Thy Spirit" was the theme of the August 3-10 Luther League camp, with **Pastor Frank Berg** of the Chicago Lutheran Bible Institute as head resource. Pastors Bill Puotinen, Karl Wilkman and Emil Paananen were also on the staff. I am personally eternally grateful to Betty, and others, who invited me to Bible Camp. There we saw Suomi Synod pietism at its best. This was the week that changed the course of my life forever and for eternity.15

The analogy of the **door** is a good one. Some doors are walnut, some are glass, and some church doors are bright red.. It can depend on your point of view as a door is a barrier to keep you out, or a door is an entranceway to bid you come in. You can look through the keyhole or peek inside but you are still outside. You can loiter mincing around outside and never enter by the door. Even a seminary education cannot do it, and sometimes galvanizes one from the real thing. A door can be opened in love and respect. A door can be slammed shut in anger. In our gated communities today a door is a sign of security. But our instruction manual, the Bible, said that an angel of the Lord rolled back the stone from the door. David said in the Old Testament *"I would rather be a doorkeeper in the house of my God than dwell in the tents of wickedness."*16

My parents were not exactly pleased about all this. Mother warned about extremism, while dad was silent. Later, I discovered what Martin Luther had preached way back in 1525 on John 2:4 (*O woman, what have you do with me?*)

For although there is no greater authority on earth than that of father and mother, yet it ends where God's Word and work begin. For in the things that are God's, neither father nor mother, let alone a bishop or another person, shall teach and lead us, but alone God's Word. I like that part about the bishop.

During my sophomore year my relationship to Betty began with earnest and we might have been termed as "going steady." I began to go to worship, and belong to the youth group called **Luther League**. It was composed of some outstanding young people.

It was the summer of 1948 that I loved Betty so much that I helped construct a basement beneath her house in Slapneck along with her uncle, Walter Oja. It was a challenge to excavate the soil from the entire space beneath the structure. And, of course I did it for gratis. That's how love behaves.

I was elected class president both my junior and senior years. Not having a gymnasium was a severe handicap although we compiled my best record in basketball with a 14 win, 3 loss mark, as a junior. I became a legend in February with a **mid-court** last second shot in a 52-51 win against county rival Munising. It was still being written about as recently as the year 2000. In short, Paul Nykänen inbounded to me at midcourt with 3 seconds remaining, and although Cliff Johnson was open under the basket there was no time for a pass. I let it fly with one hand, and *SWISH* ! Pandemonium broke out. Les Kouri was guarding me but gambled to let me shoot rather than commit a foul. I was a hero.

But pride came before the fall. I was a goat a month later, when, the day before district tournaments, waiting for Coach Mike (Mickelson) to conduct a team meeting in the English room, Arnie Ikkala and I tried to mimic our outstanding cheerleaders by flipping me over his back. The girls had made it look so easy. The result was **two broken bones** in my right hand, and only two points in the next night's loss to lowly John D. Pierce. I can recall Coach Mike taking me to the doctor in Marquette, and how much I disappointed him. In spite of that he later belonged to my Eden congregation for 17 years, and served as a "father figure" to me in my developing years.

But two months later we made up for the mishap by capturing the Class D U.P. **track and field championship** in Escanaba. Bernie Frigard, Paul Nykänen, Cliff Johnson and I dominated the field as our team had 60 and the runner-up (Chassell) had only 25. My top achievement was gold in the high hurdles. Frigard "owned" the sprints and the relays.

Things at home were not improving, but the twins became five; I attended bible camp again, and served as lifeguard at the children's camp. Although I was a big man on campus, the twins, Betty and Billy, tagged along behind me, as they were now in kindergarten. Baby-sitting them was an common thing throughout high school.

Next, came the prestigious **senior year**: again straight A's. My most serious competition for grades was Bernice Samanen and Sylvia Ollila. My second speech was the president's address at graduation class night. Pastor Armas Mäki presented Bibles to us that evening. We saw no sign of the American Civil Liberties Union. I became a fifth grade Sunday school teacher at the beginning of the school year. At the conclusion of the year the Sunday school gave me my much-cherished Revised Standard Version New Testament which I used for many years. This was also the year that a group of us would gather during our free noon hours, in (public) school, to hold bible studies with our *Pocket Testament League* New Testaments, and also prayer.

Upon turning eighteen in my senior year in February, all males in my peer group were by law compelled to register with the Selective Service Board in Munising, the board upon which I would be serving as a member in the 1960s and 1970s. Right on the heels of World War Two, which ended in 1945, came the Cold War with communism and the U.S.S.R. in particular. In March 1946 the Soviets erected the "Iron Curtain" wall not so much to keep us from invading them, as to keep their citizens from escaping communism. However, whereupon we ended WW 2 by using the atomic bomb against the Japanese, now we lived under the fear of the bomb because the Soviets had it. In reality it was all a continuation of the same war that had begun in 1914. Bolshevism, Fascism and Hitlerism were all the same basic evil.

During late high school I was able to use the family car once a week for dating. Betty and I double-dated with Nestor and Bernice so we doubled our dating frequency with two cars. School dances were nice, and sometimes I would disconnect the speedometer cable and we would take a carload to the Tri-County Luther League rallies in Marquette County. Imagine having to be deceptive in order to go to church!

In our annual battle in basketball with Munising, Nestor Salminen and I together once scored fifty-one points in a victory at which I set a new school record high of **thirty points**, previously held by Leo Lammi . The Mining Journal said the two of us were *Chatham's fair-haired boys*. In hindsight, I have thought how fortunate I was not to have had a gymnasium in high school, for it led me to Suomi College rather than a state school.

In the tourney we lost to Gwinn who went on to be the state runner-up in '49. We lost to them by only one point. My first shot in my first game from the top of the key as a freshman went in, and 677 points later I made thirteen in my final game as a senior against Gwinn. In track, I relinquished my hurdle titles for second place in both high and low hurdles. We failed to retain our U.P. Track title my senior year, taking third, and coming only 2.7 points short of a repeat championship. The agony of defeat. I added a new sport to my portfolio however in my senior year in that I was on a bowling team; our glitzy name was *Hotshots*.

On April 22, 1949 in my senior year in school my grandfather, **Henry Sipilä**, died in an auto mishap on a rainy night on the Eben-Trenary Road. It seems he had been at the New Moon Tavern in Eben with Victor Erickson. Vic dropped him off at the farm whereupon Ray Goodman, class of 1948, struck him with his car. The family curse was alive and well, as alcohol had plagued the Sipilä-Hiipakka families in Finland. The irony is that exactly sixty years later his grandson, my brother Bill, made his final call at the New Moon two days before his death in 2009. News about Henry caused some neighbors to exclaim: *"What? Again?"* as old-timers remembered that for the same reason Henry had "died" once before ca 1920 and walked out of the funeral home in Munising, and returning home. They believed him dead in 1920, but who knows? This time he died for good.

High School Graduation picture of Les Niemi, 1949.

I must tell you about our **class trip**. It was a tradition at Eben for the senior class to go on a class trip, the class deciding, within reason, where to go. And it was not mandatory for everyone to do it. Talk about freedom. The *Forty-Niners* decided to go to Detroit with a school bus. Bus driver Waino Mäki and his wife were the sole chaperones. After we squelched a trio of boys who had smuggled wine on board, the trip went without incident. And when we were to leave for home, we made a phone call to Mr. Bill Acker, our superintendent, requesting an additional day in Detroit. Request was granted. No chaperones, can you imagine that? I think it spoke well for self discipline and strong standard-setters.

And so we were graduated in the west auditorium of **Camp Shaw**. I had all my paper work done, and was accepted on a tuition scholarship to attend Michigan State College for civil engineering. Our limited curriculum in high school discouraged me from attending Michigan Tech as I would have needed to pick up a high school physics course in Houghton in addition to Tech classes. But most importantly I was not passionate about engineering. My summer job was also at Camp Shaw where I chopped wood for the kitchen stoves, mowed grass, husbanded the shrubs and trees, and cleaned the camp each week.

It was at Camp Shaw that another momentous weekend determined my life's vocation on **August 27, 1949.** The largest national Suomi Synod Luther League Convention on record was being hosted there by our local league. *"Called to Action"* was the theme for the gathering. Pastor Les Lurvey was heading up the youth work in our Suomi Synod.

On Saturday evening, Pastor Onni Koski was sharing God's Word from Isaiah 6, the call of Isaiah to be a prophet. *"Who will go for us?"* *"Here am I,"* said Isaiah, *"send me."* I felt the call into the Suomi Synod ministry and **stood up** and told them that. Within two weeks I traveled with Al Hautamäki to Hancock to **Suomi College**, a school I had not yet seen. Dad was not happy.

Once in high school, as I was constantly playing some kind of ball as an athlete, he said to me: *"You'll never make any money doing that."* I also noted that our bank balance in 1947 at the Trenary Bank was $1,829, but this did not reflect his investments in savings bonds. Mom was mystified. I had now become the black sheep of the family. But God does not call and leave us stranded or orphaned. The church set up a *Special Aid Fund* for needy seminarians and pre-seminarians. I became a grateful recipient. Fifty-eight years later I preached in Russia on the same text from Isaiah, and it resulted in my helping to lead a fund drive of $95,000 to build a church ten miles from where I gave that sermon in 3 languages. What is there about this powerful text?

This Camp Shaw event was instrumental in my life in understanding God's will for me. I have never looked back. Never underestimate the power of God's Word. *"It is the power of God and it brings salvation to everyone who believes."*[17] We were poor, but God is rich. Our school in Eben was so poor our team didn't even have a name. Today they are the *Cougars* but we were nothing . . . just Eben High with no gym. Should I have been offended because the community provided us with no gymnasium? After all, four years had gone by and nothing was done.

In review of my high school era, two major decisions were taken care of in high school. The **four major decisions** of life are these: 1. Which God do I serve? 2. What will be my vocation? 3. Whom shall I marry? 4. What do I do with my money?

To complete the answers, I married Betty four years after high school, (and Marcia in 1982). I began tithing two years later at the age of twenty. For me all four of life's most crucial questions were cared for between the ages of sixteen and twenty-two. There is nothing in this "program" in retrospect that I would have changed. I see it all as God's will and as miracles in my life, every step along the way. Only faith can see the miracles.

When I left Eben, *"the stone of help,"* sixty-seven percent of the students, by background, were Finnish, fourteen percent Slovenians, six percent were Swedes, and fourteen percent were a mix. Our "gym-less" basketball teams went forty-four wins, twenty-seven loses. These are some of the stories from my preparatory education in the geographical bulls-eye center (Chatham-Eben) of Michigan's Upper Peninsula.

To age eighteen in my life, I needed to ask: "Who 'spoke' into my life?" Everyone needs to ask that question. And one needs to determine which of them spoke only about externals, visible, trivial things, and which ones spoke of meaningful internal, invisible, even immortal things? It is the latter that is truly intellectual. What does the voice of God really sound like?

In Les Niemi's life, Hugo Hillilä, though I was too young, was the first to "speak into" my life. My mother, father, grandfather Manu and aunt Helmi spoke. That petite fourth grade teacher, Eleanor Stenstrom, spoke when I rose forth from a watery grave. Coach Mickelson and Bill MacNeil spoke. My future wife, Betty, spoke powerfully, as did other classmates. And a lay leader, Sally Lelvis, spoke into my life, especially once as a high school junior, by a written letter asking me if might consider the Christian ministry as my vocation. I was open to it, and I did.

The story is told by David Roper of how he played with his boys the game called *Sardines*, when they were little. He would turn out all the lights in the house and dad would hide in a small space, a closet perhaps. The rest of the family would then grope in the darkness, trying to find him. Each in turn, having found dad, would hide with him, squeezed into the small space, hence the name of the game. The smallest little guy would become frightened in the darkness. So when he got close, dad would whisper: *"Here I am." "I found you, Dad!"* he would utter as he snuggled against dad, not realizing that dad let himself be found.

Similarly, we have all been created to search for God, to grope for Him. The good news is that He is not hard to find. God desires to make himself known. A long time ago Dame Julian said *"There is a property in God of thirst and longing. He hath longing to have us."* So, whether we admit it or not, we grope for God in our darkness. And He allows himself to be found, saying *"Here I am,"* allowing us to reply: *"I found You!"* Someone wrote: *"Man gropes his way through life's dark maze; to gods unknown he often prays; until one day he meets God's Son; at last he's found the Living One."*

Four of the most positive things that happened in my life, happened in those first eighteen years. Someone has surmised, for example, that our chances of becoming a Christian are only 6% if we have not had this matter taken care of in our early years. A famous Finnish archbishop wrote: *"Parents cannot escape responsibility for their children. . . Responsibility extends beyond mutual satisfaction of physical needs. It includes our spiritual needs, too. Even if mother and father do not believe in God, they are responsible for the spiritual life of their child."*[18] Witter Bynner put it: *"The biggest problem in the world could have been solved when it was small."* Or, put another way: *"Milo lifted the ox when it was only a calf."*

CHAPTER SIX

Suomi College, Age 18-20, 1949-1951

The transition from high school to college was significant enough, even though size was not the factor. In my years at Suomi College the small enrollment at this very private school hovered between 125 and 183, and that included the seminary. Suomi's name was changed to Finlandia University, ca 1998 and though the seminary was moved in 1958, it now became a baccalaureate-granting four year college. This change was significant and imperative.

It was an all-day rain when I arrived at Suomi with two suitcases. My lodging for the next three years was at a private Catholic home at 615 Lake Street, three blocks downhill from the Old Main, with Mrs. Vivian Coon. She rented two bedrooms on the third floor, complete with a study room and a private bathroom. Lots of steps, but I was young. My roommate was **Tom Kangas** of Ishpeming, and in the adjacent room was big **Walt Werronen** of Fairport Harbor, Ohio. Both would become best lifetime friends, and both became fine Lutheran pastors. The room rent was $10.00 per month. Mrs. Coon was widowed and lived with her daughter, Susan.

And speaking about lots of steps, you should know that Suomi College was built on cheap land obtained from the Hancock Mining Company. Some of it was a rock pile, consisting of the "poor rock" discarded from copper mining. Later, after the campus developed there were two hundred ten steps from Quincy Street to the top of the campus. You think that was an adversity? Not at all. I used those steps with which to develop my leg muscles, and rebounding ability in Lion's basketball.

Old Main 1900.

Many of the young people who attended youth rallies, conventions and bible camps were at Suomi. It was a real eye opener as to what a Christian college was all about, and what Finnish-flavored pietism looked like. Concerning the Selective Service Board, because of my declared major of theology, my new rating was *4-D*. D for divinity.

We resident students ate **our meals** boarding-house style in Lower Old Main. The Finnish cooks were wonderful, but the fare was modest, yet

35

balanced. The house-mothers in the girls' dorm tried to instill some civility and manners into us by example. These mothers were Martha Hänninen, Lempi Auvinen and Elsa Kesätie. I usually sat at their table. Many seminarians graced the group and we said grace before eating, and gave thanks again after we were done. No one left until we did the latter. Meat was scarce in 1949 at Suomi so we thought it a real treat to have Wollwerth's ring-bologna, and we called it "Suomi Steak." The sharing at the tables was very good, both the food and discussions. It was co-ed, of course.

The concept of our Luther League back in Eben was replaced by the **Lutheran Student Association.** Even state colleges had one. Tom Kangas and I began doing evening devotions together, sometimes with prayer on our knees on each side of our bed. At this time the college was limited to two buildings, **Old Main** on Quincy Street built in 1900, and **Nikander Hall,** designed by the Eliel Saarinen firm, the famous Finnish architect, and built in 1940. College classes were in the latter while the seminary and the girls' dormitory were in Old Main.

* * *

Seminary senior **Don Lehti,** whom I met at church camp in 1947, offered me a partnership in an entrepreneurial coffee shop in Nikander Hall, by which we would split the profits. We later held a contest to name it and the name **"Nisu Nook"** prevailed, submitted by Giles Ekola. *Nisu* in Finnish was a coffee bread. We paid rent to the school for the space. Four local bakeries supplied our needs right to our door. I can still remember how good those *Persians* were. Our *Nook* also offered toast, Campbell soups, candy bars, aspirin, potato chips, tee shirts, sweatshirts and conversation. Co-eds often worked our shop just for free coffee and a roll, e.g., Myrna Marseilles worked for me in 1951, while in 1994 I worked for her in fund-raising at Suomi.

We created the very first Suomi **sweatshirt**. The shirt sold for ten dollars and displayed a wisdom lamp, surrounded by the wording: *"Suomi College, Hancock, Michigan, Verbum dei manet."* It was Latin for *"The Word of God alone."* The shirt came only in off-white. Unbeknownst to us we may have been prophetic to the successful Word Alone Network, a reformed movement in the Lutheran Church, fifty years later. The tee shirts had only *Suomi College* on them.

My **freshman** classes were: Composition and Writing, German 1, Finnish 1, Chemistry, Biology, Christianity 1, Choir and Physical Education. Our teachers were Ellen Ryynänen, E.W. Felscher, Harold Reinhardt, David Halkola, Armas Holmio, and Arthur Hill. I took eighteen credit hours each semester, and I was a "B" student. I loved my first year at Suomi. It was not easy as the competition was some of the best students from the Copper Country and the Suomi Synod across the country. Ohio came in pretty strong. Bernice Samanen of Chatham was a Suomi classmate that first year.

Meanwhile, **Betty** had enrolled at St. Luke's School of Nursing in Marquette, one hundred miles away. It was a three-year, no-summers-off, curriculum toward becoming a Registered Nurse. Science courses were taken at Northern Michigan College. She lived at the Wallace Nurses Home on West Magnetic Street. As a senior she was chosen *"Nurse of the Year,"* which included being a delegate to the national student nurses' convention in Atlantic City. The discipline was so tight that Betty had to be home by ten p.m., and an hour later on weekends. I think now that was a really good idea, but at the time I didn't.

I was invited to audition for the bass section of the **college a cappella choir**, under **Professor Arthur Hill.** Before long I was singing Johan Sebastian Bach's great cantata, *Christ Lag in Todesbanden* (Christ Lay in Death's Dark Prison). Luther wrote the words. The group consisted of forty members. I sang in the choir for three years. The Christmas and Easter concerts were a big hit locally. It was very serious business and was in the great musical tradition of Suomi, elevated earlier by Martti Nisonen. This would be the only choir in which I sang of my lifetime.

*   *   *

A huge bump in the road in my life occurred after I had been at the college for only a month. I had to go home and testify at **the divorce** of my mother and father at the Munising courthouse. The divorce was final on October 19, 1949. George Quinnell of Marquette was mom's attorney, while R.W. Nebel was dad's attorney, and also the judge. I later wondered how he could be both. I recall asking to meet with my parents, in a small room, and trying to convince them not to divorce, particularly for the sake of my six-year old sister and brother. It was to no avail. I was asked to testify. The settlement included an amount of sixty dollars a month from my dad to my mother, and they were allowed to live in the house. The house was owned by my dad, which became intimidating for mom. It seemed a tragedy that the twins were left to grow up without a father. This bump in the road was so distasteful and offensive to me that I often didn't like to go home to Chatham from college. Perhaps I was in denial. It seemed that only the positive impact of the college community of faith made this hurdle manageable for me at that time. Both my parents were devastated and the twins suffered which would manifest itself later.

*   *   *

I did not make the starting five in **basketball**. I was number six man, and had some trouble adjusting. I got into trouble on a basketball trip to *The Soo* when we played Soo Tech. Lodging at the prestigious *Ojibway Hotel* in the Soo, I played cards in the hotel with teammates. Pastor Onni Koski, Hancock congregation, got wind of it, and complained to President Bernie Hillilä that a Special Aid recipient for the ministry ought not to be playing cards. Hillilä called me into the office. I denied it. Then he said that he did not care if I played cards or not, but I should not be lying to him. It was humbling. I had no place to hide. Bernie Hillilä was right, but I was in a lose-lose situation in that interview.

Fred Vanhala of Detroit began introducing me to the game of **golf** at Michigan Tech's Golf Course and in Calumet. It was a new sport for me.

Be that as it may, we attended chapel services in the Nikander Chapel four days a week, we held noon prayer meetings, and we had weekly bible study sessions in the evenings. Despite my poverty I invested in a very sophisticated Thompson chain-reference **Bible**. I was in the "scripture-explains-scripture" mode. I had a lot of catching up to do since I was not raised in a Christian home. My favorite Bibles were my new Thompson and the Revised Standard Version New Testament given me for teaching Sunday school while in high school. I was into the Word big time.

Around this time, a verse from the Sermon on the Mount became an important theme for me: "*Above all else seek the kingdom of God, and His righteous will, so then all these will be also given to you.*"19 I was being awakened to what priorities life was about. Order is important in life. Disorder is most destructive when it involves the center of life. Dependence upon God and responsibility before God were becoming the inner core of my life. I wanted to seek first God's kingdom and his righteous will, from chaos to order. As I look back at my life, by George, if it wasn't true, and still is true. I was learning to live out of God's Word to trust Him in every need and not to worry.

I was a hundred miles from Betty, seemingly a much longer distance at that time than in the twenty-first century. We would write **letters**. To phone cost too much money so we rarely phoned. In fact I still don't phone much, except as the work demanded. I would get a letter off by 6:00 p.m. and race to the railroad a block away from Coons, and while the train slowed down a bit, I would run alongside, and slip that puppy into a "*post office slot*" on one of the train cars. Betty made several pillows later with cut-up letters for the stuffing. The written word is very powerful.

Hitch-hiking was a common thing to do at that period of poverty. I did it constantly to get home or to Marquette. I joked about challenging the Greyhound bus and beating it, often starting at the same time. I was competitive in many ways. Once some folks picked me up in L'Anse, who were intoxicated. I asked if I could drive. I drove them to the Republic junction, where they headed south. Otherwise it was very safe to hitch-hike then. Even Betty did it in inner-city Detroit during a bus strike when she and her classmates were affiliating there. When I left Chatham for college there was only one mile of hard surface (chip and tar) road in Rock River Twp., and that mile was from Chatham to within a half mile of my home. It was ideal for biking.

This was a **very pious** period in my life. My faith would not allow me to go to movies, there was no dancing, cards were taboo, nor alcohol. Drugs were unheard of. Students at Suomi were very seldom known to drink. Several years later, when seminarian Jack Hill, a war veteran who served in Burma, was seen entering the Hollywood Tavern in Hancock, it precipitated a special afternoon session with President Ed Isaac. Does it sound legalistic? Perhaps, but it was better to err on that side than the alternative, I concluded.

* * *

The school year was over and I returned to Chatham for the **summer**. My dad, who had refused to financially support me in a career which he disliked, did however offer me a summer job. I worked on installing new concrete sidewalks at Camp Shaw. But our major project was building the roof on the *Veterans' Memorial Gymnasium* at Eben High School, which was extremely interesting. We had a crew of a half dozen, I being the youngest. I received a dollar an hour about average for a family man in 1950. Dad received $ 25,000 for this long-delayed project, and that not immediately.

We made our own trusses, seven-ply doubles. I was the glue man as we assembled them on the concrete floor. Frank Salo provided a fresh spruce boom pole and Art Pelkie on his bulldozer hoisted them onto the exterior walls with only one foot of cable at the top to spare. When I was nailing the shiplap sheeting on the roof Bill Laitinen, in Finnish, said after I hit my thumb with the hammer, and did not swear: *"What kind of boy is this who doesn't swear after hitting his thumb?"* Christians do not go unnoticed. It was on this job that dad confronted me about my theology major, saying: *"Why do you want to become a minister, when you can't even talk?"* I went on to preach over 6,500 sermons in my career, and usually to a full house. I painted those eaves on the new gym carefully, standing on those high scaffolds.

I had use of dad's 1948 Chevy car and Harold Kallio and I double-dated Betty and Sally (Hostetler) over the summer. Kallio would begin his pre-theology at Springfield, Illinois, at Concordia Seminary, that following fall. He and I had previously sat on the depot platform on summer evenings pondering together what it was that God wanted us to do with our lives. What a nice memory.

This was also my last summer of playing **baseball and softball** in Chatham. Our *Chatham All-Star* baseball team was in an eight-team *Rainbow League*, and I recall one summer winning every home game except the one to the first place team, and losing every away game, except the game to the last place team. Who says God is not a God of order? My softball was played for *Mäki's Service* at Chatham Corners (Charles Mäki, manager). I was primarily the catcher for both, but also sometimes roamed the outfield. Reino Luoma claimed that he had never seen such an outstanding play in centerfield than at one Sunday afternoon baseball game in Chatham when I caught a fly ball over my left shoulder speeding straight-away, then wheeling and throwing Buzz Brisson out at home plate, trying to score from third for Trenary. Vern Richmond was the umpire, and Brisson was not a speed-merchant, which explains a lot.

But the **catcher** is rather important for nothing happens until you put those fingers down. Every play! He is the quarterback, and he calls the shots. I was privileged to catch Cliff Johnson, Nestor Salminen, Elmer Frigard, Les Latvala and John Kangas. I was a right handed hitter, but I hit to right field. It was terrific fun. I was the catcher also for the 15-16 age Junior League team where our uniforms held the name *Hornets*, and one year we won seventeen games and lost only one.

* * *

By early September I left my summer job with dad, and returned to Suomi College for my **sophomore year**. It was another overloaded year of twenty-three credit hours a semester. My courses were: English Literature, Western Civilization, German II, Sociology, Logic, Abnormal Psychology, Speech, Finnish II, Christianity II, Choir, and Physical Education. In addition to some previous teachers, new teachers were Uuras Saarnivaara, Soini Torma, and Walter Kukkonen. After the year was over I added an American Literature class at Northern Michigan University. Once again I was only a '*B*' student stemming from the heavy load. I often studied until 1:00 a.m. It was also the year, 1950, when the microwave was invented and hit the market.

I was honored as a sophomore by being elected class **president**. Also toward the end of the year I made the 1952 national *American College Student Leaders* Directory. Although college cost me only $700 per year (tuition, board and room), money was hard to come by. A cup of coffee at my Nisu Nook cost five cents a cup. Tom Kangas was my new partner. The *Special Aid Fund* came to the rescue whenever my summer jobs and the coffee shop could not underwrite it. As a result I never needed to take out a loan. Seminarian Henry Leino of Thomaston, Maine, was our new neighbor in the next room at the Coon home.

Les' hook shot against Northern Michigan University in 1952;
Note Taccolini brothers still floor-bound.

The starters for Suomi basketball that year were Walt Werronen, Tom Asuma, Carl Johnson, Warren Schultz and me. I broke into my own in February by scoring 48 points (of our team's 100) against Lake Superior State College (Soo Tech). The problem was that they had 113. But my effort was a new conference mark, and it ushered me into my first of three years on the **All-Conference Team** in the *Upper Peninsula Intercollegiate Athletic Conference* (UPIAC). David Halkola was our coach.

*   *   *

A highlight of my sophomore year came in Lent, 1951, when I preached my **first sermon** at the local St. Mathew's Church in Hancock at a midweek service. I can recall how elated I was by the experience of preaching Jesus during Lent. But during the winter I also had a mishap. I slid dad's 1948 Chevy on ice on Front Street in Marquette into another car; dad had cancelled the insurance because the car was used so seldom. I received a bill for more money than I owned. I was hitch-hiking home one day when Phil Stein picked me up; he was a Jewish businessman from Ishpeming. He told me what to do: *Write back and tell what you are doing, and how much money ($270) you have as a student. Offer it if the balance could be forgiven.* I did and it worked. Four decades later I saw Phil at his Big Boy Restaurant in the Marquette Mall, and thanked him to which he responded: *"You have made my day."*

The **Cold War** had turned into a hot war, as the United Nations police action intensi-fied in **Korea**. My high school classmates Matt Bell and Elmer Salo went there. Other class-mates were as far as Japan, namely, Don Hakanen, Ray Brisson and Arnie Ikkala. Yet others who served were: Nestor Salminen, Eugene Korpi, Les Aho, Don Bartol, and Ernie Zbac-nik. Most often they joined a military branch of their choice before compelled to being drafted. Their patriotism is to be saluted as they helped to stop communism.

My third cousin, Staff Sgt. **Kenneth L. Mäki**, grandson of my grandmother Alma's sis-ter Impi Liesmäki of Ironwood, was killed in action on December 3, 1951 in the retreat south of Hungham in North Korea at the hands of the Chinese. It was the largest water evac-uation in American military history. I have a copy of his final letter.

That following summer in August, I used the 1948 Chevy to bring five of us to the bien-nial Suomi Luther League Convention at Camp Siegel in Minnesota, the same event at which two years earlier I committed my life to the holy ministry. So my second college year was over, at a Christian college that was no party school because we took life very seriously.

* * *

Also that summer my friend and high school classmate, **Ray Lampi**, offered me a job selling **family bibles** making cold calls house to house. This bible had 400 paintings by the French artist James Tissot, (1836-1902), (Good Will Publishing Co.). It was not cheap . . .$ 29.95, three day's wages in 1951. My commission was seven dollars for an installment sale, and eleven for cash. Often I would sell three and quit for the day. I had twenty-one dollars earned. In August we operated a booth at the Escanaba State Fair. I was doing the work of an evangelist, by providing families with the Word of God. It was a great job. Only a hun-dred sales would have covered my next school year, my first year of seminary, but I far exceeded that. We worked almost totally the central U.P. cities. I think I had a talent for sales. This job and the *Nisu Nook* were indicative of it.

It was interesting after mom died in 2004 to find in mom's attic a copy of that Bible, and a Pocket Testament League card which she had signed promising to read the Bible daily, and indicating that she had received Jesus Christ as her savior dated **June 24, 1950.** That was upon my completion of my first college year.

I was going to church, every Sunday and also in between. The Lord was guiding me as I tried to walk in His will. I was not seeing my grandparents as often as before, but that was natural I suppose. Pearl began teaching Sunday school, and she attended bible study. She began to make pasties for sale to supplement her income.

I was graduated from Suomi College with an **Associate of Arts** degree in June 1951. It had been a fantastic two years. I was personally under constant pressure to catch up with my peers in religious knowledge, having not grown up in the church. I think I suffered a certain amount of resentment about my lack of church because all my friends had belonged. I had

Group of Lutheran Student Association students engaged in Christmas caroling in 1950; Les, fifth from right.

been one of those who merely peeked through the keyhole until I was age 16. Then I was able to enter by "the Door." I am confident that some youth feel this same way in 2011, but they may be ashamed to admit it. They are out in the cold, while Christian youth are enjoying the warmth of the body of Jesus Christ in congregations, including the assurance of salvation. The others obviously don't realize what they're missing. To not have assurance is to miss out on a great deal of joy.

Red Squirrel

CHAPTER SEVEN

Seminary, Age 20-23, 1951-1954

One had to be approved in order to be accepted to the Suomi Theological Seminary. Our Suomi Seminary began in 1904. Some classmates who felt called to become pastors were not approved, and entered other fields of endeavor, perhaps having misunderstood their calls.

Our **junior** class in seminary consisted of Karl Aho (Duluth), Tom Asuma (Ashtabula Harbor), Tom Kangas (Ishpeming), Rudy Kemppainen (Salo), Tom Kuusisto (DeKalb), Robert Richardson (Detroit), Richard Rintala (Warren OH), Fred Vanhala (Detroit), and me (Chatham). Walter Werronen and Martin Saarinen left us in order to obtain their bachelor's baccalaureate degrees.

Ours was the final class to be accepted into seminary with less than a B.A. or B.S. degree. The supply of clergy in our Suomi Synod had been so acute over the decades that the requirement was not raised until after 1954. We were to obtain our bachelor degrees while in the parish, which some of us did, but I did not. A bit of my father had rubbed off on me, as he often expressed his opinion that a formal education was not always necessary. In fact, he seemed to resent that this sister, Helmi, had an opportunity to go to college. Of course he would say that since he did not have that opportunity. Also, later in my dozen years in development work at Finlandia University I found countless Finns who served in high places without a formal education. A sheepskin does not an expert make. I leaned a bit toward my father's sentiments.

I sometimes minimized my seminary training by the fact that we had only four professors until I discovered that the great Finnish reformer, Michael Agricola in 1536-1539 in Wittenberg, had only Martin Luther, Philipp Melanchthon, Johan Bugenhagen and Justus Jonas. We had **Walter Kukkonen**, **Armas Holmio**, **Uuras Saarnivaara**, and **Edward Isaac**. They complimented one another nicely and were terrific by today's standards, I would add, because they "were not ashamed of the gospel. "

So I came to this point in my training with 78 credit hours of undergraduate studies, 18 over the normal. My first year seminary courses were: Greek I, Systematic Theology 1, Church History, Introduction to the New Testament, - Old Testament, Homiletics, Finnish III, and Choir. Since many of our courses were offered every third year, we had as many as twenty-four students in some of our classes. It was indeed exciting to be in seminary. In the Middle Ages theology was known as "the queen of sciences."

We had the benefit of the best Lutheran scholarship in the country, but more profound was the unique theological bent from our pietism in the **Church of Finland**. Walter Kukkonen brought new exciting life into our classes. He had been influenced by Joseph Sittler from Chicago and Finnish theologians Antti Pietilä, Martti Simojoki, and Gustaf Aulen. Holmio was our historian. Saarnivaara gave us a slant from Laestadianism, Biblical studies and deep humility. Isaac presented practical theology plus a unique evangelical fervor. Pietism believed in a living faith whereby orthodoxy seemed dry and lifeless by comparison. As Jorma Laulaja wrote: *If there is no living God in life, in His place step the powers of darkness, and false gods.* The emphasis was on the word *living*. Uuras warned us: Where the fire of faith is ignited the liberal seminary and church hierarchy, like the fire department, rushes in to put out the flames. His warning became increasingly relevant in subsequent decades.

My, O my, hadn't we seen it over and over in the Lutheran Church in America (org. 1963), and especially in the Evangelical Lutheran Church in America (org. 1988)? It prompted Professor Walter Kukkonen two months before his passing in 2007 to lament: *"I have come to the conclusion that the ELCA is a Christless church!"* And in that process our church began to dismiss her finest theologians.

*   *   *

Meanwhile, my pastoral ministry began immediately as I was invited to be the student pastor at an Augustana congregation in Skandia, 17 miles south of Marquette, **Emanuel Lutheran Church**. I held services every other Sunday for the next two years, and had a wonderful time. I taught confirmation classes and had Luther League events with attendances up to forty. Not only was this congregation mostly Swedes, but it seemed that half of them were Johnsons. While it meant I had to hitch-hike home often, I also got to see Betty in Marquette.

Skandia was the church where, before my time, a crazed man had broken into the church and with a knife stabbed Jesus in the neck in the altar painting. It was a bit creepy to look up at that painting at the altar and see that "scar" on Jesus. There was something theological about this scene. What soul-sickness might have caused this, yet an honesty as to what he had thought of Jesus. Jesus was his problem. Come to think of it Jesus seemed to be everybody's problem, if in fact a problem existed.

This was my third year in the college **choir**, and our spring tour took us to Boston and New York; it afforded Dick Rintala and me to visit the then-tallest building in the world, the Empire State Building, erected in 1931 when I was born.

I averaged 24.5 points a game on the **basketball** court, again being named to the all-conference team. My starting five included Tom Asuma, Dick Rintala, Roy Baril and Don Chaput. I would be so tired from studying to 1:00 a.m., that prior to one game I made the mistake of stretching out on the bed only to discover that I had slept through the first half of a home game. I arrived for the second half and had some catching up to do. I recall we won that game.

Tom Kangas moved out of my room and I was alone. It was my final year of operating the Nisu Nook, as the following year I "sold my franchise" to Richard and Beverly (Ruona) Rintala. During the spring Betty spent two months of affiliation at a Winnebago mental hospital facility near Oshkosh. I hitch-hiked down to see her. It was difficult to visit without a car. I can recall leaving her late that evening. I tried "thumbing" late at night, but had to rent a small hotel room in Oshkosh because no one would pick me up at midnight. I was like a street person.

The school year went by fast and the next thing I knew it was time to look for a summer job. I found a job at **Park Cemetery** in Marquette, renting a room on Fourth Street from a Mrs. Homier. I can remember studying my Greek among the tombstones. Homier had an ancient ice box which needed real ice to keep it cool. I recall buying a nice ham with which to make the ham sandwiches I loved, and not being Jewish. Soon however I noted that my ham was turning green. My room was just three blocks from Wallace Nurses Home where Betty lived. We spent much time together. Mrs. Homier was no fool as I found out when Betty once came to my room. She frowned on it. I continued to preach on alternate Sundays in Skandia.

Betty Sjostrand-Niemi, RN; 1952.

My "**middler**" year began at Suomi Seminary, my fourth year of college. I was pleased to gain ownership of my first car. Father paid half, as did mother, each donating $500. It was a used blue **1949 Chevy Club Coupe** from Frei Chevrolet of Marquette. Now I came to know the expense of owning a car. Nonetheless, I was grateful. I loved that little car.

Betty's three year course to become a **Registered Nurse** at St. Luke's came to a happy conclusion with her graduation on September 1, 1952. Having worked obstetrics at St. Luke's Hospital (now Marquette General Hospital), her first salaried job was in the same department. After leaving the nurse's home she and Lois Wiseman, rented an apartment on West Magnetic Street. She was very happy with her accomplishment. It was at this apartment at Christmas in 1952 that I presented her with a diamond **engagement ring**. She accepted it.

However, back at seminary, I needed to consult with the Seminary president, Edward Isaac, about these marriage plans. I think the seminary had a concern that all the spouses would be Christians. And well they should have. In a sense we had to get permission to get married. Sometime later that same concern might have applied to all pastors; that all parish pastors should be Christians.

My fourth and final college basketball season came and went. I again averaged 24.5 points a game and for the third year was honored to be selected to the **All-Upper Peninsula Intercollegiate Athletic Conference** team. I scored my one thousandth point in a 62-59 victory over Northland College, scoring 30. My four-year career total was **1,196 points**, which school record held until 2005. My single game record stood for nineteen years at 48. All of this was prior to the 3-point shot, the alternating possession jump balls, and the shot clock. My **No. 25 jersey** was retired in 1994 at the Paavo Nurmi Fieldhouse, and is lodged in the Finnish-American Archives for safekeeping. I also lettered in golf.

Betty and I were excitedly planning our forthcoming wedding. It would be upon us as soon as school was out. I did considerable guest preaching. Some of our sermons we preached repeatedly, for different audiences of course. Tom Asuma had the top sermon which earned him $ 210, in ten and fifteen dollar increments.

* * *

Hugo Sjostrand presenting his daughter Betty for marriage.

Saturday, **June 13, 1953** arrived, the day of our **marriage**. God had kept us and protected us and our relationship to this day. Eben Lutheran Church was the site and Frank Pelkonen was the officiant. My best man was Harold Kallio and Betty's maid of honor was Lois Wiseman. Other attendants were Bernice Samanen, Nancy Flink, and Marjorie Posio; Nestor Salminen, Ray Lampi and Toivo Rosenberg.

Since they could not figure out the transportation from Slapneck to the church, a four mile distance, Betty got left without a ride and the event began twenty minutes late. They were so anxious to get to the main event that they forgot about the bride. For a moment I was afraid she changed her mind, as I was waiting. George Wieland was the ring bearer while Susan Wierimaa was flower girl. It was the same day that Martin Luther married Katherine von Bora, June 13, but in 1525.

We rented the new high school gymnasium for the immediately-held reception and about five hundred people showed up. We greeted them all and thanked them for coming. No alcohol, no dance, just lots of food. Tired, we returned to Slapneck. Then we packed to go on our first **honeymoon**. The Detroit contingency sowed my pajama-legs closed. No problem. We went south to U.S.-2, turned left and without a reservation stayed at a small mom and pop motel on Lake Michigan, near Nahma. The name of the place slips my memory.

The following day we went to a motel in St. Ignace, took the ferry to Mackinac Island for the day. I remember the lilacs being in bloom. Our second honeymoon was to Detroit, by way of Chicago. We visited the Pelkonen sisters there (Ellen's cousins), and Eino and Mabel Sipilä. Betty wore her new pink suit. Upon returning home, we packed to drive to the West Coast. I had arranged to do **internship** at Messiah Lutheran Church in **Portland** for July, and Holy Trinity Lutheran Church in **Berkeley** for August.

Stops along U.S.-2 were in Buxton, ND, Minot, ND, Yellowstone National Park, Wenatchee, WA and Seattle. We concluded that Dan was conceived in Yellowstone Park or Wenatchee. We viewed one of the first three-dimensional (3-D) movies in Wenatchee by the name of "*Shane.*"

We lodged at the John Hattula parsonage in **Portland**, I worked hard at the church and Betty worked at Multnomah Hospital in the *City of Roses*. I conducted my first funeral; I was the first to preach in their new church, two services a Sunday, English and Finnish, directed a Vacation Church School, and began a survey of new church neighborhood (with Elsie Hjelt). I was quite surprised in the survey as I approached a small home, the door had a window into the kitchen; lo, there was a young lady milling around naked in her kitchen. I was quite embarrassed and quietly retreated. I could have been charged as a"Peepin' Tom," and suddenly realized that the ministry could be dangerous. I particularly remember Paavo Patokoski of Portland.

The trip from Portland to Berkeley with our Club Coupe was nice, including driving right through the base of a redwood tree. The Berkeley congregation was wonderful; another Vacation Church School. I met Art and Saima Mills, who later would give me $ 500,000 for Finlandia University, as a gift in the form of five charitable gift annuities. The Chevy needed a valve job, which Otto Kangas, performed for simply the cost of the parts. Don Lehti, my good friend, had a fine congregation. Betty worked at Herrick Hospital. Nurses were much in demand so she never had a problem finding a job.

Upon exit, **Harold Kallio**, from Chatham, came to Berkeley with the pastor. Dennis Marttala of Oregon met us there and the four of us took turns driving straight home in three days without stopping. There were no freeways. Kallio enrolled at Concordia Seminary, while Marttala enrolled at Suomi, both were ordained later. Betty had experienced *morning sickness* in Berkeley as she was now pregnant. It was a fine internship summer.

*   *   *

It had been an exciting summer, with the Lord protecting us twenty-two year old kids. I preached at 18 Sunday services, directed two VCSs, and learned to relate to parishioners. Later, in 1983 I would return to Berkeley to preach again in contemplation of becoming their permanent pastor; I did not accept the call.

In Hancock our new apartment overlooked the Portage Canal at **305 Water Street** in a large house owned by the Isaacsons (who owned Coast to Coast Hardware). We paid thirty-five dollars a month, utilities included. We were two blocks downhill from Quincy Street. I was back in seminary for my senior year, while Betty commuted all winter to the **L'Anse Memorial Hospital**, a thirty-five mile trip. I preached many Sundays in area churches: Chassell, Mohawk, Trout Creek, Eben, Skandia, Negaunee, Soo, Ontario, Minnesota, etc. Learning the doctrine, the system, was interesting, but it was not to be confused with lively preaching which brings about a living faith. *"Faith is born from hearing, but the word about Christ gives birth to hearing."*[20] Some of my special classes were: History of the Church of Finland, History of Missions, Practical Theology, Homiletics, Finnish IV, History of American Lutheranism, Exegesis, Systematic Theology, etc.

I recall being given as my preaching text for the homiletics class a verse from 2 Timothy 1:7: *"For God has not given us a cowardly spirit (timidity), but the spirit of power, love, and good judgment."* Later, I began thinking how appropriate that verse was for me chosen by Dr. Walter Kukkonen.

My mother's wonderful awakening in her life at age forty was followed by the first resident pastors in Eben, namely, Herb Franz, Tauno Järvinen, and Janis Dombrovskis. Under Järvinen they built a beautiful new church in Eben, my home congregation.

*   *   *

When my dad and **Lorraine Opitz** entered the New Moon Tavern in Eben on October 31, 1953, Halloween, the "regulars" knew something was up. A large surprise happened back in Munising, as my dad married Lorraine Opitz-Boucher, a native of Forest Lake. She was age thirty-five, and he forty-six. They had met at Ernie and Elsie Johnson's cottage at Lake Au Train in mid August on a blind date. Six weeks later they wed. She came with a six-year old son, **John Boucher**. Pastor 'Bud' Danner, at Eden, had refused to marry them, but Pastor Herb Ingraham performed the private event. Dad later built the first home on Sand Point Road for Pastor Herb and Earlene in 1959. They lived in the Stucco Building on East Superior Street, but soon bought a home at the corner of West Superior and Cherry Streets. They went on to have a fine marriage of thirty-seven years, and were devoted to one another. We got to be best of friends. Of German ancestry, Lorraine's father had served as a state trapper, once wintering on Isle Royale.

Love did not slow Ed down, as that same year he built the first modern motel in Munising (Alger Falls Motel), homes for Bill Cox, Jr., Charles Symon, Jack Gatiss, a new gas station for Richmond Oil Co., a cabin for Andy Stone, remodeled the Chevrolet Garage and also the Ernest Johnson cottage. When you're in love you can do a lot.

*   *   *

My campus job during my senior year was selling magazines house to house for **Crow-ell-Collier Co.**, with George Barnes as my supervisor. I had a $ 6.00 three-magazine special that sold like hotcakes, my best sales streak being in Mohawk-Fulton whereby I cleared $45 a day for 3 straight days. Not bad for 1953. Tom Kuusisto, Dick Rintala and Tom Kangas were not quite as good at sales as I was. Barnes tried to talk me into leaving the seminary and making some real money. Wasn't it Louis Aggassiz who once said: *I can't waste my time merely making money?*

By November, local photographer Carl Kukkonen dropped by the seminary to see if anyone wanted to go deer hunting. Fred Vanhala and I volunteered. And since I had just bought Eino Oja's rifle (who guarded Hermann Goering after the war), I was ready. We drove to Beacon Hill near Redridge, west of Houghton. There I was posted at a crossing of tote roads, and upon hearing a shot to the north, paid attention. Suddenly there came a **four-point buck** right down the tote road. I dropped it. It cried. I wondered why I was doing this, and felt sorry for him. But to be "macho" was so important to a young man. I went on to shoot 18 deer in my career, stopping the madness in 1980.

In basketball, our seminary pick-up team beat the college varsity, which was pretty demeaning to them. My college athletic career had now come to an end. I could not afford to continue sports in my parishes stemming from too heavy a work load. An afterthought still lingers as when high school classmate Waino Salo wrote to me in 1997 with the kind sentiment: *"I would consider you as the top* (basketball) *player that graduated from Eben."*

The students at Suomi sponsored a weekly Saturday half-hour religious radio broadcast under *Lutheran Student Association* auspices. We sang and preached and Vanhala's good voice served as the announcer. I don't see modern young people so inclined, seemingly lacking a moral compass and Christian value system. It became our practice, instead of climbing the hill to Nikander Hall and the Nisu Nook, to simply go half a block down to Ed Byron's *Corral Shop* for coffee after seminary classes at Old Main. We would discuss what we had just learned over coffee.

This entire trivia sounds pretty fugacious of course.

A big day arrived in March, on March 24, 1953. Our first son, **Daniel James Niemi,** was born at St. Luke's Hospital in Marquette. Betty suffered a hard labor which after twelve hours was solved by a Caesarean section by Dr. Archie Narotzky of Ishpeming. One forgets the pain for the joy that a child is born. Betty chose Marquette for this event because she had worked obstetrics there before our marriage. Soon they came home to our small but warm apartment in Hancock. Proud parents were we. Our friends came over to see this thing that had come to pass.

Came spring, and all senior seminarians had to appear before the Synod **Consistory** for a several hour oral examination concerning theology and churchmanship. My exam was with

Dick Rintala, my good friend. I can't recall who was present from the consistory except Dr. John Wargelin, then synod president. I liked him and regarded him as one of the very great leaders of our church. He had been a graduate of the first seminary class of 1906. This was his final year as president before his retirement. Soon he lost his eyesight completely but continued to preach. We were confident about passing the exam.

A serious aspect now confronted us (me). Where did my Lord want me to be pastor in my first parish? The synod president hinted at three congregations in the state of Maine. The Holy Spirit said "No." I loved the Upper Peninsula. I had looked at Canadian Soo, and Minnesota. "No." **Eben** put pressure on me, having been lifted up by them to go into the ministry, despite my unique socialist background. But I was uncomfortable about going to "my own country," as I remembered how they roughed up Jesus in Nazareth. I often wondered what would have happened in Chatham-Eben if I had gone there. However a fine evangelist, Herb Franz, went there a year later. He performed so well that two of his congregations, Eben and Skandia, fifty years later are able to support their own resident pastors.

I accepted **a call** from the **Trout Creek Parish**, the same congregation from where John and Gertrude Ollila worked at those bible camps faithfully, at which I was saved in 1947. They knew my background, and John Ollila wrote the letter of call. How right and comfortable it felt. God was leading me to these good people, and I would love them with the gospel for many years. I accepted Trout Creek, Ewen, Paynesville, and North Bruce, as my first congregations. We became "Creekers." It was the year that the immigration station at Charles Ellis' island in New York City was closed, having welcomed twelve million to the land of the free, my grandma Alma being one of them. Polio vaccine came out that year.

I have an amusing story about God's sense of humor. When Betty and I were having a baby in March in Marquette, a delegation from the Trout Creek Parish came to the seminary to interview the graduating class. The other five were interviewed, but I was missing. Result: They issued the call to the one who was absent! If I was one of my classmates I think I would feel offended. Perhaps they said among themselves on the way home: *Well, Niemi can't be any worse than those guys.* God has a sense of humor. Seriously, I firmly believed that it was God's good and gracious will for me to serve the fine people of the Trout Creek Parish. Besides, I knew Finnish which was necessary.

*   *   *

Now two major events in my life loomed ahead upon completion of my education at Suomi Theological Seminary in Hancock. First, I was graduated from the seminary on **June 6, 1954**, which happened to be the Golden Anniversary **commencement** of Suomi College. There were thirty-eight graduates, of which eight of us were from the seminary. We were honored to have present members of the first class of 1904, namely, Dr. John Wargelin, Pastor Alfred Haapanen, Pastor Matt Luttinen, and Ms. Minnie Perttula-Mäki. The main address was entitled *"Building God's Kingdom."*

Recall that my favorite bible verse five years ago as a freshman was: *"Above all else seek the kingdom of God, and His righteous will, so then all these things will be also given to you."*[21] The fulfillment of this promise continued right after our gala wedding. I had only fifty dollars to my name on the day of our wedding. It sounds grossly irresponsible, doesn't it? Yet, we miraculously went on three honeymoons: a. Mackinac Island, b. Detroit, and c. the West Coast cities of Portland and Berkeley. Ebenezer! The stone of help was with us!

A week later, in our nation, President Dwight Eisenhower signed an order to add *"under God"* to the U.S. Pledge of Allegiance. How do you like those apples? It was an indication of the Christian mood of the land, the best of times.

Suomi College had made a unbelievably powerful impact on my life, which would be reflected later by my service on the Board of Directors, the "no further charges" on the account of my oldest son Dan, my twelve years of saving the college by my raising over twenty-five million dollars, and my own personal estate plan with the university as a major beneficiary. It was a great festive day in Hancock, our holy city, when we were graduated. I had fallen in love with the Copper Country. We bid goodbye to our dedicated seminary professors. Little did we realize at the time that within seven weeks our president, Pastor Isaac, would die suddenly on July 29, 1954 at the young age of 54. And that many years later, at Mrs. Tyyne Isaac's ninetieth birthday event I would be giving her an award in behalf of Suomi College. My confirmation pastor, Hugo Hillilä, also died in 1954.

A major event in my life happened on June 20, 1954 as I took the oath of ordination into the **Holy Ministry** in Waukegan, IL at Augustana's Trinity Lutheran Church. John Wargelin officiated the ordination, assisted by members of the Consistory and the representative from the Church of Finland, Dr. Lennart Pinomaa. (Episcopalians would be tickled pink that my **"apostolic succession"** would trickle from his fingertips onto me.) It was a beastly hot and humid evening, and there were mosquitoes (reminding me of my roots from the north). Pastor Melvin Hagelberg, native of Kaleva, MI, place the traditional red stole around my neck, depicting the yoke of Jesus Christ. Mel was a relative by marriage with the Sipilä clan in Kaleva, and from Lapua, Finland. Later that summer, the **bishop's cross** from Finland was bestowed to John Wargelin by Dr. Eelis Gulin, indicating for the first time that the Suomi Synod was officially recognized by the Church of Finland. Now, how official is all of that?

In the light of later liberalism, it is important to be reminded herewith that my promises were made to the following serious and carefully chosen questions:

"Will you preach and teach in accordance with the Holy Scriptures and the Confessions of the Lutheran Church? "I will, and I ask God to help me."[22]

These were ordination vows, and I will later need to remember them, and what they meant in light of my church having lost its moral compass. But at the moment, and in the former Suomi Synod, it was absolutely wonderful.

The theme of the annual convention at which all of this was taking place, chosen by Dr. Wargelin, was

"I am not ashamed of the gospel for it is the power of God and it brings salvation to all who believe it."[23]

"Minä en häpeä evangeliumia, sillä se on Jumalan voima ja se tuo pelastuksen kaikille, jotka sen uskovat."

"Post tenebras spero lucem. Non me pudet evangelii Christi, potentia enim Dei est ad salutem omni crdenti."

Olavus Petri had used the same text on February 19, 1550 in Finland with "the Finnish Reformer," Michael Agricola. *"Liber Michaelis Agricolae d Torsby in Perna."*

It was the culmination, to date, of the promise that I had made to my call at age eighteen at Camp Shaw to Isaiah's question, *"Who will go for us? . . . Here am I, send me."* But it also reaches back to my "awakening" in 1947 at bible camp, when I entered the *Door* to the sheepfold, accepting Jesus as my Good Shepherd. Now, in parish life I will go, with my sheep, in and out and find pasture . . . the Word of God. It was an answer to **Sally Lelvis'** letter to me in high school when I was a junior, challenging me to listen to God's will. And ultimately, it harkens back to God's visible grace at my baptism, and Christ's command to go to all people, baptize them, and teach them all God commanded. I was by grace trying to live out God's holy will for my life, yes, even for one so untimely born to Ed and Pearl in 1931. But the *Call* was more important than the sheepskin.

All of the above seemed totally impossible. By nature we insist that we can manage without God's help. But before I can believe that for God all things are possible, even the incomprehensible, I must realize that at every turn in the road I was utterly helpless, whether I am referring to my birth, my salvation from a watery grave, my health, my monetary poverty, my moral and spiritual bankruptcy, the gifted regeneration and renewal, and my seminary education. Each of them, and more, are a grand miracle to my eyes of faith. I can see clearly now. I can possess true wisdom and intellect because of God's Spirit, and finally using the right hemisphere of my brain. God is so full of surprises. Nothing is impossible for Him. My life was a series of marvelous big or small **miracles**, it seemed.

The new synod president, Ray Wargelin, wrote: *"The past year was exceptional because of the receiving of new pastors. This is the largest number of pastors that our synod has ever ordained in one year. We wish God's blessing and the guidance of the Lord's Spirit upon all these young brother pastors in their important callings."[24]* Evidently, it was a golden era in the Suomi Synod.

Eino Tuori was elected the new synod president, but since he was loathe to move to Hancock, **Ray Wargelin** became interim president, and then was made permanent a year later. There were no women in the Lutheran clergy at this point in time. Lorraine Somers of Marquette, also in the Class of 1949, would become one of the first lady pastors in the forthcoming Lutheran Church in America. My mom was able to attend my ordination. Betty and I felt blessed indeed.

After this education and hard work, we took the month of July as a vacation month in Slapneck, before we moved to the Trout Creek parsonage. I began on August 1, 1954. It had been quite a year in our lives.

*   *   *

My deepest gratitude to all individuals and congregations who donated to the **Special Aid Fund** from which many of us drew resources in our respective needs. We will never know who they were, nor the amounts that each of us received toward our expenses. It was so simple then, compared to the indebtedness that today's seminary graduate experiences. It also always amazed me how Suomi College and Seminary could maintain such an underpaid staff with so few students enrolled. Did these people teach for free? Come to think of it, the total annual budget in the college's very first year in 1896 was a bit over $ 12,000. In 1943, during the war, the college had only forty-five students. Our Lord-Jumala must truly love Finlandia University for she is still succeeding, often having suffered persecution from her own church, which sought her demise. Suomi seems to be the apple of God's eye, which is simply another miracle.

Who spoke into my life at Suomi? Bernie Hillilä, David Halkola, Tom Kangas, Dick Rintala, Walt Werronen, Uuras Saarnivaara, Walter Kukkonen, Armas Holmio, Ed Isaac, Soini Torma, John Wargelin, Ray Wargelin, Herb Franz, Don Lehti, Norman Lund, Gusty Wuorinen, Henry Aukee, Art Hill, Toivo Rosenberg, and Betty Sjostrand.

Someone said in 2009 that the most dangerous temptations regarding one's Christian faith come in the seminary. The "historical critical" method used especially in radically liberal seminaries minimized the power of the Word of God and caused many students to doubt, be cynical, and lose their faith to unbelief. No wonder Lutheranism lost almost a million members in America in several decades. Helmut Thielicke warned, *"All this becomes impressively clear to me particularly by the way in which historical-critical study of the Bible affects young theologians. Why is it that it often inflicts upon the young believers severe and sometimes deadly wounds, while we theological teachers are unable to spare anyone these attacks?"*

Martin Luther in his *Bondage of the Will* wrote that *"here is the highest degree of faith . . . to believe that the God whose will it is that some should be condemned is nonetheless the most just God."* In my seminary experience, unlike today, I knew of no one who lost their faith while in our seminary. Our professors were all wonderful Christian men who rejected universalism, syncretism, antinomianism, Gnosticism, nihilism, and homosexuality. They were bible-believing men who knew their Lutheran Confessions and correctly taught them. But the storm in theology was already brewing, causing widespread concern among believers.

The Suomi Synod had close ties with Finnish theologians, who in turn revered **Michael Agricola**, the Finnish reformer, who had studied in Wittenberg in 1536-39 under Martin Luther and company. Dr. Saarnivaara specifically warned us about the coming wayward seminaries. And **Paavo Ruotsalainen** wrote in 1847:

"How can life be found where Christ who is life itself is not first received? For only after he has been received does life begin, and with it the doing of works of life . . . Terrible is the unbelief of the learned and the lords which deprives a man of the natural, simple ability to fall down before the Lord . . . there has now arisen a terrible controversy between the indifferent and the awakened."[25]

In seminary I majored in miracles, not mathematics. I learned that the conscience takes up more room in a human being than all the rest of a person's organs, as Mark Twain said. I learned what St. Paul wrote

"Talk about a cross is foolishness in the opinion of those who are being condemned, but to us who are being saved, it is the power of God."[26] Dr. Ray Holmes stated it well in his book, "The Road I Travel: My Journey Along the Narrow Way," *"Theological ideas are a matter of the mind, whereas religious experience is a matter of the heart."*

It has been said, if you don't remember being lost, you are. Honest preaching about the predicament of man clearly shows how lost we are. The lost don't believe that they are lost. Dishonest preaching ignores both man's creature-likeness and sinfulness. The Lutheran church's great contribution to Christendom is exactly this dimension of lostness, the doctrine of man, which is being ignored by liberal thinkers today. If you are tempted to think that I am overstating the case in these memoirs perhaps you are not yet old enough, or mature enough, or both, to understand the situation. I have been a student of history and the human condition for a very long time.

To use a sports metaphor, some forms of Christianity are able to get the runner to third base, but not home. My seminary made me a coach at third base with the will and ability to get the runner safely home. Honest preaching concerning sin and salvation, plus energetic visitation, is the success formula for most Christian pastors. But that success is not by the world's standards.

Now let's see how that simple formula worked in my career for the next three decades.

These were my thrilling days of yesteryear. And look! And here comes my first parish! Hang on!

Wasn't it Aristotle who said: *Educating the mind without educating the heart is no education at all.* But Horace countered in 68 B.C. with: *Mix a little folly with your wisdom; a little nonsense is pleasant now and then.*

Ebenezer! "Till now the Lord has helped us." 1 Samuel 7:12. "Blessed is the nation whose God is the Lord." Psalm 33:12.

CHAPTER EIGHT

Trout Creek Parish, Age 23-30, 1954-1961

A Batak woman on Indonesia's island of Sumatra wrote: *"When I wrote my thesis the pen knew what to write."* **This is somewhat my feeling as I write these memoirs: when I wrote my memoirs my personal computer knew what to write. Perhaps the Holy Spirit was the invisible part of this endeavor.**

He reminded me of the thin line between boasting and witnessing to the faith, and telling it like it was. Then there was the whole matter of knowing what to reveal and not to reveal, so as to protect the innocent. Considering the human propensity for evil, this was of course impossible, so the chips fell wherever. What will your memoirs look like?

My first twenty-three years of career preparation was now completed, and **Part II** begins right now. This part consisted of forty years of "ministry," three quarters of which were to three Upper Peninsula parishes, all located on or near Michigan **Highway-28**, extending from Matchwood in Ontonagon County in the west to Star Siding on the edge of the Seney Swamp to the east. It encompassed the area where the moose ran loose. . . Ewen, Bruce Crossing, Paynesville, Trout Creek, Kenton, Nestoria, Three Lakes, Michigamme, Champion, Humboldt, (Republic), Deerton, Shelter Bay, Au Train, Christmas, Munising, Wetmore, Shingleton, and Star Siding. It was wonderful country and had an abundance of rocks, sand, trees, animals and people.

My working years concluded with twelve years of "ministry to accumulated resources" with **Finlandia University** which effort would result in her survival in a transitional stage in which she became a full-fledged baccalaureate-giving university. The story of my preparation told you of some of the hazards of my life, my life-changing transformations in which I took ownership of the believing faith offered me. It included my call into the holy ministry and its preparation. Most of this, if not all, was not my doing, but the grace and work of a personal God. I had the powerful conviction that Someone was in charge of my life, an alien influence. The computer ran by itself and I merely moved my fingers.

In the spring of my final year in seminary I accepted the call to be pastor of the rural Trout Creek Parish. I succeeded Pastor **Arvo Korhonen**, who had been a classmate of the esteemed theologian and professor, Taito Kantonen. The parish knew exactly what they were getting as John and Gertrude Ollila had been managers of Lake Nesbitt Bible Camping for years, at which place seven years earlier I had come to saving faith. In fact, Mr. Ollila wrote my "Letter of Call."

* * *

This parish was as **rural** as any parish in the former Suomi Synod (Finnish Evangelical Lutheran Church in America). It was in the **Ontonagon Country**, a majestic river system in the western U.P. It fringed the Porcupine Mountain Wilderness State Park, where I would learn downhill skiing, and which park perennially rated among the top ten State Parks in the USA.

I was following Pastor Korhonen, who was a classic example of the goodness of **Finnish pietism** which heritage I was the grateful recipient. Arvo's only fault was his limited English language ability. I had the task of turning a basically Finnish-language parish into a modern English program. This made my new parish all the more exciting and challenging. I was hoping not to lose the piety so typical in the Suomi Synod, most of which were of the so-called *Awakened Movement.*

*   *   *

At the age of twenty-three, I rolled into Trout Creek with my '49 blue Chevy Club Coupe, nurse-wife Betty, and our four-month old son, Daniel. It was a warm day, **August 1, 1954**, and the final eight miles of M-28 was still a gravel road. We had basically nothing materially to bring; our new furniture for our nine-room parsonage had just arrived. The congregation-owned parsonage was impressively in the middle of town, having previously been the home of a medical doctor two decades earlier. *The Duluth South Shore Railroad* ran two hundred feet outside of my parsonage office window. My phone was on the wall with a crank; there were nineteen parties in the Trout Creek Telephone Co., and our ring was two short and three long.

The parish encompassed three townships: Interior, Standard and McMillan (Trout Creek, Bruce Crossing-Paynesville, Ewen and Kenton). Farming and logging were the chief employers until White Pine Copper Company opened a huge drive-in copper mine during our tenure.

So imposing was the latter that a bus ran through the parish to transport miners for the three shifts per day. The copper mines had a history of being dangerous. Marcia's uncle, Eugene Belmas, was killed at White Pine. Literally hundreds of miners died in Upper Peninsula mines, including, in Painesdale, Betty's great-grandfather. For every death there were a hundreds of injuries. The phrase, "costing an arm and a leg" originated in these mines. All mining was dangerous.

The parish was surrounded by the Ottawa National Forest, which had an office in Kenton. South Ontonagon County, my parish area, had a population of 3,500. This was the physical setting. My starting salary was $ 3,229 for the first year. A "clergy discount" gave us a ten percent discount on delivered dairy products, and the local Shingler grocery gave us a fourteen percent off. It was common to ask for a *clergy discount.* Our nearest large-town shopping area was in Ironwood, fifty miles away. This was the beautiful rural hinterland.

*   *   *

To tell the story of life in our first parish, it is best that I comment primarily on the **parish as a whole**. All four of my congregations were basically within fifteen miles on an east-west highway. Within a year the entire highway was new blacktop. The hospitals which served our members were in Ontonagon, Wakefield, Ironwood, L'Anse and Phelps, Wisconsin, the nearest being 38 miles away. I was expending 40,000 miles a year on my cars. In 1955 we purchased a new green Chevy station wagon from the brother of the first parish resident pastor, Ferdinand Kaskinen, who delivered the product from Kaleva in Lower Michigan. Next I purchased a 1958 blue Chevy station wagon from Marttinen Brothers of Mass City, and finally a 1960 Ford Falcon wagon from Walter Kemppainen of Ewen Motors. Relatively speaking transportation was a big ticket item.

The givens were further enhanced by the presence of **two sawmills** in Trout Creek, the large Abbott Fox Lumber Company, and the Nordine Sawmill. Wages in '54 were low, as it was not uncommon for a man with a family to earn only a dollar an hour, or eight dollars per day. So when we talk about spending four thousand dollars on new church furniture, as in Ewen, or building a new church in Trout Creek for $24,000, we are talking bigger money than you might think.

Betty and I continued to **tithe** our incomes, which meant giving away the first ten percent. By so doing it assured that the remaining ninety percent went further. Go figure. Furthermore, if we didn't set a giving example in the parish, we could not expect others to do so. In spirituality one cannot lead the members any higher, or deeper, than the leadership. Giving is truly the fourth of man's top four questions in life. I can recall how Nels and Ellen Tahtinen of Trout Creek were model givers, and Nels was a fireman at the sawmill.

Politically, Duncan Cameron who owned Cameron's Bar in Trout Creek was the south county "Mr. Democrat;" many Finns were Democrats.27 I inherited a Republican era as Dwight Eisenhower was president, but shortly John Kennedy ran and won the presidency. I could not vote for him. Godless Finnish socialism in the area was centered on North Baltimore Road near Bruce Crossing but McCarthy-ism and the Winter War in Finland quieted them down. Many socialists were about to become parish members. I knew of only one family, Olli Timonen, who, having gone to Russia in the 1930s, had escaped from Russian Karelia. and they were members. I voted Republican at this period in my life.

A huge and successful Settler's Co-operative centered in Bruce Crossing, headed by Eben's Carl Norberg and his wife Ida (nee: Luoma). It featured a dairy, credit union, milling, oil business, in addition to branch stores for mercantile. Ewen represented a more business type of community with a bank, MSU Extension Service, medical doctor, lumber yard, auto dealership, and numerous businesses. There was limited tourism and two of the U.P.'s finest waterfalls,

Bond Falls.

Agate and Bond, were located here. Hunting and fishing was outstanding. At the time the largest manufacturer of Finnish sauna stoves, *Niippa Sauna*, was located in Bruce Crossing.

A positive church climate existed. The parish had been blessed with a number of lay preachers and speakers, almost all immigrants from the *Awakened movement* in Finland. Among them were Herman Lindell, John Helin, John Perttula, Nestor Sjögren, Antti Asikainen, Victor Fräntilä, John Fränti, Maria Sironen and Joel Moilanen. With the addition of Covington, prior to my arrival, Pastor Korhonen and others before him were unable to be in every congregation every Sunday, so these lay speakers filled the vacuum. These speakers gradually diminished by death before and during my early years in the parish. Such lay speakers were common in the Finnish pietistic movements, as it is carried on within the Laestadian congregations still today. I was not yet a pastor, truth be told, but this outstanding rural parish would "knead" a real pastor out of me. I would forever be indebted to them for that.

*   *   *

Immediately upon arrival parish life greeted me with **tragedies**, mostly concerning youth. This was real life mingled with real death. It is true that Satan is out to kill us. Erland Perttu was my first funeral within several weeks; he died at age twenty-three from lockjaw as a result of working the farm in Bruce Crossing.

I processed the first confirmation class upon arrival. Two students, Norman Sormula and Richard Nelmark, the latter the school superintendent's son, went to Ironwood to buy new suits for confirmation. There was a car crash on the way home and Nelmark, 15, was killed. Sormula was in the hospital for six months. The following deer season Bob Mattson from the same class, was deer hunting on opening day. An unknown hunter shot him through the neck, killing him instantly. Soulcare was immediately of importance, and the perpetrator is still at large. Our local funeral home was Brown's Funeral Home in Bruce Crossing; George Brown was the son of a Methodist pastor; he became a good friend.

*   *   *

Also, upon my arrival the parish council had a special request, that I would pay special attention to the **youth** of the parish. It became obvious that my special achievements were in the following areas: solid worship, youth work, Finnish immigrant focus, evangelism, building a new church, and Suomi Synod piety. The total membership on arrival was four hundred forty-three in the parish.

Worship would in two years reach a point where I had five and four services on alternate Sundays, resulting in an average Sunday attendance of three hundred and two. Weather was never a factor and I never canceled services with bad weather as an excuse. One Sunday morning it was minus 43 degrees but worship went on unaffected.

The Ewen church, First Lutheran, was blessed with three choirs and nine organists who were Hilda Ojala, Marlys Ojala-Roberts, Gert Moilanen, Ida Fränti, Alice Fränti-Leno, Ruth Moilanen, Ruth Nordine-Chown, Senia Suomumäki, and Barbara Fleming. Other parish organists were Gert Ollila, Sandra Helsius, Marilyn Mänty, Kay Linna and Carol Linna. Lenten mid-week worship went on in three churches. For some years it was helpful when the time zone ran right through the middle of the parish. Worship was enhanced in Ewen in 1960 by $4000 worth of new church pews and chancel furniture. The old theater seats had served their purpose and were discarded. Ewen also boasted of four of the finest Finnish rag-rug makers in the entire Midwest, in Hilda Ojala, Patsy Daniels, Lempi and Taisto Holmstrom. Hilda's rug is the first rug on the jacket of a 2010 coffee table book by Yvone Lockwood entitled *Finnish American Rag Rugs*.

Youth work resulted in a Luther League of over 100 high school youth, divided among three leagues. Many youth enrolled at Suomi College, including seven from the Sanford Ojala family from Ewen. The 3-team softball league among boys was popular. Some youth attended the largest Sunday service (125,000) in the history of Lutheranism in the nation, namely the Lutheran World Federation service at St. Paul, MN, capitol building in 1957. The Trout Creek church bought a school bus for the work of youth and Christian education. *Västerås* bible study of New Testament epistles was effectively used by our teenagers. I immersed myself in being their youth pastor. I drove that bus, filled with youth, to area rallies and conventions, picnics, swimming, camping, downhill skiing, the longest trip being to the Lower Peninsula ten hours away. It was our youth who assembled our monthly parish newsletters.

Two Trout Creek young men became pastors: **Roy Tähtinen** and **David Taeger**. A Paynesville girl, **Judy Mattson**, long a lay pastor, was ordained in 2010. I baptized her when she was four. After the baptism she wrote in wet cement but we never found out what that meant. Several youth served in the Peace Corps: Robert Knivilä and Verna Johnson. Many became teachers.

Youth work had gone on previously as the following became pastors: John Hattula, Rueben Perttula, George Hautala, and Ahti Karjala. Tyyne Kaare was a child evangelist. Many became pastor's wives: Saima Kaare, Lois and Marlys Ojala, Alice Fränti. In Ewen Brian Crocker, whom I baptized, became a pastor, son of Nancy Fränti and Gary Crocker. The young man I thought might become one died young with AIDS. The chapter on our parish youth work was an outstanding chapter in this parish.

On a personal level the immigrant generation of this parish taught me both theology and the **Finnish** language. Maria Sironen of Ewen was noteworthy regarding depth of faith. How grateful I am that they allowed me to learn the Finnish language so that I could share the gospel with them. This ability allowed me to minister to immigrants in: Ewen, North Bruce, Paynesville, Trout Creek, Republic, Munising, Eben, Newberry, and Ishpeming, all on a regular basis. Ability to read and research Finnish theology was an advantage in the formation of personal spirituality.

I recall visiting Sanna Lehto in a home call who was severely ill and she thought the end was near. Soulcare dictated the agenda. Though she had been a faithful lifelong member her ultimate concern in facing death was the forgiveness of her sins. As it happened she recovered and lived much longer.

The basic task of **evangelism**, making Jesus Christ known to the point of personal faith and discipleship, in the Trout Creek Parish was as important as her youth work. In seven years I received 324 new adult members, or 46 per year. Membership classes of six sessions were held at least twice yearly; one class had 26 socialist background folks. We employed the *Preaching-Teaching-Reaching (PTR) Missions* to their utmost potential. One such series averaged 242 worshipers per evening for a week in that parish.

Isn't it interesting that Congress put *In God We Trust* on all our coins one year after I arrived in my first parish, and in 1956 it was made our official national motto? Not only as individuals but also our nation found strength through faith in God, and that it is He that bestows blessings on America, including our liberty. We need to remember this in 2011, the year of these memoirs.

My outstanding evangelism story in our Preaching-Teaching-Reaching program was when Reino Lakanen visited former classmate Ensio Suhonen to invite him to church. They were both bachelors and age 53. When Reino explained why he had come, Ensio replied: *"Why haven't you come before?"* He joined, got married, and when I left that parish Ensio was the head of the building committee. I took in 82 new members in my first year in the parish. They were coming out of the woodwork, as the saying goes. The parish membership grew to 683 which represented an increase of 47% in an area that had decreased in population by 10%. The Holy Spirit was quite evident.

Part of the Americanization process of this parish was to designate specific names for two congregations who had none. The congregation in Paynesville took the name **Our Saviour Lutheran Church**. The official name in Trout Creek became **Trinity Lutheran Evangelical Church**. (The order of that wording was by design.)

Architect **Eino Kainlauri** of KKM Associates, helped Trout Creek both move and enlarge its church building in 1959. It would be the first of two churches he would design in my parishes, Munising being the other. And he did this while living in far-away Ann Arbor. We picked up the old church, held a communion service in it while it was "on wheels" parked over Sunday by the side of the road, and planted it in the middle of the village, to become a terrific community center and church. The floor space was doubled. The dedication was on **June 12, 1960.** The Men's Brotherhood had interesting funding projects for the expenses such as a field of oats, and a pulp project of a railroad carload of peeled pulp. It was very exciting. And we did it for the price of a small automobile (in 2010), namely, $ 24,000.

After we moved the extensively remodeled church to the heart of the village, we did an evergreen tree planting project as a fund drive. We had saplings left over. Betty took those left-over starts to the old site and planted them. Today they are fifty feet high and an historical marker stands nearby with the words: ***Betty's Grove***. It is also a memorial to Betty who died twenty years later. Her trees whisper her name in the gentle west breeze.

Other ministries went on as expected; Christian education and stewardship. We had a unique young married **couple's club** in Ewen, which consisted of couples in their twenties. Largely for fellowship, it kept these young couples out of the bars and into wholesome group events such as camping in the Porkies, smelting, walleye fishing, and home events.

I remember particularly the overnight camping trip to **Mirror Lake** in the Porcupine Mountain State Park. It was a long hike. I knew there were brook trout lurking in the lake so we brought fish poles. I had been brook trout fishing just prior to this event, so I decided to include a mess of them in my backpack. I went fishing alone then pretended that I caught them from Mirror Lake. The plot worked perfectly. They saw me pull up one fish after another, while they were being shut out. Later, we ate them; someone commented on their gray eyes. Finally, I was compelled by conscience to confess what I had done. They never forgot how cunning I could be as their pastor.

At the risk of omission, some of the **great people** of this parish were: Gert and John Ollila, K.J. and Gert Moilanen (Gert was the daughter of Pastor Matt Luttinen of the very first 1906 ordination class from Suomi Seminary), Jalmer and Aileen Mänty, Wäinö and Linda Linna, Reino and Weikko Lakanen, The Ojala Family, Arne Lehto, Aileen Taeger, Jim and Barbara Fleming, Bill and Ellen Perttula, and Nels and Ellen Tähtinen. There are so many more. They "spoke into my life" in this parish.

* * *

. While in Trout Creek, our **family** was blessed with two more sons. On August 10, 1955, **Michael Jonathan** was born in Marquette, again by Caesarean section. Once Michael as a baby swallowed a 67 cents adhesive-backed price tag. But a day later as his mother was changing his diaper, there came a little hard round stool with this price tag neatly stuck to its outside: 67 cents. It seemed inflationary.

Our third son was born three years later at the Ontonagon Memorial Hospital when we welcome **Nathan Lloyd** on December 16, 1958. Betty had worked at the White Pine Hospital so long that she had confidence in Dr. Don Archibald which explains why Nathan was born in Ontonagon. This would be the limit of our family, except for one more. . . .

That one was a husky eighty pound pet dog named ***Boxer***. He was not pure but had those typical boxer characteristics. His favorite trick with Dan and Mike was to bat them down into the soft snow and just hold them there. We were sad to leave him in Trout Creek when we left in 1961. He kept strangers honest. We were a family of six, living in a nice old house with a white picket fence. Our parsonage was our only parsonage of our career with a sauna. It was in the basement of the house, and it was a joy also for our young men.

Although I was far too busy to deserve a family, at least my office was in the parsonage, making me more visible to them. After Betty went to work at the White Pine Hospital, the nanny for the boys was **Aileen Taeger**. The parish was outstandingly nice to us as a family, and in every possible way.

*   *   *

In addition to the parish schedule, I also felt it necessary to serve the **church-at-large**, beyond local parish boundaries. Social ministry was not yet what it would be in later parishes. I was elected to the board of trustees of **Suomi College** during a critical time when bankruptcy almost closed the college in 1959. At a particular board meeting I supported the motion to give the college one more chance. We called **Ralph Jalkanen** as the new president who went on to save the college, and served in the office for 30 years. It was he who later hired me in 1983. I was on the board for seven years during which time we built three new buildings (Mannerheim and Wargelin Halls and Paavo Nurmi Fieldhouse), and we fought off the adversaries (like bishops, other church colleges, and our own church hierarchy) all of whom were clearly intent on closing our school.

I had a unique experience in August of 1958, along with Ray Salim, of transporting the Suomi **Seminary library** to Maywood, Illinois, whereupon the seminary merged with Chicago Lutheran Seminary. Ray and I rented a U-haul trailer for the task. Beer-drinking seminarians and faculty in Chicago did not think highly of Suomi pietism. Else they would not have hoisted in 1960 on the campus flagpole a bed sheet with black skull and crossbones thereon and the words *"Death to pietism."* Welcome, Suomi Synod, to the world of liberal theology!

I excelled in **synod youth work**. I succeeded Gert and John Ollila as the business manager of the conference bible camping program for youth and children, located at Sidnaw nineteen miles away. It is hard to imagine that camping at that time cost only $ 9 to $11.00 for the week. Youth work was as educational and evangelistic as it had always been in our unique piety, until the time of Lutheran Church in America merger in 1963. The Suomi "men for the ministry" program was highly successful prior to church merger for raising new young pastors.

I distinguished myself in leading several **"town and country"** church endeavors in 1957 and 1960. The first was an M-28 church self-study regarding parish alignment which encompassed the Covington to Berglund area. **Dr. E. W. Mueller** of the National Lutheran Council rural church office in Chicago came as a guest resource. It subsequently resulted in my being invited to move to his Chicago Loop office as his associate. Live in Chicago? I turned down the offer, but recommended Giles C. Ekola, my friend, who served in that capacity for twelve years. I also organized a conference T & C workshop for rural churches in Marquette in 1960.

*   *   *

A somewhat related activity took Betty and me to do a survey during a vacation month to **New Port Richey,** Florida, in 1957 for our Home Mission Board. We called on every home in town. It resulted in Eli Lepistö developing a congregation there the following year and he was subsequently the pastor for twenty years. During that month we went to the Columbia Restaurant in Ybor City in Tampa. They were televising the show and I was fearful that pious Finns in NPR would see us on TV, and not understand. Our table was not far from that of Bob Hope and Miss America. Fifty years later Finnish Lutheranism is alive and well in New Port Richey at both the church and the Finnish social hall.

Now, you must not get the impression that it was all work and no play. We took our first three **vacations** to Florida, 1956, '57 and '58. Our first trip to South Miami was 19 days, and our total expenses were $ 255.40. Remember my earlier comment about thrift. On our final seven hundred dollar trip to Miami Beach we took Dan and Mike along. We were young. We also spent some time on summer vacations at Hugo and Ellen's new cottage at Lake Au Train, built in 1957. They were Betty's parents.

The Suomi Synod being a nation-wide church, our annual **conventions** were apt to be in far-away-places. It afforded us to see almost all the synod clergy and top-level laity annually. Our boys had opportunity to meet and mingle with the finest young people and clergy of our church. It was sort of a poor man's vacation. The parish usually helped with expenses.

Other **hobbies** we enjoyed in our first parish were downhill skiing, brook trout fishing, deer hunting, and golf. Trout **fishing** would obviously be very good in place called Trout Creek. The biggest trouble was coping with the woodticks. Beaver dam fishing was so good that one had to bait the hook behind a tree.

In 1958 Betty introduced us to **skiing,** by going directly to the Porkies Ski Hill on Wednesday afternoons from work at White Pine. I bought my first laced boots and steel edged Northland skis from Rudy Saari Sports in Ontonagon. President Ray Wargelin from Hancock would often meet me at the hill, as did Rudy Kemppainen from the Wakefield parish. Dan was able to conquer the Porkies from the top before he began kindergarten. The view from up there of Lake Superior was breathtaking.

Men of the parish made sure I was a man's pastor by taking me deer **hunting.** Such men were Arne Lehto, Weikko Lakanen, the Taeger brothers, Nels Tähtinen, and Wäinö Nykänen. Arne had a thing about burning white pine stumps. I shot my animal almost every year in this parish. Two deer stood outside the sacristy window one Sunday of deer season in Trout Creek, trying to distract my preaching. Often I hunted so close to home in this great parish that I could hear my dog, *Boxer*, barking in the parsonage yard.

During summers my favorite **golf** partner was Fred Bergfeld, the Wisconsin Synod pastor from Bruce Crossing; we became good friends. We did a half dozen courses but mostly Land O'Lakes WI, where one drove on the first hole from Wisconsin into Michigan. Golf is a dangerous game. One day I took John Kaare and Arne Lehto golfing. It was their first time. On the second tee John glanced his drive to the right, hit Arne on the wrist and broke the bone. From then on it was hit the ball and drag Arne. What meager night-clubbing we did, it was in Vilas County, WI, which resort area had excellent supper clubs. Although it was not far away, I felt safe there as members were not in the habit of crossing the border. Pietism might not look kindly at this. At least, so I thought. You see, in this seemingly hinterland parish in the middle of nowhere, we lacked for nothing, and we were totally content.

*   *   *

In Stannard Township, so heavy Finnish, I held two-language services in **North Bruces** to which 25 came, and we would have coffee after each Sunday evening event twice a month. In the forties **Paynesville** was once an outstanding farm parish. It was there that when I took two-year old Dan with me to call on aged Susanna Pouttu, that she looked at him and said: *"Niin pieni matkamies,"* which meant: Such a small pilgrim! In my time the power structure was Nieminen, Niemelä and Niemi, in Paynesville.

I married gorgeous June Illikainen and flashy Gilbert Kotila in Paynesville. What a handsome couple. Gil became a successful Bruce Crossing business man, manufacturing saunas (Niippa) and serving good food (*Grandma's*). When June and Gil **divorced** while I was in the parish, it was the only divorce during my entire ministry there. But here's the rest of the story: After I had left, I heard that June and Gil remarried.

Paynesville was the home of **Maija-Liisa Wuorenmaa** who lived to 104. I would visit her. Arne and Carol Huhtala, in downtown Paynesville, ran the Settler's branch Co-op. I had baptized the entire family. Arne had trouble keeping those boys from crossing the busy state highway. They kept finding them across the road, and repeated reprimands were fruitless. They insisted they were innocent and had not crossed the road. Finally, it became clear that the boys had <u>not</u> cross the road, as they claimed, but they crawled through the culvert. Very innovative. They had not lied, and we were so sure they had.

Ewen was the home of Aliina Nykänen who lived to 101. Reino Sironen's home was the site of the only time in my career that I **forgot** to show up for an engagement. We were already in bed when the phone rang and big Reino's gruff voice was heard: *"Pastor, did you forget something?"* This teddy-bear type man, whose firm built our Trout Creek Church, forgave me, and we re-schedule the two baptisms to September 5, 1957 for his granddaughters, Polly Ann Sironen and Cindy Lou Soronen.

One day in August Jim and Barb Fleming, and Betty and I, **canoed** the entire South Branch of the Ontonagon River from Ewen to Victoria Dam. The route was rapids infested. In the end there was only one dry arm amongst us. But we did it, and in time for me to appear at a Ewen evening bible study in the Finnish language at a North Cemetery Road home. I recall having had trouble staying awake.

Incidentally, the biggest **flooding** of my lifetime in the U.P. happened in April 1960 when the entire peninsula had about twelve inches of rainfall in three days, and that added to the usual spring run-off. That same river we canoed was overflowing the state highway by a foot of water. At Lake Au Train, I took notes, and when I built my cottage two years later I set the floor elevation of my cottage based on the high water mark of that flooding. One must know the history.

* * *

God gave me yet another chance, when on July 10, 1960, I was happily motoring up the Baltimore Hill, just west of Bruce Crossing, to a evening Finnish worship service at the Ewen church. The sun was directly in my eyes climbing this incline on M-28. There was a sickening **loud crashing** sound, when my '58 station wagon spun around and the next thing I saw was a man on a tractor. Mr. Lähde of nearby Matchwood was hauling a double tandem trailer of bailed hay. He had been sort of straddling the edge of the blacktop, and I drove 50 mph, without braking, into the left rear corner of his load of hay. But I had been rehearsing, not wanting to waste a moment. I had my hymnal out and singing in Finnish: *"Ei murhetta mulla oo täällä, kun Jeesus on kanssani tääll'."* (I have no worries here since Jesus is here with me...) Indeed! It's an unbelievable story to me. I see a miracle. Someone was still in charge of my life. An empty pop bottle from the back of the wagon got me in the back of the head, requiring five Dr. Hoage stitches. I was fifteen minutes late to the church, but they would not let me do the service. Oh well, that vehicle had over 80,000 miles anyway, and a leak in the gas tank. This was only one of two services that I missed in 29 years in active ministry (in the other I was so dizzy with influenza that I could not stand up, in the same parish.) Weather was never a problem. Moral: Cell phones while driving should be illegal, and singing of hymns.

Are dreams important? One is certainly a "right brain" person when one begins to listen to dreams, don't you think? The bible is saturated by stories about dreams. I had a recurring dream causing guilt. My dream was that I seldom gave my Ewen congregation enough attention. I would run out of time. I would run out of energy before I got to Ewen. And it caused me to feel guilty in my dream. Does that make sense? Yet, in reality, Ewen was a shining light of success in my first parish, and filled with great people, who got along well even without me.

Also in 1960, when I was in Duluth, chaperoning a youth deputation team which visited local Luther Leagues, I visited the **Duluth Clinic**. They generously did clergy examinations for gratis. The doctor was concerned about my weight, having ballooned to 235 lbs., and detected a slightly too-high blood pressure. Upon hearing my story, he counseled that I move from my present parish. Was he speaking into my life? In short, this, and the accident, concerned me.

* * *

65

Now a few stories about **Trout Creek**: South of Trout Creek was the Saari-Hogbacka Farm. Selma Saari and Oscar Hogbacka were sister and brother. They had **cats**. I went there to make a pastoral visit (remember those?) And at the porch screen door was a foot-long brook trout, recently arrived and flopping on the ground. It seems that this family of cats had learned to fish. A small stream ran through the backyard which emptied into Trout Creek. The mother cat would teach the offspring how to reach down with sharp claws and pull up fish of all sizes. The skill ran from generation to generation. Wasn't it Jeannie Bentti who wrote in her new book *"Accepting wisdom is as difficult as catching a brook trout with your bare hands."*28 These cats were impressive and I wished I could have done that.

When my friend Rudy arrived as the new pastor in Wakefield in the late 50s, he wasted no time in having a tall rotating TV antenna installed on the parsonage roof. A Mr. Niemi, an immigrant layman, no relation, took one look at the spectacle and said in Finnish: *"Pappilan katon päälle on pantu **pirun sarvet**."* (They have put **the devil's horns** on the parsonage roof.) The same happened to the Trout Creek parsonage in 1956. Our very first television set was a small portable black and white General Electric. Even with the rotating antlers on our roof we could barely pull in Marquette, Duluth and Rhinelander. And that layman's perspective and prophecy is truer today than we wish or dare to believe.

Another little addition was in the parsonage basement. I purchased a big heavy **printing press** from Setterlund Dry Cleaners in Ironwood for fifty dollars. We made church materials such as schedules, postcards, pledge cards, tickets, and posters. We slid it down planks to get it in, but no one ever got it out. It is still there. The youth had fun working it. It was so heavy that it might have doubled for an anchor for an ore boat. Also, once I caught a baby **woodchuck** and let him loose in that same parsonage basement. There was a crack in the southwest corner of the foundation, and wouldn't you know that little guy squeezed himself through it to freedom. In Martin Luther's time, the parsonage was a model for community and society.

I was so busy in this parish (and subsequent parishes) that there was no time to think about that notion of getting that bachelor's degree. Degrees don't mean much when hard work needs doing. Yet, I managed on a limited basis to pick up some **continuing education**. With the extension agent, K.J. Moilanen, we took several extension courses from Michigan State. I took a Northern Michigan history class held in Ontonagon. I took a summer course at Garrett Bible Institute on the campus of Northwestern University near Chicago, and at Michigan State University.

I don't remember much about the subject at Garrett, but I recall how I got home. I **hitch-hiked** home from Evanston each Friday. I pre-arranged to meet Betty in Three Lakes WI at 9:00 p.m. Dusk came late in the summers. I would begin hitch-hiking at noon from Evanston, taking U.S.-45 north. When folks learned that I was clergy, many began to confess their sins to me. I was anonymous and they would never see me again. A pastor's work is forgiving sins. It was uncanny how close I came each Friday to reaching our meeting point at 9:00. Then I'd preach four times and go back on Sunday afternoons. Hitch-hiking was very safe to do in the 50s. Even women picked me up, but they were not wild women.

Jimmy Hoffa owned a resort within this parish. It was at Tepee Lake, about four miles south of Kenton. After his unexplained disappearance his son, Jim, has continued to spend summers there. I regret not succeeding to attract Mr. Hoffa to worship at Trinity in Trout Creek. Incidentally, the first of over a thousand new adult members in my career was a simple-minded nice man named **Severi Leinonen**. He was definitely challenged. He hung out with our churchmen and came to church, so why shouldn't he be a full member? I was proud of Severi.

Not long after arriving in Trout Creek, the Midway Telephone Co. came in with a new company and system. We were fast coming of age. Bob Godell pondered: What am I going to do for an initial phone book? I volunteered gratis to print the first **telephone book** for the area with my magic mimeograph machine in my office. And Bob was happy, and I still have a copy.

Trout Creek had a K-12 school system at the time and our school under Coach Bruce Warren put out championship basketball teams. He soon became also the superintendent and one of his problems was **substitute teachers**. I did a lot of on-the-spur-of-the-moment teaching, including sometimes a month at a time. I was one of the best educated people in town. How wonderful those children and youth were back then!

The land for the first church in Trout Creek halfway between TC and Agate, was donated by John Ollila Sr. **Marissa Mayer** is often seen on national television representing *Google Corporation*, this huge information-revolution behemoth. Marissa is the granddaughter of Esther Hautamäki-Hallberg, who grew up a mile from Betty's Grove. Esther is the granddaughter of this original John Ollila Sr, who gave the land. And she was the wife of Pastor Oliver Hallberg. You never know what good genes, and a very good gospel environment can do.

It was not easy to be a pastor in a four-congregation parish. Lots of duplication, three youth groups, three congregation councils, a parish council, four Sunday and three Vacation Church schools, on and on it goes. It was not uncommon for me to have 21 straight evenings of meetings. The boys long ago stopped asking: "Where's dad?" They knew dad was at work, dad was doing soul care, dad was doing hospital calls, dad has a funeral . . .

Charles VanGorder reflected: *"If I had my life to do all over again, I'd do it the same way - - - - go somewhere small where people have a need, contribute to people who need it; help people."* My self-therapy was helping others.

Much of church work is left brain stuff, often Mickey Mouse stuff, imposed by the hierarchy. . .often only numbers and dollars and wood and cement. This is the external part. What about the internal, inward things? Is it only "head" knowledge, or does it affect the heart, the core of man? It was put well by the grand-daughter of Matt Luttinen (who was in the first Suomi Seminary ordination class of 1906); **Ruth Moilanen** said on the eve of her confirmation at age 15:"*Pastor, I know a lot <u>about</u> Jesus, but I am not sure that I <u>know</u> Jesus!*" And she was in tears. And I was listening. She was asking, or commenting, on the right question. How much truly spiritual happened in my seven years in my first parish? Soulcare demanded that I had to be able to forgive sins, to prepare an individual for death, and the here-after. Those were the *Kodak moments*.

One can pretend to be busy, but are we busy with the right things? One thing I discovered is that all the work will never get completed. Therefore I learned a phrase "**intelligent neglect.**" Be on top of it and choose what you will leave undone. Another concept that is comforting to those of us, who are not meant to serve in the plush suburbs of Milwaukee, Minneapolis, or Detroit, is that we be aware of "*psychic income.*" Psychic income is that invisible, non-monetary income, that comes when we live in God's country, where we are only 20 minutes from fishing our favorite lake trout hole or beaver dam, or a half hour from our downhill ski hill, or where our cats can catch brook trout in the back yard and bring them to the door of the house. Those suburban hotshots need to spend a lot of money and time to get to do those peaceful things that for those in rural ministry are just around the corner. Yes, for a Finnish pastor, just taking a sauna is one of those. Did you know that it is impossible to come out of a sauna angry?

* * *

So the time came that Les and Betty had to consider what God next had in store for them. A sincere "call" arrived from one of the charter congregations of the Suomi Synod in November of 1960. It was one of those "*Come-over-to- Macedonia-and-help-us*"29 calls. I would be following the outstanding Finnish-trained *Evangelical-movement* pastor **Alpo Setälä**, who had once served the prestigious Maaria Parish just outside of Turku, Finland, and who had on two separate terms served **Bethany Lutheran** of Republic.

That call was echoed by a 32-year old Republic housewife:

> "*We certainly do hold a big welcome sign to you and your family. . . . and have and do hope and pray it is the Lord's will for you to come. We have on the whole, a good group of people, but we lack good leadership and need it so desperately, old and young. We've all heard how much interest Les takes in youth work and that too would be such a blessing here! To tell you the truth, right now there's nothing to help the young folks interested in church . . . and the situation on the whole, at present, seems pretty sad! I do try to remember 'The Lord's will be done' . . . so prayerfully and hopefully, may we see you soon?*"30

In the meantime, after I had submitted my resignation at Sunday worship throughout the Trout Creek Parish, and accepted the call to Republic, the mother of future pastor **Roy Tähtinen**, her name was Ellen, wrote these portions of a 13-stanza poem. She wrote from the heart:

"A man of God sent to us in '54;
A mere boy then, no battle scars he bore;
A parish perfect was his youthful dream;
Preach Christ to all whom God in love redeemed,
To gather in those children, too, of God,
Who knew it not, yet saved by precious blood.
He found a stiff-necked people he must lead
On stewardship of treasure, time and deed. . .

The shepherd looking back upon the years
Of strife, and work, and fun, and sometimes tears,
Of confirmands, of loved ones who passed on,
Reflects, 'Those I turned well may fall away;
Those turned by God will love and serve and pray.'
When time has honor on your brow bestowed,
Your shoulders firm must bear a heavy load,
Remember then, those former grounds you've trod,
Your voice has echoed here the will of God."[31]

How touching are those words? How holy the job descriptions of those who answer the call to holy ministry? How utterly grateful to our *Jumala*-God for His grace, which alone deserves all honor and glory. This was Suomi Synod pietism, pure and simple, as expressed by a layperson. How I loved the members of my first parish, each one of them!

But now I must take leave. I must move 75 miles further east along M-28. For I can hear the call: "*Come over to help us.*" Such is the pastor's work. So it has always been, and so it is still. Did they love me too much? Was I guilty of love avoidance because of that? No, don't try to figure it out. It was the will of God, as we knew it.

In hindsight I should certainly not have needed to feel sorry about this parish "losing us," considering how fortunate they were with not only the next pastor, but the **next two pastors**. Dr. Ray and Shirley Holmes, later destined to become a seminary professor, was my immediate successor. Ray claimed that he received his "call" into the ministry at my ordination service at his home congregation in Waukegan, and while singing in the choir. A minor negative was that he did not speak Finnish. He was followed by Dr. John and Betty Linna, an Ishpeming native, who after he left Ewen served only one other congregation, United Church in Crystal Falls for the next 37 years. These folks were superior in both intellect and spirituality. The Linnas lived in the new parsonage in Ewen.

On April 6, 1961 some nice men from Republic came to move our furniture to the historic Republic parsonage. Only *Boxer* got left in Trout Creek at the Marvin and Gert Leaf home. We never saw Boxer again.

I was age 30, now a seven year **veteran** of my first parish, where I had a basket full of successes in both external and internal forms. But St. Paul warned, *"Don't think overly about yourself, more than you have reason to think, but keep your thoughts within bounds, each one within the measure of the faith which God has given him."*[32]

The temptation is to imagine great things about ourselves. Only the Holy Spirit can teach us to think soberly and humbly about ourselves. Paul and Barnabas in Lystra were greeted as gods. They answered that they were only men, human like all others. When the Spirit shows us that we are human then we are united with others at the lowest level, as mere sinners. But if believing is only by grace, then no one is more special than another. Hence we have no reason nor need to boast. *Let him who boasts, boast in the Lord*, said St. Paul. Love does not envy or boast. I will boast most gladly about my weakness. Far be it for me to boast except in the cross of our Lord Jesus Christ.

While I was pastor in the Trout Creek Parish, my dear grandmother, **Alma**, suffered a painful death with cancer, passing away in the Marquette hospital on November 5, 1957. She was age 70. Pastor John Hattula, Trout Creek native, of Marquette, officiated the funeral in Munising.

Dan began kindergarten in 1959 and Mike started the following year. They were simply able to walk one block to the school. Dan made us promise not to watch him go on the first day; he was spreading his wings. *Peace Corps* began the year we left Trout Creek on which Knivilä and Johnson-Numinen would serve.

To walk to the middle of the street in front of our parsonage in Trout Creek afforded the unique view of rotating in a circle and viewing the homes of Michigan State basketball star Bob Gale, major league pitcher Jim Manning, major league pitcher and pitching coach Dick Pole, the home of Florida State University president Bernie Sliger, and three Lutheran pastors (Hattula, Tähtinen and Taeger). Manning and Taeger coached the congregation's Little League team. How can a small poverty-ridden village in Interior Township have such results?

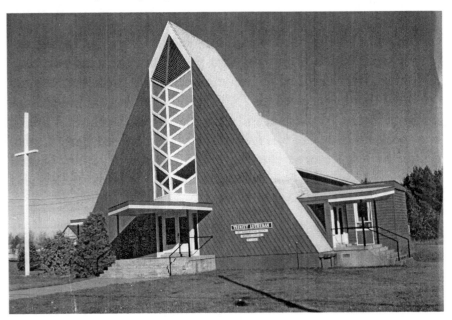

Trout Creek Church, 1961

Les Niemi, ca 1961

CHAPTER NINE

Republic, Age 30-34, 1961-1965

Why am I telling you all this? I am aware of the diversity of audiences who may read these memoirs. Once upon a time we would have understood one another perfectly; no longer! However, my story may be able to relate to your personal spiritual journey, as we engage the spiritual stagnation of our modern times. Furthermore, wasn't it Winston Churchill who wrote: *The farther backwards you can look, the farther forward you are likely to see.*

The volunteer movers from Republic, had come and gone with our humble furniture. I had to leave my printing press. I have tried to travel light. The world's goods did not enchant me. To become clergy is to take a vow of poverty. But we trusted God more than we trusted man.

*   *   *

We loaded up our "fab five" into our **'60 Ford Falcon** station wagon: Les 30, Betty 30, Dan 7, Mike 6, and Nathan almost three. As soon as the rivers started flowing south, we stopped to rest at a bridge near Lake Michigamme, around the place where the Michigamme and Sturgeon rivers had once connected (before the water went down and the ground rose up.) It was April 6, 1961, Thursday, and spring had sprung. With sadness Betty left her nursing job at White Pine Hospital where she had been held in high regard.

We enjoyed our Suomi Synod parish which set my standards for subsequent parishes and life in general. The move caused us grief. Part of the grief was that I had to make a clean break from my former friends in order to be fair to my successor, **Dr. Ray Holmes.** I had fielded job offers from many places but it was the name **Republic** with which the Lord caught my attention. I met with Bethany's church council once prior to my acceptance of the call. I think God spoke to us through Rachel Mattila and Bill Oja.

All of my ordinand-mates had already moved once, some even twice. I believed in the simple axiom that the Lord opens and closes the doors of our lives. Jesus talked about going in and out and finding pasture. I was embarking from one pasture to another pasture, exchanging copper mining for iron mining, but the same kinds of trees for logging, some farming, and both containing some wonderful people. This was the Suomi Synod where we had no confusion about what the gospel was, or if they were hearing the Word of God. When these laymen heard it, they knew it. When they no longer were able to hear it, they still tried to be nice to their pastors. Finns had high respect for the office of the pastor.

The 1960s would prove to be the beginning of some terrible times. The Korean Conflict was over, but the Vietnam War was just beginning. Make no mistake our nation was compelled to make a stand in the **Cold War** (1946-1991) because of the impending threat of communism. We lived in fear of *the bomb*, and the name of the game was mutual destruction if there was a slip-up.

I came to Republic with a track record of having served on the Suomi College board, Luther League youth work, including bible camping, a concern for town and country parishes and the immigrant generation.

*   *   *

We arrived at our new home. Actually it was a big old home, within ten feet of a handsome brick church. **Ray Wargelin**, our synod president, was born in this house, when his father was the pastor following the turn of the century. My office was in the parsonage. *School Lake* was out the back door. We were a block from Kloman Avenue the "main drag" of Republic. For the first year the boys had only to walk around the lake to school. There was excitement in the air as the "open pit" **Republic Mine** of Cleveland Cliff Iron Company, had just begun a few months before our arrival.

C.C.I. promised to be there for twenty-five years. The best of economic times were on their way, from famine to feast. By elevation this was the highest parish (1,600+ ft.) in the Upper Peninsula, the top of an ancient mountain range exposing some of the oldest rock on the planet. Because of this I would later boast of having *the top parish* in the Wisconsin-Upper Michigan Synod. The local terrain was a series of marshes and rocky ridges. They wrote that when this hinterland area was first discovered in the 1830s, men came down the Michigamme River from Lake Michigamme in canoes. As they neared present-day Republic they encountered around the next bend this huge shining **"mountain" of specular hematite** gleaming like silver in the sunlight. Some said it was *Smith's Mountain*. I suppose as we rounded the next bend on the road to Republic we too saw the spiritual mountain of hope and promise as we entered our new parish. How appropriate the words of the Psalmist, *"I lift up my eyes to the hills. From where does my help come? <u>My help comes from the Lord,</u> who made heaven and earth."*[33]

Upon arrival I soon discovered my responsibilities encompassed the entire west end of Marquette County, which would also include **Champion** and **Michigamme**. Eskil Bostrom of Ishpeming was anxious to let me "claim" Michigamme. Soon the Finns and Swedes there merged as we gathered in the picturesque Augustana church, which years later became the *Church in the Wildwood*, a favorite arts and crafts outlet. I was the *Shepherd of M-28*.

As mentioned earlier, I succeeded **Alpo Setälä** in Republic, who also conducted services twice monthly in Champion and monthly to Michigamme. Our Champion church was on Beacon Hill, adjacent to the high school. As the plan was to diminish my schedule for health's sake, my Sunday load lessened from 4.5 service per Sunday to 3.4 in the new parish. Setälä

Bethany Church, Republic.

was a wonderful caring pastor, who came out of the "evangelical" revival movement in Finland. The Republic congregation resembled the kind of **"folk churches"** that were common in Finland. Soon it turned out that 840 members belonged to Bethany in a village of only a thousand people. It was difficult to match the names and the faces at the outset. Truth be told, I never did get them all straight.

The **iron mines** were booming. The parishioners worked at the following mines: Republic, Humboldt, Champion and Randville; some men also traveled to Ishpeming and Negaunee. Mining was a high paying endeavor, and whereby something is actually produced, namely iron.

A unique feature in Republic was the presence of **Sarepta Home**, a home for the primarily Finnish elderly, which was wonderfully owned and run by Ben and Ruth Mykkänen. Pastor **K.V. Mykkänen** established two Sareptas, the other located in Sanford, Florida, where Tamar Mykkänen-Braden was the administrator. These homes were far ahead of their times in outstanding and adequate care for the elderly. Both Sunday services were "piped" into the rooms of Sarepta, and where their own doctor made weekly visits, namely the legendary **Dr. Paul van Riper** of Champion. Ben and Ruth became best of friends. As a registered nurse, Betty began faithful years of gerontology there.

The boys soon found new friends as playmates. It was here that our sons formed the fundamentals for a budding basketball careers, especially Dan. This was a great small town in which to raise our family. A year after arrival the boys had access to a brand new K-12 school in *South Republic*, three miles away. They rode a bus to get there. The mine was gradually moving the old town to South Republic. It was evidently the cost of progress, and not everyone was happy.

The head of the local mine, which had over six hundred employees, was a Finn named Evert Lindroos. The mine got the attention of the community each day with a huge **blast** at 4:00 p.m. which shook the frozen ground. Sometimes huge rocks would fly into the village. It was not uncommon to have frost every month of the year at this elevation. On windy days from the south shiny bright specular hematite would coat everything including house windowsills. It was said that Republic folks lost their hearing from iron gathering in the ears, necessitating good acoustics and a public address system at Bethany Church.

Meanwhile, back in **Chatham**, it was mostly a bad time. My brother, Bill married Judy Vartti at the age of seventeen because of a pregnancy. Fortunately for them, my dad hired Bill and taught him the construction skills over the next ten years. For most of this time they lived in my old home. My sister, Betty, immediately upon high school graduation, left to live in Milwaukee. Her best friend there was murdered several years later. She married Jacob Korpi of Suomi Location but they soon divorced. Mom had left the family house, and purchased a small house at Chatham Corners. She now lived alone starting in 1961. Alimony had ended and she worked out of the home as a cook, and began her *Pearl's Pasty* business, with a regular delivery route.

Dad and Lorraine lived on Cherry Street in Munising, dad being at the peak of his building career. A son, **Edward Paul** was born to them on Monday, June 25, 1955 in Munising. He was soon known to all as "Eddie." His half brother, **John Boucher**, was six years older. I baptized Eddie on October 24 at the home.

* * *

How Les looked preaching in Republic, 1962.

I enthusiastically seized this new opportunity to "Americanize" this new parish. This initially meant establishing a solid **worship** schedule, as follows: Finnish worship at 8:15, then race to Champion for 9:30, and back to Bethany for *10:45*. Twice monthly I held services in Michigamme. Before long the new format showed results. I average 306 per Sunday in this parish. The acoustics for speaking and singing at Bethany were outstanding. We had a forty-voice choir directed by Ruth Mykkänen. We had a children's choir. Bethany had a marvelous pipe organ. This worship average was the highest of my career.

More often than not Bethany worship meant adding chairs in the aisles. I loved that part. It was wonderful as folks responded to the Word of God, and longed to hear it. You see, the secret was never in my ability, but in the product I was "selling." Or, as Mark Finley put it: *"You can't expect help from your Bible if you leave it on a shelf to collect dust."* James Kennedy was right, saying *"Many people who go to church are not Christians, but every Christian goes to church."* However, Bethany had no parking lot for cars. **La Verne Antilla** was my office secretary at Bethany.

Worship in **Champion**, recall, had averaged 15 on alternate Sunday afternoons. It ended with 69 per Sunday on the eve of calling their own pastor in 1965. Susan Mikkola was the organist. Michigamme worship averaged 25.

* * *

Basically I believed there are two things imperative to a successful ministry: Solid honest **preaching**, and constant **visitation**. I had some gifts, but I didn't have them all. Worship was a joy and a highlight in this new parish, but also the Spirit led us in great strides in Christian education, stewardship, evangelism, youth work, the "*Champion project*," and merger into Lutheran Church in America.

In **Christian education**, Sunday church schools, and vacation church schools were maintained in Republic, Champion and Michigamme. And there were an abundance of children, which indicated young families. I initiated a **weekday church school** in Republic (which reached its zenith later in Munising), whereby students were released from public school on Wednesday mornings to attend religious classes. The concept was that as they were growing in their knowledge of, e.g. science, mathematics, and history, they would be growing simultaneously in Christian faith. Some of the classes were related to the confirmation program. E.g., in Republic I recall teaching grade eight at the Erland Keskitalo home, a half block from the new Republic School.

Since the church in Republic had no classrooms, per se, we bought the **Bice House**, three houses down the street from the church, for classrooms. And in Champion, Dr. Paul van Riper donated to the congregation the **Van Riper Hospital** building, across the street from the church in 1963. It was remodeled for classrooms. These steps were temporary at best, but answered to the immediate need for better Christian education. Confirmation classes were huge as the entire parish came together for these combined classes at Bethany.

* * *

The Cold War was beginning to escalate in 1962 with the Cuban missile crisis. In later years I met a Rock native named **Kaarlo Tuomi**, who was a double agent spy during the crisis being employed by Tiffany's of New York. I have often wondered how much Kaarlo knew and whether he helped avert World War Three.

There was still no color television or transmission of news from Europe, but news conferences had begun with President Kennedy. Tab-top tin cans had just been invented in 1962. Plastic had just made its appearance into society a year or two previous. I was becoming very interested in a mineral collection, as parish members would often offer me exciting mineral samples from the mines for my collection. Little boys have always been interested in stones. I found agates and thomsonites on the Nick Lukanich beach north of Calumet. And we adopted a stray alley cat.

Youth work was still high on my list of priorities, being on both synod and national agencies, but it was not the fever pitch of my previous parish. I had Luther Leagues in Republic and in Champion. Bible Camp participation lessened as there was not interest in going to Camp Manikiki near Newberry as there had been with Camp Nesbitt or Fortune Lake. Yet, we had outstanding local youth like Lucy Latvala, Ron Kangas, Dan and Joy Hakala, Paul Kaare, Laaninen brothers, Jon Mattila, Sandy Heinonen, Barbara Skogman,

Jim Urpila, Judy Pasbrig, Cynthia Wuorenmaa, Larry Mustama, Mike Carriere, John Bentti, the Järvi sisters and others. Many of these served as church school teachers.

Peter Laaninen, next door to the parsonage, went to seminary and became a pastor. From Champion **Michael Carriere** became a pastor in the Apostolic Lutheran Church, **Donald Mikkola,** before my time, became one of the two top leaders of the metallurgy department at Michigan Tech University, and **Bill Koski** led his family to church and gained membership in Northern Michigan University's Sports Hall of Fame with his basketball skills. In 1964, he was the point guard in Champion's dominance as the top U.P. high school team with a victory over Marquette in the *David and Goliath* game of the year. Bill became a coach and teacher. Republic youth got their festivals mixed up with a tradition of lighting numerous huge hilltop bonfires on Independence Day, July 4, instead of the Finnish Mid-summer, June 24, events.

I was honored to be picked to serve on the initial **Commission on Youth Activities** of the new merged Lutheran Church in America, 1962-65. All meetings were in Philadelphia or New York City. I also headed up the Youth Committee of the new Wisconsin-Upper Michigan Synod (WUM). This called for meetings in Milwaukee, in which case I would often walk a block from our parsonage to the depot and take the Milwaukee Road Pullman car in the evening and go to sleep, waking up in the city in the morning, refreshed for the day-long meetings, and then take the train home. It was cool. To fly North Central Air cost $67.00 at that time, forth and back.

We had now entered into our merger with **Lutheran Church in America,** and youth work was already changing. It was not the same, not as good, as it had been in the Trout Creek Parish. Both quantity and quality had been affected, and that not for the better. Life changed in the Sixties.

*   *   *

While we had taken some vacations at **Lake Au Train** with our young family at Grandpa Hugo's and Ellen's new cottage (1958), they sold us the extra lot they owned for $100.00. This lot became useable when Hugo had the road (trail) to the point moved further north. The lot was an acre and a quarter with frontages on both lake and the river.

Beginning August 1, 1962, I built a 36 x 20 foot **A-frame cottage** which cost $ 4,000. It was made from Douglas fir, with beveled redwood siding for the roofing. My dad did not know I was building it and did not see it until its completion. When he saw it he remained speechless which meant that he approved. When unsuspecting visitors came to visit, as I built it, chances were good that they were put to work.

One of the best deals I made was the purchase of thirteen plate glass window panes from Ness Glass Company in Escanaba on my dad's carpenter's discount for $ 197.00. Upon completion of my vacation month, I was able to lock the door on August 31. It being only sixty-five miles from my parsonage, I completed the interior on my day off each week. A chilling memory was the laying of my tongue and groove Douglas fir flooring when it was minus thirty degrees during the night. We had only a 2-burner hotplate for heat, and only the fire-place next door where we slept. Later, I rented the cottage at a rate of $75-100 a week until rentals totaled $4000, the initial cost of materials.

* * *

It was exciting in 1962 to prepare the congregations for the January 1, 1963 four-church merger into the **Lutheran Church in America**. The merging convention and celebration was in Detroit in June, 1962. My Upper Peninsula with fifty-five Suomi congregations became a part of the Wisconsin-Upper Michigan Synod, which had its constituting convention in Neenah. Our new leader, though a Swede-Finn, proceeded immediately a "russification" process of our congregations to kill the Finnish language and to close Suomi College. He also brought a "*social gospel*" that unashamedly took the focus off of the true gospel. Interestingly, he apologized to me for his attitude about Suomi College after he retired. Even bishops' mistakes can be forgiven. His name was Theodore Matson.

Perhaps the former Suomi Synod was overly exuberant in that instead of our congregations, wherever they existed, joining the local synods, we probably should have kept our 155 congregations to ourselves in a non-geographic synod of our own. Hindsight later suggested that might have been wiser, and thus slow down the process of losing the true treasure of the gospel. Yet we met some great new leaders, both clergy and lay, who loved the Lord Jesus because of the merger.

In 1964 I was elected by the Wisconsin-Upper Michigan synod to be a delegate to the nine-day biennial **convention** in downtown Pittsburgh, PA. The LCA was in her infancy and Franklin Clark Fry was an able leader. An interesting aside was for our family to take our lunch at our huge hotel with the Nat King Cole family, including Natalie, at the next table. After the event we visited historic sites of the Delaware Swede-Finn colony of 1638, the World's Fair in New York, and went fishing for mackerel on the Atlantic Ocean. It was a "poor-man's" vacation. We were using our Chrysler New Yorker, which we had purchase for a second car earlier.

Social Ministry, perhaps by Theodore Matson's influence, was becoming more preva-lent to me. I was the chairman of an outstanding local group called the **Republic Youth Organization**, which was our very own United Fund. Fedora Fowler, a Catholic, was a life-long inspiration of this work. We divided up the funds to various service organizations.

Bethany was largely responsible for constructing a ski hill, complete with an electric dri-ven rope tow, on *Carlson's Hill* five miles south of Republic. It was spearheaded by Elmer Heinonen, Norman Kaleva and me. Community youth made big use of it. It's only negative was that it faced south, and the spring sun raised havoc with it. Republic did not get a great deal of snow but it was beastly cold.

Our church custodian, Wilbert Laaninen, was an alcoholic. He was a "loner" **Alcoholics Anonymous** member and traveled to meetings weekly. I asked him how he could afford such long distance travel, to which he replied: *It is cheaper than drinking.* We went on to organize a local AA group, which met every Saturday night in the church parlors. Some of the open meetings had over seventy in attendance. Republic was a heavy drinking town, typical of mining towns. Some of my members for decades would thank me for helping to facilitate the AA group, claiming that it saved their lives. It was fitting that we had an AA group for on January 19 (Heikinpäivä), 1888, the first organized effort to bring together individual temperance groups among the Finns took place in Republic.

My **hospital calls** in this parish were all made in Ishpeming (Bell) and Marquette (Marquette General Hospital), 20 and 35 miles away. Home visits were important. I must tell the story of calling on a schizophrenic named Werner Niemi, who lived in a log cabin in *Hungry Hollow* (Puutteenperä), a failed farming area some six miles directly east of Republic. Werner had wild beliefs and stories. But I went deer hunting with him, and once he shot a nice deer. It took courage to hunt with a man with his malady. In the winter I would snowshoe two miles from the plowed road to have coffee with him. Werner was able successfully to live alone at home.

* * *

My hunting and fishing suffered in this parish. The only buck I shot was coming out of the woods with Dina Saari one afternoon south of Beacon Hill in Champion. My successful fishing was limited to catching splake (a brook trout-lake trout hybrid) at Squaw Lake west of Witch Lake.

I have two more **deer hunting** stories. One day Betty and I took our Falcon wagon to hunt nine miles up the Michigamme River. And it was a bitter cold day. We tried to cross a small stream. There was no bridge, but others had done it so why not us? We got into the middle and got hopelessly stuck. There was ice around the fringes and now dusk as rapidly approaching. We spun the wheels, sinking deeper. Wouldn't you know that Les Waline was logging nearby and his big truck came as darkness lurked? He pulled us out. It would have been a long hike home from so far away.

One Saturday I was invited to join Bill and Jack Oja, Emil Mikkola, and others to hunt up the Peshekee Grade near Lake Alice in the direction of the Huron Mountains. I mean this is the wildest of U.P. country. The best time to sit is just before dark, but one does not often think about getting out in darkness after one has sat. I found a nice ridge. Later I discovered from the snow that two bobcats had followed my tracks. Dusk came. I'm far from the car. Soon I heard two shots. The men were at the car waiting for me. I shot back in response. It was one miserable walk through a wet swamp to get out! They, of course, were worried that they would need to preach the next morning, in case I had to stay the night.

This was also country where the **moose** ran loose. I once questioned why a family in Champion had missed the previous Sunday services. Walt and Bertha Lindsteadt replied that they had set out, but a moose would not let them drive through on the road out from Arfelin Lake from up the Peshekee Road. In this same area a lost hunter once came upon a **gold** nugget so heavy he opted to hide it and come back to retrieve it later. He got out safely but that nugget is still out there waiting to be retrieved. He never found it. This was wonderfully exciting country.

*   *   *

With the new economic boost due to mining, I cannot tell you what a contrast the congregations made in **Christian giving**. What a marvelous time to put into practice what was called the "every member visit" which consisted of members visiting with fellow members about giving. The first year we used this, the budget tripled in one year. Members were asked to make a pledge of a certain amount or percentage per week. It made possible in Champion the notion that they could support their own resident pastor. Since there is a spiritual need of the giver to give, it did not matter whether we needed the money or not. The congregations began to support world missions liberally beyond their local borders. .

In 1963 the first heart transplants and heart valves happened. That year also I was a part of the dedication of the new **Van Riper State Park** at Champion Beach, at which the life-long work of Dr. Paul Van Riper was duly recognized. It was in 1963 that the powers from the LCA New York office, and Dr. Theodore Matson, local bishop, at a meeting in Green Bay, tried to close Suomi College (now Finlandia University). They failed. The vote was 20-1 against them, Matson being the one vote. I was a member of the board. O Lord, protect us from our friends!

Then, it was the year of the tragic **assassination** of our president, John Kennedy in Dallas on November 22, 1963. Betty and I were deer hunting east of Republic and we heard it on the car radio on the way home. Vietnam, Kennedy . . . the mood of the nation was beginning to change from faith and hope, to cynicism. Later, in 1992, when I was attending a Gift Annuities Conference in Dallas, my Hyatt Hotel overlooked the street and grassy knoll, where the deed was done. I walked over the ground in tears over the depravity of man.

*   *   *

You would think that in this folk church community there would be little need nor room for **evangelism**. Yet, the external facts show that during my four years in this parish 225 adult members were received as new members. That was fifty-five a year, which surprisingly surpasses the forty-six a year average in my previous Trout Creek Parish. By 1965 the total number of members is my congregations was 1,181. (In the Trout Creek Parish that number was 877.)

For evangelism I had again used the *Preaching-Teaching-Reaching* program. While I lived in Republic I went to two PTR missions as a speaker, to Soudan, Minnesota, and Lake City, Michigan. The former was in the dead of winter when the temperature dipped to minus 40 degrees. But evangelism is more than adding numbers; it is also warming the hearts, reaching deeper in our inner life of the spirit and soul, now known as spiritual formation. Important is what is happening that is spiritual, not merely a numbers game. The world is concerned primarily of the latter. We opted for a first-hand, rather than a second-hand, faith. If Champion entertained wild thoughts about calling their own pastor, it would have 329 members for openers.

* * *

Champion was the recipient of a 1964 summer ministry in the form of **Roy and Nora Tähtinen**, Roy being on the eve of his ordination. It gave this young and enthusiastic group a taste of what it might be like to have a full-time pastor. Roy, whom I confirmed in Trout Creek in 1954, and Nora made a fine team together. Nora was extremely talented, and would later work full-time in youth ministry. Roy, after serving Embarrass, South Range, Wakefield, and National Mine, died of cancer January 10, 2003. I have his final email testimony of faith in my files. In the fall John Wargelin, who came to Champion at age five from Finland, was the guest preacher at the seventieth anniversary of the congregation. He spoke about the cross of Jesus Christ.

And so it came to pass that Bethlehem of Michigamme merged with **Our Redeemer** of Champion and they voted to call their own pastor, effective 1965. The first pastor was **Harlan Haack**, with his wife Lydia. Their first task was to obtain housing. Enthusiasm was high. (Six years later they built a remarkable contemporary new church on M-28 near the Peshekee River under the tutelage of Chesmond Bade. It was such a source of satisfaction to me to see the surge of faith in Champion. I simply needed to get out of the way.

As if I didn't have enough to do serving an over 1,100 member parish, I must relate what involvements I had in the **Lutheran Church in America**. Starting in 1964 I served nine years as a member of the executive committee of the WUM Synod; all the meetings were in Milwaukee. Simultaneously I was a member of the Lutheran Social Services board for three years. Also I was on the Examining Committee of our synod, whose task it was to orally examine seminary graduates coming to serve in our synod. A far cry from Suomi Synod pietism, I can recall rejecting only one young man who attended Princeton Seminary. We should have rejected far more, some of whom seemed faith challenged. I was still on the National Lutheran Council's Town and Country committee. Betty also served as delegate and was on the Lutheran Church Women's synod board.

What did I do in my spare time? I **skied** in winter and played **golf** in summer. Betty and I obtained season's passes at Cliff's Ridge Ski Area in Marquette and enjoyed it. This time it was Nathan who tagged with us before he began kindergarten, bombing down from the top. Fred Vanhala was my primary golf partner at the Mather A golf course in Ishpeming. Classmate Fred was living in Palmer.

* * *

I have several seemingly interesting incidents and stories of things that happened while in Republic. Regarding **continuing education**, I had an opportunity to participate in a three-summer program at Michigan State University of two weeks each. Their intent was to keep pastors aware about what changes were to transpire in the very near future in areas like communications, travel, birth control, agriculture, information revolution, and the like. It was extremely helpful.

I have a story about running **out of gas** in mid-winter while hurrying to make the 10:45 Republic service after Champion. The car stopped for lack of petroleum about a mile south of Koski Korners. Because of the shortness of time I never disrobed from my vestments between these churches. So I got out of the car, fully vested, and waved my arms up and down in the middle of the road for the next car that came along. It was Bill and Inga Oja who were heading for worship. Inga saw this apparition on the road, and for a moment thought it was heralding **the end of the world**. I left the car, jumped in, and we hardly missed a beat. Incidentally, for some reason, when I later left the Champion congregation I was given as a going-away gift a five gallon red gas can, filled with gas, and an appropriate poem entitled *Ode to an Empty Gas Tank*. They were so loving, and accepting of crazy pastors.

A small story is: Pastor's kid breaks **stained glass** church window. It is still unclear who (Dan or Mike) threw the baseball. But through Bethany's window it went. The new stained glass pane was replaced, at the pastor's expense.

Mike, however, came down with a planter's wart on the bottom of his right foot. It was almost the size of a dime. The pastor told him: Go and take school caulk dust and go to the top of one of the hills surrounding Republic. Wet the caulk from a pool of water in the rock, and apply. Your planter's wart will go away. He did, and it did. In a week it was gone. Another **faith healing**.

Dan saved a kid from drowning in Cedar Lake just east of Republic in the spring of 1964. Dan was ten years old. It seemed that this boy who could not swim drifted away from shore alone in an empty rowboat, minus the ores. He panicked and jumped into the water, at which point Dan swam out to get him. Knowing they could both drown in the panic, he would not allow the kid to touch him but merely told him what to do. The parents gave Dan a bicycle carriage rack for a gift. Word spread at school the following day, but Mike blew it off with the words: *"Yea, but that was yesterday!"* Isn't there a saying? *Yesterday's editorial masterpiece wraps today's fish.* Dan and Mike belonged to Cub Scouts. Nathan ministered to Sarepta men by playing cards with them.

On one of my trips by plane to a Milwaukee meeting, I was on a late night plane to Marquette where my car was waiting. I was to transfer in Green Bay. But I fell **asleep through the transfer**, and the staff did not notice it. I ended up in Menominee on a dead-end run. The plane went no farther. I was stranded. What to do? Meanwhile, the North Central plane I was to be on was still behind us, so they phoned the plane. The plane came down, picked me up, and off we went. So the plane was five minutes late, but I was most pleased.

Kookery? A UFO? It was February 1965. The boys normally call to their mother when in need, not their father. But this early morning around 2:00 a.m. Dan is screaming for his dad. *"Come quick!"* Out the east side upstairs bedroom window he is pointing to a football shaped strong white light in the NE sky moving slowly to the southeast. We both saw it. The other three saw it also. It moved behind the roof line of Laaninen's house, next door. We raced to another SE corner window to see it come through. It never came. So what was it? Why the unusual circumstances? It was large, moon-sized, but only a solid white light.

*   *   *

Joe Crites was now the Republic Mine superintendent, succeeding Mr. Lindroos. He was feisty and sharp tongued. One day I drove my Falcon up a back road from town, up the big hill and to the edge of the pit, an act of trespassing. There I gazed at the gigantic shovels and Euclid trucks down below. It was fascinating, and I had done it before. I was alone. Lo, here comes a pick-up. Out jumps the head honcho, yes, Joe Crites. Oh, no . . . *"**What the hell are you doing here?**"* I was speechless, and apologized, and went away. I don't know if he knew who I was. Years later, Joe, a generous man and friend of Suomi College, would give me checks of $3000 each for the school. He had retired to Ishpeming. I visited him and we became good friends. His bark was bigger than his bite.

What the hell are you doing here? And, well, I left Republic for a new parish after only four years. Was he a prophet? Was it the voice of God speaking to me? Would God talk like that?

Be that as it may, two spies came from **Eden Lutheran Church** of **Munising** to attend a service and hear a sermon. They were Harold Pirlot and John Toebe. That Pirlot fellow was so sneaky that he lifted the lid of my garbage can, evidently, to see what I drank. They reported back to the church council at Eden.

Shortly thereafter I received a "letter of call" from Eden in Munising. And quite suddenly, Betty and I agreed that we would move. I suppose we prayed about the open door. Our sons would have grandparents as close as three, and eighteen miles away. That weighed important. Betty and I would be near our parents. My dad called me and said: *Aren't you coming?* Deep down that felt nice to me. I was wanted. Munising was my birthplace, yet it was not my home congregation. Then, the convenience of my new fine cottage on Lake Au Train, built three years earlier. It certainly seemed convenient, but did any of this matter to God?

Martin Luther, on the *Lord's Prayer*, once wrote *"Good occasionally allows comfort to come to the conscience and fills us with cheerful confidence in his mercy to strengthen and inspire us with hope in God even in times when our conscience is fearful. On the other hand, God at times saddens and terrifies a conscience so that even in happy days we will not forget the fear of God."*

Have you ever pondered how seemingly little decisions can change your entire life? It certainly seemed like the will of God. I followed Pastor "Bud" Danner, who had moved to Red Oak, Iowa. Mrs. Danner had recently died in Munising at age fifty. It was the year that Medicare began.

The Republic Parish has been very good. How could it have been better than Trout Creek? But it was. In a way, but maybe more from the external impact, it was the "highlight years" of my parish career. It was so comfortable that I could have stayed in Republic a long time. Whose life took on new and eternal meaning in Republic and Champion because of my ministry and the Holy Spirit?

*   *   *

On March 1, 1965 we left Republic for 210 Spruce Street in Munising. It was a Monday. This time it was a moving van that moved us, including heavy boxes of rocks, mineral samples. The snow banks were high in Munising, much higher than in Republic. The boys did not want to leave. I had to bait them with things like the football program, and the movie theater. And yes, I would like to believe the words of my friend, **Mary Ann Voegtline**, one of my faithful Sunday school teachers in Republic, who said in 2007: *"When you were in Republic it was the golden era at Bethany congregation."*

Flattering, yes, but how much did God's work really get accomplished? So you see, repentance and forgiveness is forever necessary. And again, Dr. Kukkonen's haunting words: *"Don't stay too long, for you cannot correct your many mistakes."* **Stuart Koski**, a good and humble lay leader, preached a wonderful sermon at my farewell service. In both parishes there had been not merely a party, but a worship service at the very end, conducted by the lay members.

My three sons, Michael 15, Nathan 12 and Daniel 16.

For this young pastor from Eben (Ebenezer), the Lord had again been **"the rock of help."** That mountain of specular hematite on the Michigamme River had been the solid rock of the gospel of our Lord Jesus Christ. God knew all about my move to Munising. This was no accident. God knew from the beginning of time that I would survive abortion, be born as a "depression baby," be His child by faith, go to seminary, marry, have three sons, and write these words on my computer. And that you would read them. He knew every sin, and forgave them for the asking. He was my firm, and loving Jumala/God.

It had been a joy, a privilege, and a life's high and holy moment to serve Republic, Champion and Michigamme. No parish is exactly the same as the previous one. We oughtn't expect them to be the same. Each parish has its pros and cons and not one is perfect. Each is filled with ungodly sinners who have been redeemed by Jesus the Christ. Now we needed to point the car further east along M-28 to the city of my birth. . . Munising . . . *the place of the island.*

Our Flying Squirrel

CHAPTER TEN

Munising, Age 34-52, 1965-1983

As my ministry at Eden Lutheran Church in Munising encompassed eighteen years, I will divide it into three 6-year segments. In a sense everything I experienced in my first two parishes, over eleven years, was preparation for my final concluding congregation in Munising. Each was different; each a *Kodak moment* of its own. Eden-on-the-Bay Lutheran Church became my prime-of-life parish. It was the Camelot of my life, in a sense that legendary fleeting wisp of glory.

There was an excitement in arriving at each new parish. How many souls would I help in the days ahead? What would endure into eternity? Our furniture had arrived, and we arrived on Monday, the first of March, 1965, in two cars, our Chrysler New Yorker and our 1960 Falcon station wagon. Six of us, including our long-haired calico alley cat. He didn't like it, and he left us immediately. Having been an alley cat he was in his own element. It was still the dead of winter and we were surprised at the huge snow banks on Spruce Street. I was born 34 years earlier, three blocks away.

Our new **home** was not ours, but the congregation's parsonage. It was a small brick house with four bedrooms, an incomplete basement with a fireplace but it had a spring in it that fed a small stream across the basement floor. There was a fireplace in the combination dining/living room. The yard was so small that the outside clothes lines were on the neighbor's property. We were nestled near a huge hardwood-forested hill which produced sunsets as early as 3 p.m. (in winter), and also hindered antennae TV reception. But we were not from the "want generation." We accepted what God gave us. We lived here, gratefully, for ten years before we moved to our Au Train lake property.

We knew that there must be some reason why these Swedes named this congregation "Eden." And we knew the scriptures: *"The Lord God took the man and put him in the Garden of Eden to work it and take care of it."*[34] *"(B)efore them the land is like the garden of Eden . . ."*[35] *"You were in Eden, the garden of God..."*[36] We were on the southernmost extremity of Lake Superior, an area endowed by God's creative magnificence, complete with lots of clean water, rushing waterfalls, sandstone cliffs, sandy beaches, and green hardwood hills and forests. It was a city of 4,000. The big lake was 382 miles long and 160 miles wide, covering an area as big as Massachusetts, Connecticut, Rhode Island, Vermont and New Hampshire combined, or 31,700 square miles. Its three quadrillion gallons if spread over North and South America would be a foot deep. Its 2,725 miles of shoreline contained ten percent of the earth's surface fresh water. It was **Eden!**

Swedish Lutheran Church, Munising, Mich.

Old Eden.

From Eben to Eden. I had not really come very far. My new "rock of help" would later be to gaze from the nave of Eden-on-the-Bay Church at Pictured Rocks National Lakeshore. Years later if your eyesight was especially keen you could see the visitor's viewing ramp which my brother Bill erected on top of the famed Miners Castle. Such was the natural setting in our new congregation.

"By the shores of Kitchi-Gummi,
*By the shining big-sea waters . . ."*37

The old church was very much a different story. It was the original building built by the immigrants in 1907. The chancel was dated, the floor squeaked, the roof leaked, and the sewer was persistently plugged. And they had incurred two "roughing the pastor" penalties before I arrived. Some years earlier the congregation purchased the home across the street from the old parsonage which was now used for much-needed church school space. Munising was an idyllic community nestled between the hills and the lake. The church served a six thousand population base. The backbone economy was furnished by the **Munising Mill** of Kimberly-Clark Corporation, but supplemented by Northern Hardwoods (Hartho plant), logging, tourism, and some farming. It was a county-seat town with a large Roman Catholic base.

*   *   *

My first service was an **Ash Wednesday** event attended by one hundred sixty souls. The small church held a hundred and fifty persons if you squeezed them. My Lenten theme was *"What Language Shall I Borrow?"* lifting a line from the great Passion Chorale *"O Sacred Head, Now Wounded."* (Clairvaux, Gerhardt, Bach)

"What language shall I borrow to thank thee, dearest friend,
For this thy dying sorrow, Thy pity without end?
O make me thine for ever, and should I fainting be,
Lord, let me never, never outlive my love to thee."

These words set the theme for my 18 years at Eden in Munising! The cross of Jesus.

On the second day in Munising, **Dan** happened upon an intra-school spring basketball tourney between local elementary schools. He scored eighteen points, all in the second half. It was a harbinger of things to come as seven years later he was chosen to the State of Michigan Class C basketball All-State team, from Munising.

It was nice of the congregation to receive us with a welcoming program. Superintendent of schools, Bill MacNeil, was present. He asked my sons if they would be as good basketball players as their father. Dan responded: "*I will be better.*" Looking in the rear view mirror, he was absolutely correct.

We were all pleased to be a part of a new adventure. We were close to our families which felt comfortable. The enthusiasm which we felt in the congregation was encouraging. Getting to know these new Christians at Eden was an absolute joy. It was Lent and we were together going to Jerusalem with Jesus, going to the cross together to die to sin, and to rise again on Easter morning.

*   *   *

There were two things I tried to do at Eden: (a) to maintain a healthy balance of emphasis of **inner faith** and **outer service**, and (b) to be an enabler to the members to use their **gifts for the common good**. These gifts would vary. For some it was to be an example. For some it would be generous giving. For others it was leadership in the congregation and/or community. I would try to be an "enabler" to them so they might fulfill their unique role in church and society. Soon even the mayor belonged to Eden. I would be their pastor, and deny no one of their given role in the congregation and to community institutions. I felt I needed to lead individuals into his or her own growth maturity. We were successful in this endeavor, which made me proud of each of them.

I was careful of the trend in liberalism of the swing from the inner faith of piety to the other extreme, social gospel but devoid of the gospel. Either extreme alone spelled a sick church. Already two generations earlier the eastern elite seminaries were laughing at fundamentalism. They became enamored by the social gospel and politics. I believed if you didn't have both inner faith and outer service, you had neither. But with a balance of inner faith and outer service, you had everything and more. And only then did God appear. Without the inner experience of Christ you had nothing. After merger I am sad to report there were two bishops from whom I seldom heard the true gospel preached. I felt my primary task was to preach the Word faithfully and honestly, to proclaim the law and Gospel correctly, and to hold forth the cross and the empty grave, so that in worship one knew that he had been in church. The two emphases were to be held in balance and in tension. Inner faith came first, followed by loving outer service.

The Spirit would produce the results, for the **Word** would not return empty. In service to others, I found it therapeutic also for myself. First and foremost my job was to lead men and women to primarily the one thing most needful, to lead someone to Jesus Christ. This was my plan, presented by St. Paul when he wrote: *"There are many kinds of service tasks but the Lord is the same. The vehicles of God's power are of many kinds but He who in us enkindles all is the same. He allows the Spirit to reveal Himself in each one in various ways for the common good."*[38] This was my **job description** for eighteen years. I spent my first 6-year plan building **trust** and establishing solid basic programs. **Preaching** and **visitation** were primary concerns. Regarding the latter, the greatest ability was availability. The small budget I inherited at Eden was $ 11,883 in 1965.

* * *

For almost all of my Eden years I conducted three weekend **worship** services, which were amazingly received from the very beginning with a two hundred fourteen average weekend attendance the first six years. Early I was approached to conduct worship at the **First Presbyterian Church**, which I sandwiched between my early and late services, and which averaged thirty-five. As in my previous parish there was no time to vest or unvest, so I simply marched down the streets for three blocks to the nearby church. After three years, a notion to merge the two congregations was considered, but it failed.

An immediate result upon arrival was the absorption of the former Suomi Synod congregation in Munising into Eden. It had been organized in 1925 and had twenty-five members, having been served from Marquette. The once-a-month **Finnish language service** I continued for the next eighteen years under the name *Suomi Seura.* I also supplied Finnish worship in Eben until 1967 when they left the *Lutheran Church in America.* I supplied Finnish four times a year in Newberry for a quarter of a century. They were a wonderful group. The Eden Finnish group met in homes or at cottages, as it was a long Finnish tradition from Finland, and they were called *"seuroja."*

The **church schools** were bulging. We immediately lost our first family, the Elmer Johnson family, over a difference of opinion on how the Sunday school should function, and Elmer had been the director. **Vacation** church schools were held for two weeks. **Released time church school** was begun in which grades 5-9 came out of public school on Wednesday mornings for instruction. I began a **School of Religion** program for adults held in the evenings. We had the unusual dilemma of an almost all-male church school teaching staff: eighteen men teachers and three lady teachers. It had a huge impact on male students. **Confirmation** programs encompassed three years and worked quite well.

Youth work did well, although a noticeable diminishing into the 1970s. The names of our senior group evolved from Luther League, to Senior High Youth (SHY), to Youth Ministry. By this point in time, we were no longer attracting the brightest and the best of our church youth to our own youth meetings and events. They did, however, attend worship regularly. Some of our outstanding youth leaders were Blaine Barabas, Debbie and Jeff Kouri,

Carrie Lehto, Scott Lindquist, Lisa Männistö, Pam McCollum, Dan Niemi, Bonnie Pirlot, Denis Skoglund, David Saylor, Mark Tanis and Carol Toebe. We began a Junior Luther League with lay advisors. More and more youth went to college with outstanding success. One of Eden's confirmands, however, became a national leader in the anarchist group by the name of *Posse Comitatus*, and spent time in a federal prison.

* * *

In addition to worship and Christian education, in the first six-year plan I tried to bolster this tri-legged stool called Eden, so it might stand upright. Some of them were stewardship, social ministry, and evangelism.

One of the biggest miracles at Eden was **Christian stewardship**. The immediate use of the "every member visit" and the impact of the building program which began in 1970, catapulted the budget from $11,000 to $100,480 by 1981. (In 2011 the inflated dollar figure would compare to $ 274,400.) Proportionately Eden had the third highest per capita income in the entire Wisconsin-Upper Michigan Synod in 1981, not bad for a poverty-rated county. The 1973 church indebtedness of $210,000 was erased by 1987. In 1979 the congregation gave twenty-six percent of its operating budget to world missions. Congratulations are in order to Eden members for a miraculous stewardship response to the gospel!

* * *

In **social ministry** the inner faith/outer service policy was not easy to put into practice. Outer service was initially done on an individual basis, and Edenites served as paper mill managers, mayors, on school boards, hospital boards, development groups, county-township boards, union members, and the like. *"Prove the Word with works and do not merely hear it. Don't fool yourself."*39

The parish also allowed me to set an example by my various involvements. In addition to the many L.C.A. committees, I **personally** served with the following groups out of love for my birthplace community and in behalf of the parish. I was on the Alger-Marquette Community Action board (AMCAB),40 Action Housing Board,41 Alger-Delta-Marquette Community Mental Health Board,42 Michigan Clergy Counsel for Problem Pregnancies,43 Selective Service Board (No. 2 and 54),44 Alger County Alcoholism Council,45 Alger County Historical Society,46 and the Rotary Club.47 That's considerable.

It was an honor for me to deliver the invocation and asking God's blessing on the new **Pictured Rocks National Lakeshore** (Park) at its dedication banquet in 1966. This magnificent area could be seen from our new church windows, infringing on our city. I sat with, and got to know, **Stewart Udall**, the nation's Secretary of Interior. My blessing held firm until 2007 when two deaths occurred in the Lakeshore, one near Grand Marais where part of the Au Sable sand dune collapsed on a little boy, and the other a murder by a husband as he pushed his wife over the cliff near Miner's Castle. And the promised road between Munising and Grand Marais finally materialized in 2010, thanks to hard work on the part of Doug Miron. Without a doubt the Lakeshore has been a blessing and a wonderful concept.

Nathan got into the act regarding **social action**, when at the age of nine he and Mike Beauparland, emptied a three-pound coffee can full of dead sea lampreys into the city storm sewer in 1968. When the city workers, cleaning the sewers the following day found them, excitement ensued. They and biologists concluded that they had aggressively come up the storm sewer from South Bay. It was front page news, and the end result was a $250,000 special grant for local **lamprey control**.

What had happened was that Tim Bonner brought the lampreys to my high school Sunday school class, held in the parsonage living room. He wanted me to realize how they were spawning in the Au Train River, and then he forgot them. Sunday evening I asked Nathan to try to get rid of them. One by one, they dropped them down the manhole grate at Spruce and Superior. Voila! We told no one.

Someone said it looked like the Pied Piper leading the rats to the lake. It was one of the first **Earth Days** in April 1973, an emphasis on the first article of the Apostles' Creed and the environment. I marched the congregation down to the outlet pipe where spring run-off untreated city sewage on our church property poured directly into our pristine Lake Superior. We went there to conduct our corporate confession of sins on Earth Day. It was part of our worship in very visible and dramatic terms. Later, extremist *tree huggers* went off the deep end underscoring the first article, at the expense of the second and third articles (Christ the Redeemer, and the Holy Spirit), and environmentalism became a new false religion for some.

*   *   *

My next two stories cannot make sense until I share what kind of **tumultuous climate** governed the late 1960s. 1968 was the turning point in our nation. After President Kennedy was killed, his brother Robert also was gunned down, the Vietnam War was in full swing. The Beatles had landed, and Woodstock gathered thousands of counter-culture Hippies and Yippies, drugs and sex driven. A black clergyman civil rights leader, Martin Luther King, Jr., was shot in Memphis. Cuba had gone communist, ninety miles from our shores. Materialism and hedonism were claiming our youth. Abortion had become the birth control of choice. Our cities, led by Detroit, were burning down. But yet, ironically, Holy Scripture was read from the moon by the first men who "discovered" it, and the Green Bay Packers ruled all of football. The average wage was $ 6,772, and a gallon of gasoline cost only thirty-four cents.

Let me tell you two more exciting "churchly" stories before sharing more personal insights.

The **civil rights** movement for African-Americans was in full swing and I was looking around where I could get involved in it, without leaving Eden, my paradise on the northern fringe of American society. Trends always reached us a bit later, allowing us time to go to school on the others.

As the Civil Rights movement arrived, I began to think how I could get involved in it, being located so far from a major city. The city came to me. I began a four-year commitment to primarily African-Americans at Camp Cusino. This chaplaincy was my answer to the movement, and it was spiritually rewarding both to them and to me. A third of the camp came to church, sixty percent being Black.

I had the opportunity to become the **Protestant chaplain** at Camp Cusino in Shingleton, a state trustee prison camp. Every Saturday evening, after my Eden service, I would race to Cusino to do a Bible study, worship service, or a religion course. Pay was poor, but it was a wonderful experience. Along with the Rotary Club, I sponsored a ten-man basketball team in the Munising city league, eight blacks and two whites. Blacks being *"sinkers"* we almost lost one in the school pool as permission was given to allow them to jump in the pool after a game. All-state football linebacker Luther Collins, from Saginaw, fished him out and he spent three days in our hospital. No more pool! One of the Detroit Mafia was a regular attendee, namely, "Little Jack" Giancolone.

I did baptisms, a few weddings; it was evangelism and social ministry. Herman Denson whom I baptized went to the Detroit Bible College upon leaving, and Mr. Hairston went to law school at the University of Michigan. A Mr. King asked me to find a home for his sheepdog-looking terri-doodle, named Shag. As a result **Shag** lived with us for the next seventeen years. I wondered how many more members Eden might really have had, since Shag, coming from a bad neighborhood, sometimes bit folks at the church when he was afraid. But bitten people could get free tetanus shots from our Dr. Neil Grossnickle, who was an Eden member. One Sunday someone sneaking into my office, left the door ajar, and Shag came up during the opening liturgy to lie down under the altar. The usher, Denis Harbath, came to fetch him, and he bit him, with the saints looking on. But he was stepping on his tail. If someone was stepping on your tail wouldn't you bite him? Shag was a loyal and loving pet to our family.

Along the way, our two automobiles got old, and so we gave our smooth-riding Chrysler away. But since *"all things were being added unto us,"* as Jesus promised, a **Nash Rambler** Ambassador with only 27,000 miles was given to us by an Eden member. It was our primary car for the next eighty thousand miles. Actually, the giver was a relative of Betty, via her grandmother Mary Oja. Jacob Ulvila died in 1966 and Hilda did not drive so it was revealed to her that she should give the green Rambler to her grand niece and pastor husband. By and by Mike took it over and sold it to his future wife for fifty dollars.

Now, entering my mid-life crisis, we bought an orange 1972 **Dodge Demon** from (Norm) Methot Motors for $2400. It had a devil in front of each front fender. I sported my clergy collar with an orange clergy shirt and my orange pipe. I was so very impressive that one day tooling up Elm Avenue little Nicole Dionne, 4, saw me from her sidewalk and called out: *"Hi God!!"* Expectations were high in this parish. Meanwhile, as Dan reached the teens, he invested in a Honda motorcycle, then a German Opel, which I later "totaled."

I'm leading up to the story of how our family took that Nash "Green Bomb" and drove it all the way down to Atlanta, Georgia, in 1968, where I was a delegate to the biennial **convention** of Lutheran Church in America. I know going to Atlanta was downhill, but this economic Nash with a huge gas tank was gassed up only once (Kentucky) along the way. We visited **George** Wieland at Ft. Campbell, KY, along the way, where he was doing basic training, having been drafted. The car resembled an upside-down bathtub.

I served on the resolutions committee at this convention that was bombarded with resolutions about war and Vietnam. On a Sunday we worshiped at a black church where **Coretta King** was the preacher. Her husband had been assassinated five months earlier. We met her, and our sons played with the four King children. Staying at our motel was the famous Black singing group, *The Platters*. As the boys were frolicking in the pool with them, ten-year-old Nathan sent out a shrill challenge: *"Last one across the pool is a dirty Nigger!"*

Dan and Mike hastened to put their fists down their brother's throat and get him to his room. The Platters were nice about this stupid white kid. When I sang with the Platters in Branson in 2007, as an audience guest, I asked them if they could have been in Atlanta around 1968 and they said: "Yes." I dropped the subject right there.

On the return trip we picked up some outstanding staurolites (fairy crosses) in northern Georgia. Later they would grace the large stucco wall in the lobby of the new Eden church. All in all, it was a great family trip.

*   *   *

A Ball for Each Season.

During these early years in Munising our sons were living out their junior high and high school years. They rotated the kind of ball they used with the seasons. As parents Betty and I were privileged to attend all of their games. I helped Bernie Aken coach their Little League baseball teams. Nathan excelled at football (quarter-back/ linebacker), basketball (point guard), and golf. Mike was the only football player (linebacker/OT) among them to be team *"Most Valuable Player,"(MVP)*. Dan was into football (QB/ safety), basketball

(All-State Class C), and softball (pitcher). Hunting birds, deer and lake fishing was popular, Nathan in 1976 shot a nice buck on Grand Island.

I was justly proud of the accomplishments of my athletic sons in sports, especially on the football field, as well as in basketball, softball, and golf. They worked hard at it and were good examples for other youth.

We had some fun with a lemon-looking two-motored vehicle called *The Jiger*. It went everywhere with its six balloon tires, and it would float. But the rig wasn't lemon color for nothing, the two motors being troublesome. A good deal of our free time was spent at our new A-frame cottage at Lake Au Train. But in 1966 we took a camping trip with the Chrysler and the Jiger trailer around Lake Superior. The gas tank leaked, but we took turns chewing gum, which would stop the leaking for a while. The boys got caught by the Canadian Mounted Police for throwing firecrackers onto the recently-opened new *Circle Route* near White River, Ontario, from a rock cut, while Betty and I searched for mineral samples. The trip was memorable.

Kissa.

The boys had a white pet rabbit named **Bun-Bun**. He was housebroken and tame, jumping onto one's lap on the sofa and licking your hand just like a cat. He came to church on Easters. Stretched out on the floor, he and Nathan were about the same length as they watched the *Bugs Bunny Show*. We also had an affectionate Persian cat named *Kissa*, which sadly died of distemper. Kissa once was trapped across the street in Mr. Parker's garage. Later that evening with the garage doors shut, Kissa projected her voice in such a manner that it penetrated both the garage walls and our brick parsonage walls in her call for help. We immediately went to fetch her. This powerful form of communication still remains an unexplainable mystery to us. Kissa was a beautiful, blue-eyed Persian.

In 1967 I built our five-person **A-frame sauna** at the cottage, but six fires threatened its existence due to structural errors. Sauna-ing was a powerful form of therapeutic well-being, and attracted many friends to visit us at the lake. Rolling naked in the snow, cooling down in minus fifteen degrees, and making a hole in the ice with a chainsaw to jump into, was not unusual behavior for us Finns in our northern sauna culture.

The John Pirlot farm in Bark River furnished the outstanding barnboard at my sauna, while the first exceptional stove came from the Leo Nippa firm in Bruce Crossing. A paraphrasing of the forty-fifth rune from the Finnish national epi, *The Kalevala*, goes like this:

Steadfast old Väinämöinen Produced honeyed vapour, Through the glowing stove stones, He speaks with these words: "Come now, God, into the sauna, to the warmth, heavenly Father, healthfulness to bring us, and the peace secure to us."

Welcome löyly, welcome warmth! Welcome healing power! Löyly into the floor and ceiling, Löyly into the moss in walls. Löyly to the top of the platform, Löyly onto the stones of the stove!
Drive the Evil far away, Far away from under my skin,
From the flesh made by God! (Sauna Spell)

Why I'm A Piscatologist,

The **hunting and fishing stories** could go on endlessly. I caught my first **lake trout** in 1966 in Au Train Bay with Frank Doucette. It was sixteen pounds and 45 years later I was still waiting to surpass it. It was also the largest laker caught that year in the central Upper Peninsula, and merited a *Master Angler Award*. Frank taught me the art of catching lake trout. I did **brook trout** fishing and **smelting** as well. Our largest northern **pike** was also sixteen pounds in 1983, fishing with Marcia. Prior to 1981 I was often a guest of Dr. Neil Grossnickle for lake trout fishing. I became so proficient that for almost twenty years on the *Koskela Flats* I caught fish every time I went out except thrice using my lunar major/minor feeding period system. My finest brook trout fishing after childhood was the Slapneck Creek, Sturgeon River and Addis Ponds. For decades after retirement my calling card identified me as a **Piscatologist** (fisher of fish and men). Marcia in 1983 took brook trout Master Angler honors with a speckled trout of nineteen and three-quarter inches on the Sturgeon River.

My largest whitetail deer of the **eighteen deer** of my career was a 10-point behemoth that scaled at 245 lbs. on the hoof. It was shot just north of Bullshit Hill, south of Lake Au Train in 1966 in the company of the Reverends David LeLievre and Paul Landstrom. I once shot a deer with a well-placed shot without benefit of seeing it in 1968. Our lake cottage served as a deer camp, and once I counted 13 hunters asleep there. My favorite rifle was a .722 Remington bolt, with a Weaver scope, and which shot a .300 Savage cartridge, which I had purchased for seventy-five dollars. My favorite haunts were the Au Train River valley and hills, Grand Island "thumb," and Chaney Lake near Wakefield.

* * *

In addition to deer, I joined hunting parties for **moose** in Nakina, Ontario, and Robb, Alberta, and **antelope** hunting near Casper, Wyoming (1972-74). I enjoyed the hunting of ruffed grouse in the Seney Swamp area with my 1946 Jeep. A good day would produce an array of partridge, sharptail and woodcock. A good amount of the above was done with my sons and parishioners.

I have a moose hunting story from the Nakina trip. Actually it is not so much about hunting as it is about the true meaning of grace. I used it in my sermons several times for an illustration of grace. I joined a six-man hunting trip in September 1972 (Neil Grossnickle, Bill Tidd, Richard Nebel, Ed Myler, Bob Neale and myself) I brought with me our cool Rupp mini-bike onto which handlebars I strapped two guns, my .722 Remington rifle and my little .410 shot gun/.22 combination.

On the first day of moose season in 1972 I was tooling to the campsite for lunch. The shotgun was empty, but I left three cartridges in the bolt action rifle. I came speeding over a ridge on the two-rut sand road, and whoa!, right before me was a **Conservation Officer** checking out six Canadians. He motioned to stop. I was in deep trouble, and I knew it. I let the bike fall to the ground still running. It was a distraction attempt. *"May I check your guns?"* I handed him the shotgun. As he was checking it, I turned and with my back to him I ejected three shells from the rifle. Why? I felt that if he didn't see them in the gun, my chances were better. All this was while the Canadians were watching, standing in a row.

He looked at me. I looked at him. I had a gut feeling that the first person who speaks loses. He said: *"It was loaded, wasn't it?"* Silence... Then there was a seemingly long moment of silence, like an eternity, and finally he said: *"I will give you another chance, since it is the first day of the season."* Then I spoke and said: *"Thank you; you are a good man."* I breathed relief, remembering the stories of how tough Canadian COs were. He left. I went over to the Canadians, one of whom uttered: *"Isn't it nice that there are some decent people left in the world?"* I should say! Then, I collected myself and sheepishly, yet elatedly, drove back to the campsite and to my buddies. I told them the story, and they were amazed. They had never heard of such leniency in Canada. Grace is undeserved favor.

Yes, I will give you another chance. That sounds like the story of my life in my relationship to my God. My very first chance was merely to be born, you recall. My life has been one of falling down (sinning, breaking bones and covenants, forgiveness), and getting up again. Life is a struggle for wholeness.

*   *   *

In 1965 and 1970 I lost my final two grandparents, **Maria Sipilä** and **Emanuel 'Manu' Niemi**, the latter being eighty-eight. The former had been unbelievably longsuffering in a family and culture of heavy drinking. The latter had become enamored by a godless socialism, even Leninism. He spoke of having been a *"Progressive,"* which term is interestingly and unashamedly being used by leftist liberals today. Let's be very sure we all understand what that word implies. *"Well, that's not so bad...."* is heard from surprising sources regarding current conditions. That's the culture I abandoned, thankfully. However, I thank God for having known my immigrant grandparents, and for my numerous trips to Finland. Many people have neither of them.

Ed Niemi

Prior to death grandpa bequeathed to me $2000 which I used to take the family to look at our roots in Finland in 1972. He seemed to rebound back to Christian Faith as he attended worship with me in Newberry prior to dying. I remember some of his last words as I prayed and sang hymns in the hospital to him; *"Leslie, minä rakastan sinua."* (Les, I love you.) It is uncommon for a Finn to talk like that, stoics that we are. *"Minne Manu meni?"* (*Where did Manu go?*)

My **dad retired** from a forty-year construction career in 1971 due to arthritis and a parting of ways with my brother Bill, who had worked with him for a decade. Ed built an unbelievable number of new structures (264), plus all the remodeling jobs, peaking in the 1950s and 60s. His finest display of new homes can still be viewed on East Varnum Street and Sand Point Road in Munising. Forty-four percent of his jobs were in Munising, while thirty-three percent were in Rock River Township. He trained Charlie Vartti, Oscar Olson, Bob Oas, Bill Hautamäki, and his son Bill, all carpenters. His final project in 1974 was a small equipment barn at Eden Church, which he donated, as if a stamp of approval. Andy Stone was his assistant on the structure.

I feel fortunate that my dad by example taught me values, which builds character, patriotism, democracy, and stewardship, preventing waste not only of money but also time, thought and effort. Thrift perhaps prompted him to say of my playing ball: *"You'll never make any money that way."* The wartime and childhood purchasing of ten cent saving stamps which resulted in twenty-five dollar savings bonds was instructive. The evils of materialism and consumerism have now wreaked devastation to this millennium.

Betty Niemi-Marlow, sister.

My brother **Eddie** completed high school in the same class as son Michael. **John Boucher** went to Minneapolis to work for Augsburg Publishing House of the American Lutheran Church. Both are retired now.

Sister **Betty** in Milwaukee divorced **Jacob** Korpi, moved to the Detroit area and married Trenary native, **Stanley** Rämä. **Bill** also had an awful time, went through an alcohol-induced separation and divorce from **Judy** Vartti, who moved to Durango, Colorado. But not before they received four daughters Janice, Christine, Suzanne, and Patricia. Their Christian training would cease when my mom no longer brought them to Sunday school in 1969, and the family curse continued.

By 1970 Bill married **Pamela Fitzgerald** of Gladstone, and they had a son, **Brian**, born October 21, 1970. At this point hard feelings ended Bill and Pam's residency in dad's house causing a long estrangement. Bill moved to Gladstone, worked for Schwalbach Kitchens, and then moved to Chatham Corners.

The times they were a changin.' Cable TV appeared as did calculators. Allan Shepherd had hit three golf balls on the moon, and they lost them. You have heard that in the history of man, the more upscale and older he gets, the smaller his balls get: basketball, football, soccer, softball, tennis, baseball, golf and ping-pong. It's a natural evolution. My favorite lake trout lure was a McMahon No.7, 50-50, of brass and silver. In January 1973 the Vietnam War ended with the Paris Peace Accord when Richard Nixon was president. That same year abortion became legal in America with the *Roe vs. Wade* Supreme Court decision. Most of us know however that legal does not make anything moral. Was there any difference between the German Holocaust and the silent holocaust of our abortion clinics? In both cases an entire class of humans were declared legally expendable.

*   *   *

The primary focus in my second **Six-Year Plan**, was to build a **new church** in Munising. which task would consume most of the 1971 to 1976 period. This challenge would be one of the highest achievements of my pastoral career, yet, of course, a building, however lovely, is merely a visible left-brain item.

To find a suitable **site** was not as easy as one might think in a place like Munising. It called for great patience. The site was very important. God answered this prayer by sending us Bill and Lois Ryan. Bill bought a half mile of South Bay frontage in order to build a new marina. He sold Eden 500 feet of it for the same price, per foot, as he paid Kimberly-Clark Corporation. We paid only $26,229 for 5.3 wonderfully-located acres. The site, going backward, had previously been owned by Ford Motor Co., Jackson-Tindle Sawmill, Superior Veneer and Cooperage Co., and Northwestern Cooperage Company.

We hired a professional **funding** service whereby Clifford Kent (not Clark) came to help us raise $ 103,817 in three years. The second similar campaign raised an additional $ 89,077. Edenites learned about stewardship.

We needed an architect. We interviewed three architects and the members hired Finland-born **Eino Kainlauri** of KKM Associates, who had designed the Trout Creek church in 1960. We gave him our ideas through a self-study called the *Written Building Program*. We maintained function before form. Eino drew up a three-sided building which looked like a ship upside down, and also reminded us of the Holy Trinity, Father, Son Jesus, and Holy Spirit. It would have a radical functional design, complete with a Finnish sauna. But it would cost us $ 291,000. The view of Munising Bay and Pictured Rocks was unbeatable from the new site.

So now we needed a loan. God sent us **James** McKenna from Green Bay, a banker I had met on the Lutheran Social Services board, and who looked like the singer, Eddie Arnold. Three banks shared the loan. Our monthly payments until 1987 would be $ 1,941 per month. We never missed a payment! Members were so excited they almost jumped out of their skins. Groundbreaking services were on Pentecost, May 21, 1972, with the *Whole Truth* junior choir singing and huge icebergs floating in the bay. The pastor wielded a golden hard-hat and a golden shovel. City manager Royce Downey was present and spoke.

Caspian Construction Company of Iron County took the job, led by Jerry Wrate of Gwinn, and Edmund "Eb" Oas, of the Seattle World's Fair fame, was our building manager locally representing the architect. In December the cornerstone was laid at which former member Arthur Nieman preached, in a sizeable snow storm.

Natural materials from the surrounding area graced the church, like sandstone quarried near Onota, driftwood pilings, staurolites, cedar, agates, a mineral display, a waterfall, cor-ten steel, a driftwood crucifix, fishing nets and floats. At every turn the right "angels" appeared as if programmed. I think every congregation has its own angel.

Eden-on-the-Bay Church, 1973.

When it was done, and dedicated on **October 7, 1973**, the new church building was accepted as one of 28 world churches entered in competition by U.S. architects. The winning church was in Switzerland, however.

Wait! What do we do with the old church at Spruce and Onota? It was sold to the local Grand Island Masonic Lodge #422 for $ 10,000, provided they remove the steeple. Many of our members were also Masons, so it was a win-win situation. Now, here is where it gets spooky. Two weeks after the sale, an early morning **lightning** strike put a ten foot hole in the steeple, but it did not burn. The timing was uncanny. It was a "sign."

The old church building and those who invested their faith and life in it, are to be gratefully commended for their decades of service and deep devotion. The church building and the longtime members had served faithfully.

New Eden was a refreshing radical concept which freed members toward better relationships to both God and man. We understood what Paul Tillich meant when he wrote

"Luther did not reject church buildings but he devaluated them as the holy spaces..."[48] Or, what Harold Wagoner meant when he said: *"Before any church builds, they might do well to ask 'Do pews keep people apart?' If they do, should they not seek another type of flexible arrangement more suited to seeing Him in the encounter between man and man."*[49]

The building of this exciting modern church was truly a marvelous experience for the congregation. The oneness of spirit was uplifting. A goodly portion of the interior work was done by the members. We enjoyed large donations of both time and materials. The multi-use concept of space was most refreshing.

*   *   *

New members and vacationers began to flock to the new ***Eden-on-the-Bay Church***. **Counseling** opportunities were overwhelming, evenly split between members and non-members, and of necessity tightly scheduled. In this connection I tried not to let the pipe go out, remembering the counseling adage that if the counselor's pipe goes out he is doing too much of the talking. Several community schools and groups began using/renting the new facility.

The new church immediately prompted the offering of new programs. Worship increase was important primarily because more folks were able to hear the Word of God. Anticipating the times, e.g., we offered a class for young married couples entitled *The Marriage Enrichment Course* with Urban Steinmetz as our resource. A highly successful youth offering was *Love, Sex, and Life*, with up to 45 youth attendances in repeated course offerings, all part of *School of Religion*. *Family Night* special events were held once monthly on Sunday evenings to packed houses. Eden-on-the-Bay enjoyed a decade of superb programming.

The six-person **church sauna** was installed by Eb Oas and Walfred Mickelson. Jim and Nancy McClurg gifted the electric *Ilo* sauna stove which was manufactured in Dollar Bay. We were likely the only church in the nation with a sauna, and it was much more than merely a publicity stunt, albeit the Wall Street Journal featured it.

The 3-room sauna became both an evangelism and social ministry tool. During one year over a third of the new members began coming to our building initially because of the sauna, then later to worship and followed by membership. Motels sent their guests; wrestlers from the high school came to "make their fighting weights." Buildings are external activities, and I needed to reach to the inner man. While it may seem strange to the uninformed to fathom a church to house a sauna, one must recognize how enormous the *sauna culture was* in Michigan's Upper Peninsula. Before long the Eden sauna competed for the most frequented rooms in the building. Beside sweating out the impurities in the skin, it also energized one's mind and one's soul. It unified parents and children, helped folks socialize, and alone aided in contemplation and meditation. Status and rank tended to disappear in the sauna.

Average Sunday **attendance** during the second segment was 214 with 649 members. One Christmas Eve a vacationer from Ohio who knew the violinist begged to get through the crowded narthex door because his friend was playing. The building was literally filled to capacity. They let him in. During summers when weather allowed we would hold the worship service at the lakeshore, where we had electrical power for the organ. Also weddings were enjoyed there, including our son Michael and Patty's wedding, in October 1980.

But, we found that we had moved from a 'safe' neighborhood to a bad neighborhood. On the dark side, **thieves** failed to open the church safe one Easter evening where the large offering was stored. Neighborhood thieves, who will go unnamed here, habitually raided the donation honor box in the sauna and stole the money. They stole also the sacristy communion wine. My *Sea King* rowboat was stolen from the beach and also my silver-copper "half-breed" nugget from the church office which Frank Rader (who had survived the Calumet Italian Hall Christmas Eve massacre in 1913) had given me. Once the acolytes stole the offering after a service and buried it in the sand at the top of one of the hills surrounding the city. All of this mayhem, of course, simply clarified our reason for gospel's existence in the community, namely sin and brokenness.

Our new Au Train home.

In 1972 and '73 **Dan** enrolled at **Suomi College**, excelling in basketball and serving as a hall resident assistant; he transferred to Northern Michigan. **Mike** enrolled at NMU but dropped college after one year. In 1975 I added a wing to our cottage and we moved to reside at Lake Au Train with the aid of a housing allowance. The new wing was an $ 11,000 item. Leftovers built a small garage. With the encouragement of funeral director Richard Hallifax I began a 25-year career of **jogging** for health reasons. It was a good move. **Betty** became the office nurse for Dr. Neil Grossnickle in 1974. It was also the year that Dr. Ralph Jalkanen contacted me about joining his development staff at **Suomi College**. Earlier I had received "inquiries" about moving to Negaunee, Glenwood Springs, CO. Ashtabula, Ohio, and Allen Park (Detroit). My classmates, Rudy Kemppainen went to Negaunee and Fred Vanhala went to Allen Park. Negaunee was additionally interested in the athletic prowess of my sons. The Lord had not spoken to me about these places.

To close out **the second Six-Year Plan**, I relate the following two items, both of which also deal with buildings. It seems that the owners (Dennis and Bonnie Stirler) were transferring from Hiawatha Forest to a similar job in Ketchikan, AK. Dr. Grossnickle and I purchased the two-unit **apartment house** on 801 West Superior for $ 25,000. It merely demanded the doctor to wheelbarrow his bars of silver to the bank as collateral. In 1976 I remodeled the lower unit into two rental units. But it was not all peaches and cream. Some renters were loathe to pay their rent, and some lived slovenly. The doctor finally gave me the entire business, and finally I gave it to the bank after ten years. Easy come, easy go. I was too sympathetic regarding unpaid balances, (e.g., one of them still owes me $ 1,800 dating back to 1984). Let's simply say: we furnished affordable housing as a service and as a social ministry experiment.

By July 1975, after I added a 24 x 22 foot addition to the Au Train A-frame, our family of three **moved to the lake,** ending our 21 years of parsonage-living. Wasn't it Ralph Emerson who wrote: *"In the woods, we return to reason and faith. There I feel that nothing can befall me in life which nature cannot repair."* Well, faith might argue with that, but it's a nice thought. The parsonage that we left was rented for income for the congregation.

The **chisel design addition** cost $11,000, whereas the initial cottage cost only four thousand dollars. Shortly we purchased an experienced pontoon for $5,000. Our initial year-round neighbors on North Shore Road were Larrabees, Ronns, Wilsons, Clarks, and Browns. We had longed to have a home of our own for quite some time.

At this point a word might be in order about the name *"Au Train."* It is French and the word *"train"* is from *"trainerant,"* which means "drag." So much sand formed at the mouth of the Au Train River that the early voyagers had to drag their canoes over a shoal. Early forms of the name Au Train had left out the "au."

The Native-Americans had the words *"Madabon ingk"* which meant *"where the trail comes down on the beach,"* or, "end of trail." The trail was the Bay de Noc Trail, a major "highway" of twenty-two miles between Lake Superior and Lake Michigan. Lake Au Train was *"Madabon sagaiigan,"* or *"on a river in a canoe to the lake."* Au Train Island was *"Madabon miniss."* Munising got its name from *"Kitchi minising."* Ten thousand years earlier when Lake Nipissing was of much higher elevation the primary river south from this lake ran right through Lake Au Train, as is evident from a satellite photo. About 7,500 years ago the land began to rise and the water receded to how we see it today. There are no natural rocks in Lake Au Train since it is all sand beaches. It's a wonderful place.

So in **review** I have not gone very far. I moved sixty-eight miles from Hancock to Trout Creek, sixty-four miles from Trout Creek to Republic, eighty miles from Republic to Munising, twelve miles from Munising to Au Train, and (in the winter) 2,330 miles from Au Train to Lake Havasu City, Arizona. Now, let's move on to my **third 6-year plan** for Eden-on-the-Bay Church and our family.

* * *

The chief components of the final segment of **eighteen years** as Eden's pastor was highlighted by The *Bethel Series* (bible study), *The Partnership Conference* (social ministry), the death of my wife Betty, my exit from Eden, marrying Marcia, and my summary of parishes.

When Eden decided to adopt **Bethel Series** in 1975, one of the first tasks was to carefully recruit eleven potential lay teachers. Responding to this call were: Evelyn Balko, Skip Bray, Denis Harbath, Elwin Huck, Lois Lehto, George Männistö, Millie Männistö, John Nadeau, Lynn Nebel, Richard Oas, and Scow Seglund.

I taught this class for two years on a weekly basis on the Old and New Testaments. Bethel employed huge paintings, one for each lesson. We read the entire Bible. The congregational phase was to offer classes of no more than thirty members each. They would meet simultaneously on Wednesday evenings. The maximum Wednesday attendances were one hundred forty and this went on for two years. It was very exciting. Bethel was the most successful Bible Study program in the world to date, originating out of Madison, WI. What it meant to Eden was that in 1978 we had the highest church attendances in the history of Eden . . . 228 average on Sundays, and one hundred twenty-five average at Wednesday services. Enthusiasm, and hopefully, spirituality had never been higher. Bethel had been a great blessing to Eden. After we completed the program we kept offering Bethel to all new members who joined.

We were bold to dream of continued membership growth. We toyed with the theme: *"1000 by 2000."* A net gain of only twenty members a year so that by the year 2000 A.D. Eden would be a thousand members. Little did we know that within five years the congregation would be in decline (and the weekend attendances finally dropped to as low as 40-60.) Church sociologists had predicted that attendances would decline by a third every generation, which meant that Eden was ahead of schedule. We once joked while building the church that its radical form could easily lend itself for a hamburger shop if necessary. Around 2009, that didn't seem so funny any longer.

An interesting project which I undertook for the 1976 Bicentennial Year of our nation was the organization and editing of an All-Alger County **Pictorial Church Directory** in color. It held the names of the sixty-three percent of the county population who belonged to one of our twenty-four county churches. This project was a nice bit of ecumenism in our two hundredth anniversary as a nation.

* * *

In 1978, Betty and I joined a Catholic **pilgrimage to Rome** . . . thirty-six Catholics and four Lutherans from Munising. Cost: $ 575 each, flight included. We communed all over Rome including St. Peter's Cathedral. It was a wonderful trip. Other vacations in the late seventies were taken were several to the middle **Florida** Keys, namely Marathon, as well as Tampa where Dan and Ann lived.

I was **honored** in 1979 by both Suomi College and Northern Michigan University on the twenty-fifth year of my ordination. I received an award from Suomi and served as the master of ceremony at Suomi's seventy-fifth Diamond commencement banquet. On that same program was Ernie Montgomery, Suomi's finest basketball player ever, having had a tryout with the NBA Golden State team. (Earlier I failed to mention that while in high school I was "scouted" by Michigan State University in February 1949. They didn't call me, perhaps because we lost the game 47-43, although I made seventeen points. If it has seemed like an unusual amount of ink on basketball, I warned you that basketball was my game. But when you get older the ball gets smaller . . . golf. Fortunate is the person who is able to play games for its therapeutic value.)

On August 4 Northern Michigan University invited me to participate in their summer commencement exercises and luncheon.

*   *   *

The impact of building the "inner man," by preaching and Bible study, was balanced in 1978 when Eden adopted and helped develop **The Partnership Project** for "outer service" in social ministry. These two must be kept in balance, we felt. The success of this program distinguished Eden as one of the top social action type parishes in the entire WUM Synod. This became evident by invitations to appear at regional events in the Midwest where we were asked to tell "**The Munising Story.**"

It was a community development effort for the purpose of improving the communities and the way of life of local residents and it qualified as social ministry.

It began by Eden spearheading the holding of **seventeen forums** in the county. Over six hundred citizens came to these. Some were village forums like Au Train, Christmas, Shingleton, Chatham and Munising. Others were industrial, retailers, tourism, churches, city hall, etc. So successful were these that the program expanded to two additional counties, namely Schoolcraft and Luce. It was now the Tri-County Partnership Conference, with visible results especially evident in Germfask, Seney and Newberry. Joint county meetings were held at the Seney Wildlife Refuge.

Some of the most immediate results were: Christmas Civic Club, Shingleton Civic Club, Au Train Civic Club, (each had their respective lists of accomplishments), The Munising Visitor's Bureau (still powerfully operative in 2010), Redecorating City Hall, New Munising High School on the first ballot, a boxed firewood industry (now defunct), Annual Ecumenical Church picnics, and enabling citizens to run for political office. Other spin-off: Munising Ice Arena, Au Train community building, blacktopping of the Forest Lake-Au Train Road, etc. The *Putting Life into Au Train Now* (PLAN) group was an outstanding civic group that endured for a decade. The Partnership Project was incorporated.

The dynamic looked like this: six thousand area population base, six hundred forum participants, sixty on the advisory council, and twelve on the "Glue" (board). The listing of more minor "miracles" would take too much space here. (We called the results "miracles.")

Some random **observations** from our model:

1. We conceptualized a congregation's role.
2. We tried to know the trends for the future.
3. We looked at society as a "bottom-up" society, rather than top down.
4. We recognized the inherent depth of community negativism and drag.
5. We acknowledged how congregations could be segregationist.
6. We urged congregations to specialize in various ministries, using their gifts.
7. Congregations can maintain a low profile in social ministry (Lone Ranger).
8. We maintained a future-orientation: global, futuristic, and intentional.
9. We produced maximum results with very little cost due to volunteerism.
10. We emulated America like it was initially at its birth.

The Partnership Conference was America as the founding fathers had envisioned it, with the grassroots taking the initiative. We operated on practically no money and did not depend on government entitlements, albeit our synod gave us a $2000 grant. In 1831 Alexis de Tocqueville visited the infant America and wrote: *"I confess that in America I saw more than America; I sought the image of democracy itself, with its implications, its character, its prejudices, and its passions."*[50]

Yet there was resistance from our own Edenites to our **social ministry** by folks who thought "inner faith" should be our sole concern. There was less than adequate enthusiasm from some who had inherited the business from the previous generation. They were suspicious of losing control. The Partnership Project at Eden revealed to the community that Eden and other congregations were caring communities.

*   *   *

Meanwhile important things had been happening with our Niemi family. On July 5, 1979 our oldest son, **Daniel James**, married **Ann Brisson**, daughter of Bernie and Donna, nee, Morrison, at Sacred Heart Church. The ceremony kept being interrupted by fainting of some men in the wedding party. They were honored by a buffet dinner at our multi-use Eden Church, and then they danced at a roadhouse in Christmas. Incidentally, the name Daniel goes back to 530 B.C. and the prophet; it means in Hebrew: *"God is (my) judge."*[51] James was an "apostle and a brother of Jesus, who wrote the epistle. St. Paul called him a pillar.

Next, **Michael Jonathan** on August 30, 1980, **married Patricia VanLandschool**, daughter of Francis and Janet, nee, Lezotte, of Bayview Location, on the Eden Church shoreline lawn. Betty was ill but insisted on attending the gala event. The father of the groom was the officiant. The reception was at the Moose Hall. There are ten biblical Michaels, but ours was named after the angel. The name means *"Who is like God."*[52] Jonathan, 1050 B.C., was the son of King Saul, and a loyal friend of King David. Pat and Mike lived on East Munising Avenue, later purchasing the Oscar Olson home on beautiful East Munising Bay.

105

Finally, **Nathan Lloyd** was wed at Gethsemane Lutheran Church in Virginia, MN, to **Sandra Fox** of Midway Location on October 16, 1982. The father of the groom participated in the service as did the Rev. George Wieland. Sandy was the daughter of Frank and Ardys, nee, Johnson, Fox of Virginia, and they were in the business of flower shops. This wedding had the most flowers of any wedding I had ever seen. Betty was absent for this wedding. The biblical Nathan was a prophet in King David's time, not afraid to accuse the king of sin.[53] Lloyd is English (whereas Leslie is Celtic.) They lived in Virginia MN, before moving to Kincheloe, MI.

Given names serve as a "life map," or "life scripting," and thereby we try to figure out what our parents (or our God) expected from our lives. If "plan A" is rejected we must listen for the word "recalculating" in our guidance system. Ideally our life of faith is one of commitment to God's will.[54]

While there may have been some disadvantages to being a "preacher's kid," **the advantages** were outstanding. They included exceptional opportunity to hear and receive the way of salvation, forgiveness of sin, and grace; the security of a relatively solid home life; exposure to ethical and moral concepts and vocabulary; exposure to social awareness, equality, concerns such as violence, drinking, drugs and peace; wide exposure to fine people, places and ideas. Only 10-15% of PKs have trouble with that role. Some PKs will try to disprove that they are in fact pastor's kids by excelling in evil. Sometimes a loving father must say to his sons: *Son, I leave you now so that I needn't leave you in eternity.* Al Capp said: *"Don't be a pal to your son. Be his father."*

*   *   *

An **ordination service** was held at Eden Church for **George Wieland** on June 29, 1975, son of Orville Wieland and Ella Steinbach. George was a foster brother of Betty since he was age six months. He transferred to Eden in 1966, attended Northern Michigan University and was drafted into military service in 1967 when his girlfriend, Bonnie Pirlot, died, and George dropped school. He served as a chaplain's assistant in Korea, returned to NMU, had the call into the ministry, and enrolled at Lutheran School of Theology in Chicago. After ordination he served congregations in Falun and Siren, WI, Chassell, and Bark River and as interim pastor in greater Aberdeen, SD. He married Kay Torson, an outstanding and talented musician, in Fort Dodge, IA, and who worked as a parish director of music.

Two other Munising men were ordained Lutheran pastors, namely, **Raymond Johnson**, son of George and Lempi Johnson; Ray had a distinguished pastorate in New York Mills, MN, and was a noted painter and cartoonist on a national and regional scale. He passed away in 2005. **Mark Tanis**, son of Larry and Phyllis Wys, one of my confirmands, was ordained on January 13, 2001 in Grand Forks ND, and served as a U.S. Navy, Army, and Coast Guard chaplain, which included several tours to the Iraqi War.

My friends thought it was easy to be Eden's pastor because I made it look easy. But as a workaholic I needed to limit my hours to fifty-five a week. I had some **hobbies**. I was in the golf league, hunted deer and birds, fished and pontooned; took hot saunas at church and at home. I went lake trout fishing with Frank Doucette, Neil Grossnickle and George A. Bush (on his wooden sloop, named *"Sisu."*) I followed the sons in each of their athletic careers.

In every family there are skeletons in the closets. One of those around 1980 was the outright **murder** of my cousin, Darlene Erickson-LaChance, who lived with her family in Trenary, the wife of Peter LaChance. Her decomposed body was discovered in the forest near the Hoy Road, two miles north of Trenary. The murder was never solved, though there are suspects. It brought much sadness to my mom's family. But out of this home arose a wonderful Christian girl named **Lisa**, now living in Louisiana.

In Munising the new church in the decade of the seventies was an outstanding blessing to the work of the gospel in Munising. Three consecutive Kimberly-Clark Mill managers belonged to Eden: Bill Beerman, Richard Boehm and Ed Masak.

* * *

The twin thrusts of **law and gospel preaching** and continuous visitation was effective. I might have been one of the last pastors in the LCA to believe Martin Luther who said: *Preach the law so well that the Gospel comes alive.* I used four different formats for sermon presentation: "envelope notes," "oral writing," "Evanston outline," and manuscript. The most effective seemed to be the first two. With the first I stood loose as a goose at the middle aisle. While some may have thought of the sermons as dull, the proof of the pudding was not the delivery, but the faithful content that mattered most. We moved the furniture around a great deal, sometimes to a church-in-the-round setting.

Visitation consisted of two kinds: crisis and non-crisis. Crisis calls resulted in massive numbers of new members because I focused on soulcare. I normally visited the hospital thrice weekly. I conducted 190 funerals among the Rock River Township folks, the majority of them being of socialist background, which seemed to be my second (invisible) congregation. Once I visited every Eden member home in a two week period. Soulcare of the burdened, ill, grieving, and those who didn't think they were lost, was priority. Soulcare focused on unburdening guilt and declaring forgiveness of sins, creating new hearts in Christ, deep counseling, and always employing the Word of scripture, the chief means of grace. It also employed laying-on-of-hands, prayer, and administering Holy Communion to believers.

The problem with a rapidly retreating **Evangelical Lutheran Church in America** is not only heretical doctrine, but total lack of home visitation by most pastors, and dishonest preaching by many of the clergy. Forsaking the true doctrine of man is dishonest and such pastors ought to be tried for malpractice.

Although **Eden attendance** took a downturn in 1982, for eighteen years our Sunday average was two hundred nineteen. December 21, 1982, upon my departure, was the final monthly Finnish language event at Eden, which had been held for fifty-seven years. Our largest attendances at Eden were in July and August when we were brushing up against four hundred a Sunday. By design we did not do services at campgrounds, but sent messengers out on Saturdays to invite campers to Eden's great liturgical worship setting, complete with rowdy singing of hymns. And those vacationers responded beautifully.

With several other congregations, Eden sponsored a family from Vietnam. Marcia became intimately acquainted with Sieu in the fifth grade, teaching him English. Avery Color Studio hired the oldest son. At one time Eden had seven women's circles, meeting monthly. Our seven standing committees all met on the same evening and the pastor simply shuffled from one meeting to another. I trusted my members because I knew God spoke through them. We even had a 4-H club in the parish, and Sharon Eklund was the leader. She was also an office secretary, as were also Karen Johnson, DeeDee Wilderspin, Brenda Pirlot, and Sandy Shaw.

Although we never had a strong church choir, our junior high age choir was outstanding. We had a Men's Club. Our church organists were Linda Montcalm, Lillian Johnson, Patricia Erickson, Ken Ericson, Gretchen Ericson, and Paul Nybeck. The church custodians were: Ole Peterson, Dan Niemi, Ernie Schultz, Pearl Niemi, and Richard Oas. My mother traveled from Chatham to the job for seven years.

* * *

Two terrible things happened in my final two years at Eden. On May 27, 1981 my wife **Betty died** after a ten month illness. It was early Wednesday morning. She died at the Marquette hospital, where she had trained to become a nurse, of a liver failure resulting from the use of alcohol. And if that wasn't enough, her father, **Hugo** Sjostrand, died on May 31, four days later, from an aneurysm following heart surgery. Ellen Sjostrand lost both her husband and only child within four days. And I lost my wife of twenty-eight years. My conscience attacks me when I read quotes like

> "Clergy spend their love on their parishioners, and they get depleted. The spouse feels rejected, and the rejection is so overwhelming because clergy are married to the church. A clergy spouse is up against a very alluring, tempting rival."[55]

Betty became ill in July 1980, and during the next ten months went into a number of comas. She was hospitalized half of that period. It was very stressful. I continued to perform my parish duties as some parishioners tried to walk with me.

We took a **vacation trip** to the Florida Keys in March 1981, accompanied by newlyweds Michael and Patricia. While in Marathon she suspected another coma approaching. We hustled to fly her by private plane to St. Joseph's Hospital in Tampa. As an aside, while in a coma I happened upon the soloist from the Columbia Restaurant in Ybor City in the elevator, who promised to go sing to her. Although she was in this coma, she later told me about his visit, which said much about patient's ability to hear while in a coma. I had always believed this, and conducted devotions for her (and others) even while in a coma.

We flew home by commercial plane the following week and Betty was entered in Marquette General Hospital in Marquette, Michigan. She spent only ten days at home between then and when she died. She expressed fear that she would inevitably die in a coma, and so it was. I recorded her last prayers before the final coma arrived. The hospital phoned me in the early morning of **May 27**, and I hurried to see her. In another coma, her heart was racing. Michael was with me when I conducted the "commendation of the dying" liturgy and sang hymns. And then her heart stopped. Betty was a registered nurse.

It is still difficult to write about this thirty years later, which indicates the depth of denial. A **funeral** was held with the synod bishop, Robert Wilch, as preacher. The area clergy choir sang two rousing anthems as a strong witness of faith. She was brought to the Pine Grove Slapneck Cemetery just a mile from her former home. The grief was numbing. Pastor Rudy Kemppainen conducted Hugo's funeral, four days later. And I sandwiched the Henry Strand funeral in between the two. It was a difficult time for many of us. But Jesus rose again for our salvation.

As Betty prepared for dying the following hymn became dear to her, which also defined her faith and who she was:

Betty.

"If you but trust in God to guide you and place your confidence in him, You'll find him always there beside you, to give you hope and strength within. For those who trust God's changeless love build on the rock that will not move.

What gain is there in futile weeping, in helpless anger and distress? If you are in his care and keeping, in sorrow will he love you less? For he who took for you a cross will bring you safe through every loss.

In patient trust await his leisure in cheerful hope, with heart content to take whate'er your Father's pleasure and all-discerning love have sent . . ."

On the road of grief which followed, I would cry and wail while jogging North Shore Road. My preaching allowed my members to walk the road of faith with me as they pondered, "How does our pastor deal with loss by death?" "Is he not just like us?" In the midst of death and the grave I tried to set an example of faith in the midst of life's realities.

Angelo Patri wrote

"In one sense there is no death. The life of a soul on earth lasts beyond her departure. You will always feel that life touching yours, that voice speaking to you, that spirit looking out of other eyes, talking to you in the familiar things she touched, worked with, loved as familiar friends. She lives on in your life and in the lives of all others that knew her."

But of course there is death, real death. But Jesus Christ is the real resurrection from the grave and the dead. *"Death, where is your sting? Sin gives death its sting, and the Law gives sin its power. But thanks be to God who continues to give us the victory through our Lord Jesus Christ,"* reminds St. Paul.

*　*　*

A small social ministry project spearheaded by Eden was the purchase of a **Parcourse Fitness Trail**, which was erected around Munising Memorial Hospital. Parish and community men volunteered to do the installation, some of whom were Jim Landfair, Dick Bowerman and David Cromell. The concept, however, was underwhelming and not used as much as I had hoped. It was removed before the new hospital was built in 2007.

In 1982 the parish embarked upon a new program called **Stephen's Ministry**. The $ 4000 from Betty's memorial gifts were given to subsidize it. I went to St. Louis for the briefing. I recruited ten members whom I trained. Upon completion these ministers were to adopt a needy person within Eden or beyond, with whom to carry on a long-term caring ministry.

Marcia Belmas Niemi, 1983.

After a year, starting in August 30, 1982 some laymen, who shall remain nameless, had several clandestine meetings about my behavior which primarily meant unhappiness over dating Marcia Ericson, who had divorced her husband Ken in April 1982. Ken, my outstanding church organist, had some years earlier encountered serious multiple sclerosis which rapidly worsened.

Some in the parish evidently hoped I would remain celibate. Marcia continued caring for Ken's affairs after the divorce. Facing reality there was seemingly no animosity amongst us. Committed pastors begin each parish as if they would remain there forever. I believed Eden could be a thousand by two thousand and with weekend participation well over three hundred. Whether in congregations or in college funding they will do what you ask. My expectations were obviously unrealistic. And as a result some could not handle it.

Be that as it may, the Lord was closing and opening doors. The bishop interceded to solve the unhappiness. The options were clarified. **I resigned** as Eden's pastor, effective December 31, 1982, after which I took a four month sabbatical. In addition to our faith, there were some things worth dying for. I also understood more clearly what Pastor Bud Danner and Pastor Herman Larson had endured, who had preceded me at Eden. It had been a golden era nonetheless.56 Ironically, in God's mysterious ways, three pastors in succession lost their wives by death at the age of fifty, while serving the Eden congregation. And life continues.

Marcia taught fifth grade at Central School. Having invested so heavily in both Betty and Eden, the grief of losing both in a year was heavy. God knew our every step of the way, and He picked us up and carried us when discouragement threatened. But I refrained from dignifying the rumors. Wasn't it Julia Roberts who said about keeping one's mouth shut: *"It is far more dignified and deserving of respect than to put it out there and to allow people to give their opinion of it at lunch."*

Author Frank Clark wrote:
"If you can find a path with no obstacles, it probably doesn't lead anywhere."

Spoof Wedding Picture, 1983.

In a bit of uncalled-for flamboyancy Marcia and I were **married** on Sunday evening, December 26, my final act at Eden Church after eighteen years.. Our children served as our wedding attendants: Kristine, Gretchen, Dan and Michael. Pastor Rudy Kemppainen, in his Finnish tabs and coat, performed the ceremony with our families present. Only three other Eden members were allowed to attend. My eldest grandchild, Amanda, 3, signed our wedding certificate.

We went to San Francisco for our **honeymoon** and spent New Year's Eve at the Fairmont Hotel on Nob Hill. Since some parishioners said *"Go fly a kite,"* we bought a Chinese kite in Chinatown and flew it just north of the Golden Gate Bridge. I preached in Finnish at the *Lutheran Church of the Cross* in Berkeley, who then gave me a call to be their pastor. I turned down the call.

Normally it is not a good idea for a pastor to resign without a call unless he possesses unusual confidence. I spent the next few months in grief over no longer being at Eden. Ralph Jalkanen heard about my availability. I trusted that God would open the next door. I was very thankful to God for sending me **Marcia**. What a way to conclude my third Six-Year Plan at Eden, some of which was a surprise and unplanned. There was a fresh new wind blowing in the trees.

* * *

As I look into my **rear view mirror**, in summary, Eden was my crowning congregation of nearly thirty years of parish ministry. It was the same duration as that of St. Paul, but his was more successful and more strategic. I had been blessed with three wonderful parishes for twenty-nine years to which I had been called. So that we can say *"I have endured the good struggle and I have run to the end and have protected my faith."*57

Statistics are left-brain rational trivia. But in summary I can disclose that in those three decades I had a total of **3,455 members.**58 I received 1,109 adult members into church memberships. I blessed 685 persons in death, and I baptized 640 in the Name of our Triune God. Imagine the anticipation concerning those 338 marriages between a man and a woman, as it should be. Not a single same-sex marriage did I have. The Word of God and prayer was present in each and every instance. I preached over 6,500 sermons at services, plus over a thousand funeral and wedding sermons. Dad said: *"Why do you want to become a minister because you can't even talk."* But I think dad was proud of me, and I had the last word as I preached Jesus also at his funeral. I also contributed twenty-seven articles for publication in books and periodicals.

All of us well-organized clergy kept a personal record entitled *My Pastoral Record*, which contained all of the ministerial acts, new members, sermon titles, written articles, even salaries, and summaries, of one's career. Should you, or other researchers, be interested, mine was placed in the safekeeping of the *Finnish-American Historical Archives* located at Finlandia University in Hancock, Michigan. When pondering, *What did he do?* visit the FAHC at F.U.

We sometimes made a big issue about church attendance. Why? It is quite simple: attendance brings one in touch with the Bible, which both is, and contains the Word of God, and which in turn, can introduce one to Jesus, who alone can offer us faith, forgiveness and discipleship. I worry and pray for my six previous congregations which I served. They sometimes today seem like they are trying to warm themselves with a few glowing embers from the past, whereas, truth be told, we need a new present roaring fire which no church hierarchy nor seminary can extinguish.

Seven of my youth became pastors: Roy Tähtinen, David Taeger, Peter Laaninen, Michael Carriere, George Wieland, Mark Tanis and Judy Mattson. And one Sunday church school student became a lay youth minister. **Sixteen** from my little villages of Chatham-Eben, Chatham population 226, to date, became pastors and missionaries.

* * *

Some of the folks **who spoke** into my life after church merger were: Ray Wargelin, Carl Manfred, E.W. Mueller, Ted Matson, Ben Gjenvick, Bill Genszler, Walter Helwig, Clarence Schnorr, and Rudy Kemppainen.

I cannot begin to name all the fine laymen from **Eden-on-the-Bay** who spoke into my life, but that list would include folks like Brooks Hamilton, Min Scott, Harold Pirlot, Harry Nelson, Neil Grossnickle and Jack Krueger. It was like a Camelot situation to me in that *"once there was* (this) *fleeting wisp of glory named Camelot" (Eden).*

Summarizing my eighteen years as pastor of Eden Church, the umbrella-like emphasis was the magnificent shower of the Gospel for almost two decades through God's Word. My *six year plans* were divided (1) building foundational trust, (2) building the new church and (3) the inner faith/outer service theme (*Bethel Series* Bible study, *Partnership Conference*, etc.). Yet, noticeably, fate has not been kind to the Eden congregation in the new millennium, as the shower of the Gospel seems to have moved on. But we claim God's promise: *"So is my Word that goes out of my mouth: it will not return to me empty, but will accomplish what I desire and achieve the purpose for which I sent it."*59   And, *"I planted, Apollos watered, but God gave the growth. The planter therefore is nothing, nor the one who waters, but all is in God's hand, He brings growth."*60 Did not Isaiah remind us that even *a dimly burning wick he will not quench?*

As somewhat of an aside, a half dozen years after I left Eden, in 1990, I was interviewed by *The Wall Street Journal* (Paul Ingrassia) for the Midwest Edition, resulting in Eden making the front page of the Wall Street Journal. Paul was interested in saunas, Finns and Finlandia University. The dateline went: Munising, Mich. —- and the article began:

Eden Evangelical Lutheran Church here has two things most churches don't. One is an inspiring view of Lake Superior. The other is a sauna in the basement. There's nothing incongruous about the latter, not around here. Michigan's wild and remote Upper Peninsula is the heart of the "Sauna Belt," the center of Finnish-American culture. . . A small map depicting Munising and Eben Junction also graced the front page. (Friday, July 20, 1990)

The obvious downturn at Eden in the last two decades was not primarily the fault of Edenites. It was a combination of a number of factors, not the least being the foundering of the Evangelical Lutheran Church in America, including her bishops and seminaries. Errant pastors were a factor, who appeared increasingly more errant as time moved on. There may be only two valid reasons for leaving a congregation (or church body), namely, if the teachings of the Bible are abandoned, or if either bows to cultural demands. God's truths do not accomadate culture; it boldly confronts culture. Was the situation really as bad as it seemed?

Though it may seem that my tenure at Eden was her golden era, I was quick to confess my human frailty and wasted opportunities. One of our past presidents said: *An error does not become a mistake until you refuse to correct it.*

Dietrich Bonhoffer, the German martyr of the *Confessing Church*, when national social-ism of Nazism tried to extinguish the church, wrote as a young theologian: *"Have (we) really remained the church of Christ? Has it not perhaps become an obstruction blocking the path of God instead of a road sign on the path to God? Has it not blocked the only path to salvation? Yet no one can ever obstruct the way to God. The church still has the Bible; God's word will never be denied (Isa. 55:11), whether it be preached by us or by our sister church . . . We do not, however, want to deny any-thing that we have recognized as God's word. The important thing is God's word . . . God has given everyone a conscience. We can and should desire that our sister church search its soul and concentrate on nothing but the word (1 Cor. 2:12-13). . . As long as we let the word be our only armor we can look confidently into the future."*[61]

I vowed never to leave the Upper Peninsula, so I sauntered among three parishes along Michigan Highway-28. I was from Eben (Ebenezer), which means **"the stone of help."** I perceived my call primarily to be that of a parish pastor.

Vladimir Nabokov said: *"One is always at home in one's past."* Remember that *"history is a vast early warning system,"* as Norman Cousins put it.

To some young radical modern clergy, and laymen, in this age of post-modernism and licentiousness, my memoirs may seem like those of an obsolete, old geezer who is unable to keep up with progress. Remember that I too was a young radical at one time, perhaps a bit more moderate however. I assumed three parishes for a duration of almost thirty years which were in dire need of change. E.g., Finnish to English in language, modern methods of stew-ardship, new curriculum materials, Lutheran Social Services sexuality sessions, the liberation movements, numerous fads, and all the rest. So much change. Some called it progressive, whereas in reality it was regressive. Sandra Pantti, of Rumely, said, when I asked her how she lived to a hundred: *The world changed and I changed with it.*

And yet, in an increasingly hostile culture, some of us discovered that the Gospel of Jesus had the power to change individuals, families and the culture. The meaning of the Cross and suffering gave the Christian faith its power. The church and the congregation could only live and breathe at the cross, for without being brought to the cross there was no life and no rea-son to exist. We still preached, taught and confessed that Jesus Christ was Lord of all. Jesus was in control of every renegade molecule. The church is still where the Word was preached and the sacraments were administered.

The Great Commission of going and making disciples was still the calling and purpose of the congregations of Jesus. The basics had not changed, and God's home address and phone numbers were still the same. The way of salvation had not changed. Mass media today unwittingly succumbed, to save its own skin, the promotion of licentiousness, rife with flip-pant comedy referances to adultery, fornication, and homosexuality. Even the churches joined in. Modern churches caved in, replacing justification of the sinner with justification of sin. In other words if you can't beat 'em, join 'em. The indwelling Jesus could not conform to this world, but looked to both the present and the future to be transformed by the Holy Spirit as the Word had promised.

Veni, Vidi, Velcro.

A half dozen unrelated quotes for contemplation:

"Better to do something imperfectly than to do nothing flawlessly."

- Robert Schuller

"I have known them all already, known them all, have known the evenings, mornings, afternoons, I have measured out my life with coffee spoons."

- T. S. Eliot

"One path leads to discouragement and despair, and the other path leads to total destruction. Pray that we make the right decision."

- Woody Allen

"Not everyone who goes to church is a Christian, but all Christians go to church."

- James Kennedy

"Eden is "so modest and minor-key that the emotional bruise it leaves may take days to develop."
- Jeanenette Catsoulis

"If you are going to be a Christian you have to be born one."

-anonymous

CHAPTER ELEVEN

Finlandia University, Age 52-63, 1983-1994

"Wretched is the mouse that hath but one hole," implies that it's nice to have some options. From time to time since 1974 Suomi College president, Ralph J. Jalkanen, had made overtures to me about working for the college. While Marcia and I were on a spring vacation to Florida, Ralph again made an attempt to contact me in March 1983. Upon our return I drove to Hancock to meet with him. In quick order I would be *Director of Special and Planned Giving*, effective May 1, 1983. I left the parish ministry for "*a ministry to accumulated resources.*" My primary concern was estate planning and larger gifts specialist for "the little college in the North country."

This college was the only one in America founded by Finnish immigrants. The name was changed from Suomi College to **Finlandia University** ca 1998. She had been founded in 1896 and *Old Main* was built in 1900 on land purchased from the Hancock Mining Company. Much of it was a rockpile.

Ralph Jalkanen, 1960-1990

A peak enrollment of 715 was reached in 1985, my second year in her employment. I worked three-quarter time and I was allowed to perform the job from Au Train. I was oblivious to the fact that maybe I was not able to do this job. I simply assumed that I could, and I was right. I was given the freedom not to decide until I attended two four-day seminars in Denver and Washington, D.C. I was trained four days by the Rev. Merritt Bomhoff of Wartburg College, who was subcontracted by the *Robert Gronlund Associates* of West Palm Beach, Florida, our development consultants. Bob suggested **my goal** be $ 10,000,000 in my first ten years. Ralph Jalkanen, as time went by, was an excellent tutor for my new task. Among other things, Ralph said, e.g., there were three things in my work that I should not talk about in my visits: Politics, religion and sex. It took most of 1983 to prepare for this new and unique ministry.

St. Paul alluded: *"Is there reason to boast therefore?"* It may appear that reporting tangible money might seem like boasting. Writing memoirs can so easily turn to boasting and boasting can take on spiritual dimensions. Ultimately we have the best basis for boasting because we have a God who loves us through His Son. He is worth boasting about. *"Let he who boasts, boast in the Lord."*[63]

*   *   *

I was into **philanthropy**. It wasn't merely about *obtaining* money for the college, important as that was, but even if money was not needed, there was the spiritual need of the giver to give. Money can be good or evil. Greed today is the last socially "acceptable" sin of the so-called *Seven Deadly Sins*. I quickly learned to love this new ministry, for I met some of the finest giving people with their hearts in the right places. My primary audience was the immigrant Finn and the next generation. Rarely did the former have any amount of money, but the second generation did very well.

Bomhoff taught me a **color-coded system** of how to work a deferred giving program. In brief, I carried 200 primary prospect folders: ten *red-hots*, forty *yellows* waiting to be upgraded, and one hundred fifty *greens*. Concentrate on the top ten until they became **"Expectancies"** when they placed the college in their estate plan. When they died they became **"Maturities."**

My new life for the next twelve years consisted of primarily **traveling** to the fourteen states where the Finns lived, the top seven areas being: The Copper Country, Marquette County, Detroit, Northeast Ohio, Northern Minnesota, Florida, and California. I used my automobile in the Midwest but I flew to the others. I logged over a quarter million air miles on this job. I would make at least seven trips annually to various areas, usually of two week durations. In winter I spent considerable time in Florida's Palm Beach County (Lake Worth).

Les Niemi in 1987.

I participated in the **"annual fund"** events, because from these crowds surfaced the special gifts and deferred givers. My annual fund gifts averaged $ 369,539 annually, while deferred gifts averaged $ 677,167 a year. ($1,046,700 total). My cost factor on this kind of cash income was 5%, which was a pretty attractive return for the college.

In addition to the annual fund, I published a quarterly estate planning newsletter, conducted seminars, organized a "class agent" program, recruited a planned giving committee, filled in for a "church relations" person, worked the annual *Finn Fest* public relations, served on the administrative cabinet, served as interim department head, liaisoned with Finland, and more. I had the gifts of being clergy, speaking Finnish, extroverted, and unafraid to ask for money. Ralph once called me tenacious. I guarded against over-stepping my authority and knew when to defer to the president. Over the years I saw over thirty department staff that just did not have what it took. I can recall how badly I felt for them as they were hired and fired. But this unique ministry was exciting to me.

Over the years my **department heads** were Douglas Tieman, John Goltermann, Art Koszalinski, Myrna Marseilles, and myself. College **presidents** were Ralph Jalkanen, Sidney Rand, and Robert Ubbelohde, who served eight, one and three years, respectively, during my time. All were good, but none was perfect. All of them made mistakes, and sometimes we lost money because of them. They had a hard task. I am grateful for their leadership. I had wonderful friends on the Suomi staff. The college board was made up of outstanding people, chosen by the presidents. Generally speaking, some outstanding folks were helping Suomi College.

When I arrived I knew of forty-two matured deferred gifts until year 1983. When I left the number had grown to one hundred fifty-seven and they averaged $ 153,765 each. Interestingly, I kept averaging a million dollars a year for another 14 years after I retired, because the clients were now becoming "maturities," i.e.. they died. Folks were beginning to understand that *"the only thing that you can take with you is what you leave behind,"* in deliberate estate planning.63

Quite naturally the most common **products** used by deferred givers were a simple will, a trust, insurance policy, and a Charitable Gift Annuity. I created a club known as **The Second Century Club**, composed of all known estate planning "expectancies." When I retired I had 256 members. However for every deferred gift that we knew about, there were two that we did not know about. I averaged two new "expectancies" per month. I have many funny and interesting stories. Whereas I was primarily a self-educated specialist I tried to attend a good three-day conference every other year. The finest of these was the Gift Annuities Conference which met every third year. For it I went to Denver, New Orleans, Toronto and Dallas. There Winton Smith of Nashville spoke loudest into my life. It was a wonderful job. Bomhoff warned that lifelong friends would result, and so it was.

Some of my **largest** gifts (with my fingerprints them) were: Earl Forsyth ($5,100,000, Lily Jutila ($3,100,000), John/Sofie Smith, Sulo/Aileen Mäki and Lillian Karey, all of one million dollars each.

Others over $100,000, Arthur/Saima Mills, John Niemi, Gordon Elson, Mary Jean Nelson, Thomas Niemi, Jean Hill, Lydia Sjögren, Donald Kenney, Joel Lempiainen, Voitto Mutka, and Aune Koski. There were others of which I was unaware.

Two of the above gifts named buildings: *Aileen Mäki Library*, and the *Lily Jutila Art and Design Center.* The large Forsyth gift paid some huge bills, and in the nick of time.

However, I lost the very first check given me in Marquette in 1983. It was for $50. At my retirement I presented the check, which I later found between the pages of a book, with six percent, interest to the college.

As of this writing, having been retired from Finlandia for seventeen years, I am aware of just under **$ 25,000,000** that I helped bring to the school. When I retired on June 30, 1994, President Ubbelohde expressed, though he must have been exaggerating, that I helped "save" the school. I hasten to add that college development work is seldom a one-man activity, but is a team effort. Someone asks, another cultivates, someone else harvests. Perhaps the day will come when someone can again become the Director of Planned Gifts at Finlandia University for that's where the really big money lurks. But college administrators are sometimes suspicious because it appears so elusive; but God works on his own time and not ours. Pietist-rooted Finlandia ought to know that after 121 years!

I have stories. Let me merely relate three:

She called the police. Yes, Lily Jutila was having a bad day in Hanover, MA, the day I came to visit. She lived in a barn-like house with eighteen cats. They smelled. Ernie had died. I heard they may have had an estate of a half million and had no kids. One day she would not let me in the house. I pleaded. No. She called the police. The police came. And he said: *"It looks like she doesn't want to see you."* I agreed, thinking how lucky I was not to be arrested. I left my material on the porch and left. Lily left the college over three million dollars and the *Lily Jutila Center for Art and Design* is named for her as a result. She was a big surprise. But it required many visits. . . and all those cats. Also with the company two for one match each visit was worth three thousand dollars.

Win some, lose some. Ralph said: *"Go see Kaarle Lehtinen in Newport, NH."* I flew to Boston, visited others also (including Ernie and Lily, above), and drove up to scenic Newport. Kaarle was about 96. He was a nice, cordial man who spoke only Finnish. He agreed to give our college a third of his million and a half estate. I translated the documents into Finnish and I gladly loaned my pen for his signing the documents. Mr. Lehtinen had been subject to wrongdoing by a John Fairbanks of his town. This attorney had cheated some other elderly. Before his arrest, he escaped to Montreal, Canada, where he reportedly owned one or more apartment buildings. He was later found dead in a Las Vegas hotel, having committed suicide.

A lady from Wisconsin, got acquainted with Kaarle, invited him to live with her for a time. When I met her at a subsequent Finn Fest after Kaarle died, she understandably avoided me. Suomi's portion in Kaarle's plans had interestingly been reduced to only five thousand dollars. Win some, lose some. Time and again it became evident how vulnerable these more well-healed folks were. There were *advocates* and there were *adversaries*. Sometimes it resulted in figurative hand to hand combat.

The anchor held. Tom Niemi of Ironwood returned a coupon from one of my Planned Giving newsletters. I called immediately. He said: *"Come see me."* On a stormy winter's day in March, I drove from Hancock to Ironwood. We spent three hours together as the storm raged, and at the end had his Michigan Statutory Will notarized by his bank. Tom died in 1994. His niece's husband, an attorney in Wausau, contested the "home-made" will. They failed. And Suomi received another $ 128,000. Total effort: three hour meeting plus travel.

I could tell dozens of stories. Here are a few one-liners:

+ Once, when I was in Florida, Marcia had received **fifty-three inches** of new snow in a three-day period at Au Train. Florence Snow, next door, had to shovel out her door of snow so Marcia could open the door to get out.

+ On a Tuesday morning I drove to Hancock to spend three days on campus. As I bypassed Covington, I was aware that on John Tusa's farm in Amasa that morning, 28 miles away, it was a **minus fifty-seven degrees**. This was the North Country and it was not for wimps.

+ Several times upon returning to my car at the Marquette Airport, it was awful. Once, the car was coated with a half inch of **ice**. The State Police saw this and said: *"We'll take you home."* It was forty-two miles, and we gave one ticket along the way.

+ Again, I got off that plane and went out to get the car. I could not find it. My little Honda CRX was totally **buried** and showed only an inch of the antennae. A man with a jeep saw me clawing the snow dressed in Florida whites, no socks, no gloves. He said: *"Let me help."* He hooked a chain in the proper place and yanked that baby out of the snow just like magic. I was on my way.

+ More airports: In 1989 after a couple of teenagers on ice **totaled** my Honda now looking like a "Smart Car" from the rear. I drove it to the airport, and took a plane to work in Hancock. That's the last I saw of that car as someone from Green Bay bought the salvage and trailored it away. This was my third *"totaled"* car.

+ The first time Ralph was really angry with me was when I brought **Aileen Maki** of LaJolla, CA, to the campus. He became angry when she said "I'll think about it," to Ralph's bold question for one million dollars. The next day Ralph said to me: "If she ever gives us a million I'll eat my shirt." But alas, in 1995 Aileen indeed gave the million dollars. I don't know if he ever ate the shirt, but it named the remodeled library, making possible the college to become four-year institution. It was redirected from naming the heritage center.

Les' Retired Jersey.

+ In 1991 during an alumni game, I was honored by the "**retirement**" of my *basketball jersey* (No. 25) from my 1949-53 college playing days. The shirt is safely in the archives where some new coach or athletic director cannot discard it from hanging in the gymnasium. Coaches see only their own records.

+ One of my pet projects, work related, was the ***indexing*** of the annual directories of both the Suomi Synod Almanac (*Kirkollinen Kalenteri*), and the directories of the Finnish Temperance Society. This work is on file at the Finnish American Historical Archives and Museum at the college, and on internet through Finland's Genealogical Society of Turku, Finland. (<genealogia.fi>) It is valuable for researchers. The job afforded me to meet some **noted Finns**, like Greta Peck, Taina Elg, Dick Enberg, Matti Nykänen, Jorma Kaukonen, Joyce Randolph-Charles, Eino Grön, Jean Auel, Coretta King, Miriam Hoover, Lasse Virren, Arto Härkönen, Urho Kekkonen, Paul Kangas, Archbishops John Vikström and Jukka Paarma, Kaarlo Tuomi, to name a few, all in the course of my work.

But mostly it was hard work and long hours of visitation late into the night. A rule of thumb: Big money is raised when "the ask" is made by the right person, for the right amount and at the right time. The asker needs to give first. People give to people, usually face to face. If you don't ask, you won't get. Do the homework. Ask for a specific amount. Be persistent (tenacious?) If they say "*No,*" they may really mean "*Later.*" For example: "*I've been thinking about asking you for a big gift.*" Then come back and ask. Be nice to givers after the commitment is made. All *Thank You* letters must be sent out within seventy-two hours.

In May 1990 **Ralph Jalkanen** was asked by the board to retire from the presidency when the college went over two million dollars "in the hole." Shortly he had a stroke, and died in 1994. I did soul care with him the evening before he died at the local hospital. Ralph was a wonderful and talented man, and he saved the college in no uncertain terms. Most of what I knew about raising funds for Suomi, I learned from him. Some of the development counselors who were also helpful to me were Winton Smith, Merritt Bomhoff, Frank Habib, and Gary Quehl.

Sidney Rand from St. Olaf College came to serve as interim president for one year until the board hired **Robert Ubbelohde**, who served for the next eighteen years. I was grateful to Syd Rand, who loved us so much that he came to help. Bob ably led a name change from Suomi to Finlandia and transitioned the school to become a baccalaureate-giving university.

Bob was the right man for his time period performing a tremendous task in perilous times. Ralph had saved the school during his thirty years at the helm, warding off the unfriendly Church and other adversaries. The **Työmies Society** publishing house in Superior, WI, went out of business, and they donated the **Finnish American Reporter** monthly periodical to Finlandia University, which currently is thriving under the leadership of David Mäki and James Kurtti. Presently the multi-gifted **Philip Johnson** is the university president and near record enrollments are again with us.

*　　*　　*

Les on a 5-K in Hancock.

Now, while all this was going on in my second career, a ministry to accumulated resources, what was the **new marriage** doing? Marcia and I lived at my cottage on beautiful Lake Au Train. Our front all-glass wall gave one the impression of living right on the water. What a view! Marcia continued to complete her fine teaching career until her retirement in 1995, enduring the rigors of winter travel along the most treacherous piece of state highway in Michigan. She never missed a day of work, unless of course school was cancelled due to storms. Finally, much later in 1998, she was in a seven-car white-out crash which hastened our retirement move to Arizona in 1999. A white-out is when you see only two cars though there are seven cars in the crash.

Our hobbies in our second marriages were cross-country skiing, downhill skiing, jogging, brook and lake trout fishing, sauna-ing, sailing, pontooning, photography, and fall excursions to Mackinac Island's *Grand Hotel*. We lived with our two dogs, her *Lily* and my *Shaggy*. They were quite compatible, like us. Season passes at *Marquette Mountain* cost only $299 for the year, and Marcia became an excellent skier. To keep in condition we did our X-country trail all winter and jogged all summer. Marcia, at age fifty, debuted in the Pictured Rocks Road Race, and excelled in her age bracket for over a decade.

In 1992 I invested in a hydraulic-principled weight machine, *The Trimax*, the solution to many bodily ills of stiffness and arthritis. In the cold of winter we hunkered down next to our Vermont Castings **Defiant** wood burner which totally heated our small house. In 1985 my brother Bill remodeled our kitchen bathroom and bedrooms; I repaneled the house interior with western cedar.

In 1987 we purchased a used *Northport* pontoon for only $5000, and in '89 we invested in the Cadillac of fishing boats, an eighteen foot **Crestliner**, fully equipped. Its 115 Mercury could whoosh us across Lake Superior at 51 mph. I obtained my first personal computer in 1986, a Korean made *Leading Edge*, with which I began to write some memoirs. Marcia sold her house in Munising in December of 1986.

We began our marriage with another honeymoon, taking our mothers with us, to the **Scandinavia**n capitals for fifteen days in 1983, Copenhagen, Oslo, Stockholm and Helsinki.

After a horrible seventy-year experiment, **communism** failed in the U.S.S.R. in 1989, and down came the Berlin Wall. Godless socialism and communism took a huge blow, but now has surfaced in Central and South America. Almost all socialist Finnish halls closed in the USA. Perhaps you've noticed that soft and hard communism and socialism usually fails.

What kind of **car**s did we drive? I could afford only economy cars. We drove four Hondas and a Nissan. For second cars we bought a used Ford, and Marcia bought a Pontiac. Also we went with two experienced four-wheel-drive Chevy Blazers.

* * *

And now a word about our immediate **families**: There is that old saying about being able to pick your friends, but you can't pick your relatives. They are a given. Jesus alluded to this problem when he raised the question of who were His brothers, sisters and mother? His answer was: those who did the will of God. Like it or not, people of faith are closer than a family with a secular worldview, that does not know the mystery or secret of faith. Perhaps one day the younger generation will again begin to ask the significant questions about life, to which one can respond. The problem is not uncommon.

My dad, **Ed Niemi**, died on December 20, 1990 at his home. His first stay in a hospital was five months earlier with pneumonia. **Ken Ericson**, Marcia's first husband, died at the Tendercare Nursing Home on April 15, 1991. The Upper Peninsula lost one of its finest jazz pianists, our church lost a good organist, and Alger County lost its premier builder of four decades.

Marcia's 20 Inch Brook Trout, 1983.

Dan and **Ann** lived in Tampa and to whom were born two daughters, Amanda and Kristen, born in 1979 and 1983. Dan worked as a financial planner. **Michael** and **Patricia** lived on the East shore of Munising Bay, to whom was born Nicole in 1983 and Jaden in 1988. Mike worked for Northern Hardwoods and then for the City of Munising. **Nathan** and **Sandra** moved from Minnesota to Kincheloe where they both worked for the Michigan penal system. They had sons, Brandon born in 1983, Jason born in 1984, and Nathan born in 1989. Nicole became a teacher while Jaden captained boats for Pictured Rocks Cruises out of Munising.

Kristin Ericson, Marcia's daughter married John Madigan in 1982, living in Beloit, Virginia, San Diego, and back to Munising; they had a daughter **Kathleen** born in 1991. **Gretchen** married John Marks of Beloit, WI, in November 1989, where she worked as a nurse; they had children Alexandra and John. These were Marcia's highly talented grandchildren.

My brother **Eddie** worked at Northern Hardwoods, remained single, and medically retired in 2009. Sister **Betty** divorced Stanley Rämä and Bob McComb, married Dan Marlow, and lived in Carleton south of Detroit. Brother **Bill** married and divorced Pamela Fitzgerald, and they had a son, Brian, born in 1970. Next Bill married and divorced Yvonne Yeadon; alcohol continued to curse his marriages. Bill medically retired and died in May 2009, having a multitude of maladies. He enjoyed a significant building career. Marcia's sister **Cheryl**, a registered nurse, lived in Muncie, Indiana. (See appendix for a brief genealogy.)

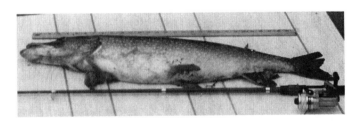

The Great Northern Pike Lunker, 16 lb., of 1983.

Regarding our health, I began to encounter problems with my eyes in 1988. A virus scarred my cornea, necessitating a **cornea transplant** done by Dr. John Kublin. A twenty-three year old African-American from Detroit donated a cornea to me, after his demise on a weekend. I also began to battle glaucoma from that date forward requiring attention.

Four years later I needed **gallbladder surgery**. The bladder burst in surgery requiring additional days in Marquette General Hospital.

Marcia had terrible right **wrist trouble**, starting in 1986, when she fell in the Central School unkempt icy parking lot. And she re-broke it in 1994 while running in the Mather balcony during school. The external fixator and pain made it *her summer from hell*. This was the summer that I retired, enabling me to help her. Later she was seen racing downhill with her skis at Marquette Mountain. When will they ever learn? She retired as a teacher in 1995.

*　*　*

Meanwhile back at the college, enrollment difficulties placed added stress on the need to raise money for the budget. Vast reorganization needed to happen, e.g., becoming a four-year institution inasmuch as a private school could not compete economically with community colleges. **Bob Ubbelohde** ably helped us over these hurdles, which also included becoming by name *Finlandia University*.

*   *   *

But for sundry reasons I decided to **retire** effective June 30, 1994. To my surprise my income increased $3000 a year with retirement. (See *Why I Cashed in My Brown Stamp Book* in my longer memoirs.) It had been a marvelous twelve year ministry for a great cause. To be able to raise money one needed to believe in the product. Suomi had been tremendously important in my life, starting in 1949. I had hoped that my efforts had helped her get over the hump. I am thankful to the hard work and dedication of the colleagues with whom I toiled. Some of those favorite people at the office were Olaf Rankinen, Doreen Korpela, Sue King, Jim Boggio, John Blohm, Doug Tieman, John Goltermann, Bill Olson, Bill Givens, Don Haines, Jim Greenfield, D.J. Boyd, Myrna Marseilles, Jan Gustafson, Dick Lantz, Anne Miller, Martha Puska, and John Gagnon. The first year that our department broke the one million dollar mark in cash gifts was 1988. Then we accelerated.

Olaf Rankinen once said: *A normal person cannot work for Ralph for more than three years.* Again, I must have been abnormal for my years added up to twelve. Living off campus may have been an asset, although during the final six years I spent Tuesday, Wednesday and Thursday at my campus office, when not traveling.

Upon my departure the staff honored me with a nice afternoon reception, at which **Jorma Kaukonen,** of *Jefferson Airplane* fame, played his guitar. At the following board meeting, nice things were said to me, and I was presented with the copper *Suomi Lion Award.* Upon leaving the staff I continued to be a member of the **Finnish Council in America**, which I helped organize in 1983. That group focused on keeping the goodly heritage alive at the college.

Speaking about normality, I found out in 1992 that I was one of only a few extroverts in the administrative cabinet.[64] I had always worried about my *introvertishness.* I am more intuitive and feeling, as opposed to data and logic based. I can be moved by a great story better than cold facts. I find that a strength; others may see it as a weakness.

I sometimes joked about what epitaph would be an appropriate engraving on my stone at the Slapneck Cemetery. Perhaps the following: "and then the beggar died."[65] When you love what you are doing it hardly feels like work. God gave me two types of ministries, a two-pronged ministry, both meaningful and exciting. With the new name at Suomi, we must learn a new song, which concludes:

"But the Rock of our foundation, ever sturdy solid ground, Finlandia, Finlandia our song we sing to thee. Finlandia, Finlandia our hearts we give to thee."[66]

In my fantasy moments I would like to believe that I saved the college, as the president suggested in 1994. Actually it was our Jumala/God who did it for He is the one who specializes in saving both men and institutions. Finlandia has been "the apple of God's eye" for a long, long time. I pray that it will continue as a special place, a special place in the north country. I believe Phil Johnson will continue to make it happen.

At this juncture at the conclusion of **forty years of ministry**, it is meet and right to share my greatest spiritual temptations. They had to do with **soul**, the most significant part of man, and conscience, man's largest organ. In hindsight the battle was fierce during the final half century of the previous millennium. Should you take your eyes away from **Jesus and his cross**, "fads" of every sort surrounded the average pastor. The devil wants one to dabble with anything which could detract man from the central focus of his cross. Alternatives came attractively packaged.

Some of the main packages, which were not only suggested but promoted by our seminaries and leaders, were: The "social gospel," rationalism-intellectualism, ecumenicalism, politics, drama, Christian psychology, liberation theology, self-absorption, and naturalistic materialism; the list is endless. Many were the avenues available for how one could be "ashamed of the gospel." **(Romans 1:16-17)** They all had one thing in common. With all of them **the power of God** was usually depleted. Any one of the above, or a combination thereof, meant shipwreck to an authentic and successful clergy career. Though each of them might contain an element of truth (which is how they got their foot in the door), the devil wishes us to excess in them, with the logical result of forsaking **the true gospel**. Recall that prior to Paul being shipwrecked at Malta, they were required to throw overboard all unnecessary baggage and supplies. So with us. In our desperation on the sea of life, the very last thing remaining aboard ship is our God. **(Acts of the Apostles 27)**

At the time of my ordination in 1954 the "**moral rearmament**" kick was emerging with headquarters right in my back yard, on Mackinac Island. Liberals were boarding the bandwagon, of course doomed to fail as it was dependent primarily on merely human effort and morality. It was "law," but very little gospel.

In my early parish years, I imagined myself to be into **Christian psychology**, somehow viewing my worship events as therapy sessions. My counseling sometimes eroded to being neither Christian nor psychological. But I received *Psychology Today* for many years. I boarded the *Transactional Analysis* train (T.A.), with its heretical theme *I'm OK, you're OK*. Luther would say that neither is true.

Naturalistic materialism, promoted by Germany, Russia, Heffner, Kinsey, Darwin, Sanger, Mead, and Freud, took its toll. It became the pop culture. What could be worse than what happened in Germany? The answer is easy: Russia. And the jury is not yet in concerning America! God will not be mocked, remember.

Liberation theology was next. Pick your wagon: Slavery, race, women, ethnics and homosexuals. The gospel took a back burner, if not totally off the chart in most of these.

Rationalism-Intellectionalism. These were the "head faith" sophisticates. Once I loved the philosophical gospel of Paul Tillich. Today I abhor liberal rationalism as cheap grace, if it can be called grace at all. *Historical criticism* falls under this umbrella, which proved to be a very slippery slope. Later, with each new generation, new literary criticism of every shade so confused theology that it gave new meaning to our Lord's Prayer, *lead us not into temptation.* The final erroneous result was that there could be no one legitimate interpretation of Scripture, and it was every man for himself, that is, you can believe whatever you want.

More recently **activism** has become fashionable under the guise of Christian love and caring, or tolerance, or fairness, or equal rights. But we are not to assume activists have the true gospel. This emphasis has also been called the *social gospel.* By itself activisim is shallow, however noble. My leadership in *The Partnership Conference* in Alger County, a successful community development experiment in the 1970s and 80s, was activism, in the attempt to improve the community, and retain in our congregation a balance between *"inner faith"* and *"outer service."* It could have easily been misunderstood, and was.

All these **fads** also wormed their way into my sermons, counseling, and parish activities to some degree. Sometimes they replaced the real gospel of the saving work of Jesus Christ, who came to fetch the ungodly, forgetting that our greatest "political action" is to bring someone to Jesus Christ. These were my **temptations** in my work, but concerning which I have already received forgiveness, as a child of the Almighty. I was not the pastor I should have been.

Hopefully Jeannie Bentti was right when she wrote: *In the time it takes for an apple to rot, a fad will fade.* (from her book *Dust Off Your Brain*)

The apostle Paul defines the spiritual enemies thusly: *For we are not fighting people but against spiritual rulers and powers, against authorities of this dark world, and against the evil spirits.* (Ephesians 6:12) The foe is formidable. The sin is serious. But **the Savior** is merciful, if asked.

* * *

+ You see, the basic problem of those who are spiritually challenged, was to truly realized how lost they were, namely, the doctrine of man.

+ Sin is an **inherited** condition, having a two-way sway of pride regarding the soul, and lust of the flesh regarding the body. We are powerless to help ourselves.

+ Following the first man, all subsequent sinning of humanity was the result of corruption of human nature. We are sinners and therefore we sin, not the reverse.

+ For by **grace** we have been saved and even faith is not our own. It's the gift of God for us and not the works that we have done. We cannot boast of it. Humans cannot even choose to believe, yet they are able to become open to the possibility.

+ From experience it can be pondered whether all people can receive grace, and whether God gives grace only to those whom he chooses. E.g., Judas from Keriot seemed condemned to be eternally damned. Or what did Luther mean when he wrote regarding the bondage of the will: *"Here is the highest degree of faith, to believe . . . that God whose will it is that some should be condemned is nonetheless the most just God."* It doesn't sound like *universalism* to me!

+ Happily, our guilt was removed by justification by faith and we are given a new heart, with which to do good. Luther said it was liberating and exhilarating: *"I felt exactly as if I had been **born again**, and I believed that I had entered paradise through widely open doors...."* That's exactly how it was for me in 1947 though I had never read Luther say that. I had read only his *Small Catechism* in 1946 in confirmation class. Jesus is the "Door." The new heart can then promote acts of faith, acts of love, and putting the gospel of Jesus into action in big and small ways. Suomi piety believed that the new heart and the indwelling Christ went together, and were in fact inseparable. Luther said before we can ask whether we should love our neighbor, or who in fact is our neighbor, the indwelling Jesus has already done it. Why should that concept be so difficult for some?

+ It was immensely important that we became sufficiently aware of how lost we were? It was Lutheranism unique gift to take this "lostness" seriously. It was followed by how saved we are. Big sinner, big Savior. I didn't, of course, realize the dynamics of the above theology at age sixteen. In a way I didn't understand what hit me, but whoever said that my understanding and reason would make it any more true than what it was? Conversion is infinitely deeper than merely a "head faith." It is doubtful that salvation is based on upon one's IQ. We needn't explain it, merely believe it! There is something in the steadfast form of Finnish piety causing the young Finn to affirm, *Min*ä, *poika, uskon vain!* (I will merely believe.)

The core Christian beliefs, raw material, continue to persist despite a hostile culture. They are the *regula fidei*, the canon of truth, normative Christianity, that form the starting point and the ending, considered to be universally held from the era of the apostles to the end of all things. Faith is the true apostolic succession. These indelible convictions include monotheism, creation, the redemptive death and resurrection of Jesus, human redemption/salvation, and eternal life. They are expressed in the general creeds of the church. They demand, not the ability to define the *how*, only the necessity to believe that they are. Else Luther might not have written *"Ich gleube das ich nicht aus eigener vernunfft noch krafft . . ."* (I believe that I cannot by my own reason or strength believe . . .)

Martin Luther explains this secret beautifully in his exposition on John 14:

There are two kinds of sight and of hearing. The one is performed with physical eyes and ears, entirely without Spirit. That is the way all of his countrymen looked at Christ, only with their five senses, thinking that he hailed from Nazareth and was Mary's son... But Christ cannot be recognized in this way, even if we saw him every hour before our eyes and heard him. The second is a spiritual sight, which only Christians have, and which takes place by means of faith in the heart. With this, if we are Christians, we must also view and recognize one another. . .You must also look at Christ this way if you want to recognize him and know who he is . . . Then you see not only his form, as your physical eyes do, but also the power and the might of his death and resurrection. Then you do not call him a son of Mary and Joseph from Nazareth, as his countrymen did, but our one true Savior and Lord over all.
This way of looking at Christ is far different from the way all the world does . . ."[67]

+ Since my rescue from the clutches of colon cancer in 2004, I became less ashamed of the gospel of Christ but felt the need to tell the truth both of man and of Christ as long as others could bear it. There have been some happy results. .

+ **Paavo Ruotsalainen**, the peasant Finnish awakenist wrote in 1847: *When without thinking about the consequences you have fellowship with the indifferent, you then become frivolous, and the guide, the Holy Spirit, must leave the heart and you have nothing left but head faith and an accusing conscience . . . For in this time of great light people are terribly deceived. They become satisfied with an outward head faith without true inward knowledge of Christ.*[68] This can happen to congregations and synods as easily as with individuals.

+ Two years later, Paavo wrote: *Place before the all-seeing Savior all the accusations of your conscience, your piety and your wickedness which bother you, and practice yearning trust in the Savior revealed in the Word. Read in the New Testament how the thief* (on the cross) *didn't need a lengthy repentance but upon a single word received a precious single word, "Today you will be with me in Paradise." Take courage, friend, for I too, an old man, must put up with my wretchedness and from now on give the Lord the glory..... With all your unfaithfulness be faithful in begging for mercy from the Lord . . . How can life be found where Christ who is life itself is not first received?*

+ As I cited earlier our theological roots originated in the **pietism** of the (Lutheran) Church of Finland. Almost all Finnish-American Christians shared in these roots. This unique faith was our contribution to the American scene. It was a living faith, deeper than orthodoxy, and wherein loomed large names which included Augustine, Luther, Spener, Francke, Mikael Agricola, Paavo Ruotsalainen, Hedberg, Laestadius, Simojoki, Thielicke, Niemoller, Bonhoeffer, Barth, Kantonen, Kukkonen, Holmes and Saarnivaara. Our concept of life and godly piety had minimal acceptance by majority Lutherans, who surprisingly expressed opposition leaning to hostility.

+ On my final ride to **Slapneck**, bury me in the rich tradition of Finnish pietism. So in closing this spiritual autobiography, I have painted a rough picture of my two-way ministry regarding congregations and accumulated resources. I quote the words of the "father of pietism," Philip J. Spener (1625-1705) of Germany:

"Let us remember that in the last judgment we shall not be asked how learned we were and whether we displayed our learning before the world; to what extent we enjoyed the favor of men and knew how to keep it; with what honors we were exalted and how great a reputation in the world we left behind us or how many treasure of earthly goods we amassed for our children and thereby drew a curse upon ourselves. Instead, we shall be asked how faithfully and with how childlike a heart we sought to further the kingdom of God; with how pure and godly a teaching and how worthy an example we tried to edify our hearers amid the scorn of the world, denial of self, taking up of the cross, and imitation of our Savior; with what zeal we opposed not only error but also wickedness of life; or with what constancy and cheerfulness we endured the persecution or adversity thrust upon us by the manifestly godless world or by false brethren, and amid such suffering praised our God."[69]

Are you with me?

+ In many ways what was important to early pietists Philip Spener and August Francke was also important in the life of the Suomi Synod as I remember it. The latter sent Henry Muhlenberg to organize the early roots of our church.

+ As defenders of the faith, let us guard that the congregation, the body of Christ, not become a "ship of fools," as Sebastian Brant's poem, *Narrenschyff*, suggested:

"Seldom is the truth now heard,
For men pervert God's Holy Word."

And

"Seeing the like I'm bound to say
We're not far off the judgment day."

In 1988 there was another Lutheran merger of church bodies, as the **Evangelical Lutheran Church in America** was formed. A question needs to be raised, in hindsight: What made the ELCA merger go so badly? Why did its first bishop claim that it was doomed from the very outset? Contemplate what it was that was the dreadful foreign element in this merger that spelled disaster in future decades. As an heir of goodly pietism from my relationship to the Church of Finland, I think I know the answer. Isn't it important that you also know the answer?

* * *

Ultimately, in the very final analysis, it's about Jesus, isn't it? It's *only* about Jesus. I heard a cute story, a truism however:

A Jewish businessman in Chicago sent his son to Israel for a year to absorb the culture. When the son returned he said: "Papa, I had a great time in Israel. By the way, I converted to Christianity." "Oy vey," said the father. "What have I done?" He took his problem to his best friend, Sam. "Sam," he said, "I sent my son to Israel, and he came home a Christian. What can I do?" "Funny you should ask," said Sam, "I too, sent my son to Israel, and he also came back a Christian. Perhaps we should go and see the rabbi."

So they did, and they explained their problem to the rabbi. "Funny you should ask," said the rabbi, "I, too, sent my son to Israel, and he also came back a Christian." What is happening to our young people?" And so they prayed, telling the Lord about their sons. As they finished their prayers, a Voice came from the heavens: "Funny you should ask," said the Voice. "I, too, sent my Son to Israel . . "

Les' Cedar Log Cabin built in 1996.

CHAPTER TWELVE

Retirement, Age 64 ff, 1994-2012

Several indicators made clear to me that after a forty-year career in Christian ministry that the door was open to my retirement. The doors open and they close. This ministry took two forms: (1) to three parishes and (2) to the only church-related college in the Upper Peninsula of Michigan. Some determining factors were health and the uncomfortable new circumstance in the development office at the college. This decision, with its pros and cons, was a difficult one. But I made the decision to now leave despite my deep love for the college.

These concluding three brief chapters will simply reflect upon the golden years of retirement, on our travels, and the promising future which also increasingly contains suffering for the truth.

Maxfeld.

These golden years were immediately blessed with a Golden Retriever by the name of **Sunnyridge Maxfeld von Bairn**. It has been said that the addition of a pet in old age extends one's life five years. "Maxie" was that therapist, joining our family from 1995 to May 2008. He was a blonde Golden given as a birthday present for birthday number sixty-four by my son Nathan. Pedigree, bred to be a show dog, he loved to pose for photos. His mom was a *Meadowpond* and his dad was a *Lislone* from the United Kingdom.

He replaced a mutt named **Shag** (a terri-doodle) whom we had from 1971 to 1988; Shag had resembled a mini sheep dog, black and white. Shag bit, but Max wouldn't hurt a fly. It is impossible to describe the love and devotion that transpired between Marcia or me and this outstanding animal, Max. He made twenty and a half trips, all in Cadillacs, 2,340 miles one way, between Lake Au Train and Lake Havasu. On his final trip, tired at age sixteen and unable to go further, he died in Raton, New Mexico. So our first item of retirement was the new member of our family. Our Max-memories are endless and which we will cherish. Das *Bairn* is a bear in German. Perhaps Anotole France is right in that *"until one has loved an animal, a part of one's soul remains unawakened."*

Max sat only on leather seats in our series of **Cadillacs** which began in 1995. We purchased only experienced Cadillacs, and always at fewer than twenty-one thousand dollars each. Truth be told, it would have been counterproductive to drive a Cadillac in either fundraising or the parish. Only upon retirement did this become a possibility. It was simply a matter of common sense.

*   *   *

Retirement is viewed differently by various people. Some continue to work as if they had not retired. Others totally leave what they were doing. Yet others dabble only slightly in related tasks. I chose the latter, to maintain a membership in the *Finnish Council of America* at Finlandia University, in assuming some tasks in the *Suomi Conference USA*, a special interest group led by Ray Wargelin, Olaf Raninen and Antti Lepisto and, in some supply preaching majoring in the Finnish language since few others could do Finnish. The latter took me primarily to Newberry and Ishpeming, ending with 2010. Interestingly it was easier to preach the gospel in Finnish than in English, the words being considerably richer and more profound and colorful. Why was that?

I succeeded the talented Karlo Keljo as the president of the Michigan Area Suomi Conference USA, one of a half dozen special interest groups in the Evangelical Lutheran Church in America. This carry-over from the Suomi Synod days did exceptional mission work in **Namibia** and **Russian Karelia.** But, whereas hearing the true gospel in the ELCA was becoming in short supply, I aimed to make sure it was heard at our spring and fall festivals. My emphasis was: preach Christ first and mission will follow.

Unable to handle the doctrine of man, modern spineless preaching could conveniently overlook the need for Christ's redeeming death and resurrection. Liberalism ran rampant in mainline churches. However since we know that all things work together for good for those who love God, He knows how to convert whatever would hinder and harm us into that which furthers and helps us, . . . and God can change sadness and all heartache into sheer happiness, as Luther once wrote.

Continuous "maturities" (because they died) regarding planned estate giving commitments at the college doubled my production at the college to approximately twenty-five million dollars encompassing the next fifteen years of my retirement.

Retirement meant plenty of time for various **hobbies** like travel, serious reading, downhill and cross-country skiing, pontoon-ing, lake trout fishing, senior slow-pitch softball, ample sauna events, and especially golf. I became sufficiently adept so as on occasion able to "golf my age."

Our annual downhill skiing membership was at *Marquette Mountain*. We had our own cross-country ski trail at Lake Au Train. Marcia became a fine runner from which we retired

Violinist Marcia.

twenty-five years later. Marcia picked up her violin again, and was a member of the Marquette Symphony and the Lake Havasu Regional Orchestra and the musical pit orchestra.

We invested in our second pontoon, a *Weres*, for Lake Au Train, and I continued to excel catching lake trout on Lake Superior with our *Crestliner* fishing boat. Like my father, I loved reading in retirement, mostly history and theology. I was "discovered" at a karaoke bar in Cozumel, Mexico, in 1993 whereupon the *Grace Song* from the *Luther Opera*, became my signature song in churches. And I would never forsake my tri- or bi-weekly sauna. Where Christ dwells there is fullness of life.

A year after retirement I was musing in my cedar swamp between the lake and the river, taking note of the abundance of fifty-five-foot dead standing cedars. Upon reading four books on log buildings, I decided to cut down seventy-two of them for a sixteen by twelve foot **cedar log cabin** on the river frontage. This I accomplished in 1996 complete with a roofed front deck. I began pouring the footings at the end of May and completed it on December 31. I shortened one of the longest winters on record by felling and peeling cedar trees.

One of the fascinating studies I conducted was the behavior of my swamp **mosquitoes**. These critters are the world's deadliest insects, claiming 2.7 million painful deaths a year. But not in Au Train. I "tamed" them. They would arrive each day to see who I was. Then, without damage, they would go away. But a stranger visiting me they would bite and suck blood. They did not hinder my project. The log cabin cost $ 4000 but had a value of $ 25,000. It serves as a place to read and soothe the introvert in me. The project was a source of tremendous personal satisfaction. Maxie was my constant companion during the project, announcing every intruder. That was his job.

The Deadliest Insect On Earth.

I engaged in considerable reading in my rocking chair at *Pöyröönpesä* (Nest of Pöyröö), on my camp deck overlooking the Au Train River. However, as my boardwalk signs suggested, it also included a goodly amount of Finnish mythology. The Finns rivaled the Greeks, Romans and Vikings with outstanding mythology in the *Kalevala*, compiled by Elias Lönnrot as late as the mid-nineteen century. Hence my path to the camp displayed names like *Mörkölä*, *Hiisi*, *Tapio*, *Näkki*, and *Pöyröönpesä*. The Greek and Roman myths are better known due to age and they being more noisy people than the Finns. I became a student of Finnish mythology, which revealed deep ethnic values. The modern invention of the St. Urho myths also indicate how myth-prone Finns are.

* * *

Meanwhile, my **sons** were each married and by 1989 they had presented seven grandchildren. My prodigy carried names like: Amanda, Nicole, Brandon, Kristen, Jason, Jaden, Nathan, and Jaydon, the latter a great-grandson. Each of them is a gift and creation of our Creator God, as described by Job in the words *"the Spirit of God made me, and the breath of the Almighty gives me life,"* **(33:4)**. It is my desire that each of them now come to know the inner experience of Jesus Christ.

At the time, **Dan** and Ann (nee, Brisson) lived in Temple Terrace (Tampa), **Michael** and Patricia (nee, VanLandschoot) lived on Munising Bay, and **Nathan** and Sandra (nee, Fox) lived in Kincheloe, south of Sault Ste. Marie. Each of these families had above average problems. Dan was a financial planner with Pennsylvania Financial Group, Mike worked for the City of Munising as their water technician, and Nathan was a counselor at one of the Michigan Kincheloe maximum state prisons near *The Soo*. I admired their staying power to perform their respective jobs. Only Dan, to date, was a member of a Christian congregation, Messiah Lutheran Church, serving on the congregational council in Marquette. The jury is still out on the spiritual fate of my family, but the Judge is patient.

In time **death** took my family members one by one. My stepmother, **Lorraine**, having once survived cancer, died in 2002. My mother, **Pearl**, lived to a long life of ninety-four, passing away at home on Reformation Day, October 31, 2004 at Chatham Corners. She had been a so-called prayer warrior on that Corner. She began praying for me in June 1950 when she embraced Christ as Lord. She prayed me through my cancer surgery a half year prior to her death. And when she died I wondered who would pray for me now? Christian mothers pray for their children. Some years earlier I was very impressed when she told me her favorite book in the Scriptures was the epistle to the Romans.

I was blessed with two wonderful mothers-in-law, **Ellen Sjöstrand** and **Mae Belmas**. The former, widowed in 1981 and living in Slapneck, died in May 1997 at age eighty-nine. Mae, widowed in 1982, and of unique Sami heritage, moved to Munising from *The Soo*, where she died in September 2006 at age ninety-four.

Helmi Niemi-Kaiser, 1908-1997.

My favorite aunt, **Helmi** Niemi-Kaiser, Ferris State graduate, former teacher and secretary, died at age eighty-eight in Newberry in May 1997, following a stroke and six years in a nursing home. Uncle **John** died at home at Chatham Corners in May 2000 at age eighty-seven, leaving me his home for charitable distribution. Something wonderful happened to John in the week prior to his death as a result of having heard two sermons at a Suomi Conference festival. Before that for over six years he joined me in devotions as we visited his sister in a nursing home. His legacy is a respectable endowed scholarship fund at *Finlandia University*, joining his parents and sister Helmi. His was a happy ending. My brother Eddie continues to be generous to Finlandia.

Cousins Joyce Anderson-Joel, Bill Niemi, Les Niemi and Jimmy Sipila.

And finally, death crept closer when my brother **Bill**, sixty-six, a carpenter by trade, died in March 2009 of multiple frailties. He left five children from three marriages. His claim to fame may yet be the scenic platform at Miners Castle rumored to be struck on a future U.S. quarter in the year 2018. *"Swift to its close ebbs out life's little day,"* penned Henry Late in his great hymn *Eventide*. Most died as believers and we grieved each departure.

The harbinger of death is **illness** and **accident**. They serve us as loving warnings to guide our lives. Suffering ironically becomes a blessing to many. I have already alluded to my auto accidents, my bouts with my gallbladder (1992), my thyroid (2002), my cornea (1988), and finally my colon cancer of 2004.

* * *

I celebrated my seventy-third birthday on February 25, 2004 with colon **cancer surgery** performed by Dr. Nick Rizzo, once an elementary student of my high school classmate Bernice Salminen. It was a Wednesday. It developed into a double-whammy as Dr. Alexander Zilberman a week later redid the surgery due to methicillin-resistant Staphylococcus aureus, abbreviated as **MRSA**. To me healing from both of these seemed nothing short of a miracle. The MRSA was later related to a needed major **hernia** surgery on April 26, 2005 which, come to think of it, was my baptismal day, and also performed by Dr. Rizzo. It was interesting how my golden retriever, Max, detected my MRSA infection the moment I got home from the hospital by bolting away and refusing to come near.

Of our pets, Shag lost his eyesight and Max lost his hearing, both in old age.

*   *   *

Our God is full of surprises in other ways. In 1997 we began in retirement to enroll in *Elderhostels* which brought us to Williamsburg, VA, and Arizona. While at the latter we visited my high school classmate, **Harold and Joy Kallio** in Lake Havasu City, Arizona. The next year, 1999, we rented a house there for three months, which resulted in purchasing a lovely six-year old home at 3730 Northstar Drive for only one hundred thirty-five thousand dollars. It consisted of eighteen hundred square feet, a walled yard and was fully landscaped. It had a small grass lawn for Maxfeld. It harkened back to God's promise that if one gets his priorities straight, all other things are added to you. Faith sees it as grace. We suddenly found ourselves with a winter home in Arizona, and helping a Missouri Synod Lutheran congregation to get started in addition to attending our own Mount Olive congregation gatherings. Marcia joined two choirs and an orchestra, while I sang and preached occasionally. The climate offered daily blue skies and lots of golf.

In Havasu I spearheaded the annual March 16 *St. Urho's Day* picnic at the *London Bridge Beach*, attended by as many as seventy-two Finnophiles. Our hobbies included walking, slow-pitch softball, and reading. I avoided novels and fiction. My dad mentioned how often solutions to problems associated with construction would come to him in his sleep and early morning hours. In early morning insomnia I experienced the same, and also used that time for prayer. Sometimes I placed a pen and paper on my nightstand with which to write things. We annually attended the retired clergy retreat near Phoenix where I began to participate in the *Caring Team* of retired clergy within the local synod.

Retirement summers in Michigan found me heating the sauna. Finnish people know how to bathe better than any other people in the world. Aleksis Kivi, in the first novel in the Finnish language, *The Seven Brothers*, wrote about the hot steam in the sauna as being *"the best physic for body and soul."* In fact, in Finland, people were birthed, healed, and died in the sauna, and whether there or here it was felt that a farm without a sauna was no farm at all.

For most of our retirement years, our spiritual needs were cared for at Mount Olive Lutheran Church of Lake Havasu, in Arizona, and whose pastors clearly proclaimed the

Word. In 2001 I helped adopt a constitution for a new more simplified church body named *Lutheran Congregations in Mission for Christ*, which, at this writing, is the fourth largest Lutheran synod in the nation. In 2011 Elisabeth Zant accepted the call to be Eden's pastor in Munising, where a portion of the former parish left to join the Association of Lutheran Free congregations in Shingleton, while many others transferred to Sion church in Chatham.

Thank you for reading *the road Les traveled*. By now you have surmised that this road is not merely about my body but also about my soul, as the story of my faith. Like with that Batak woman, the computer simply wrote it on its own. What will *your* story look like?

Experts have revealed that Lake Havasu City, Arizona, is the warmest place in the nation, at night; Death Valley by day and Havasu by night. City blacktop retains heat after the sun sets, which is the cause of this phenomenon. Havasu's "lows" average 63.8 degrees, beating Death Valley by more than one degree. E.g., in 2010 Havasu's highest low at night was 98 degrees. Toasty.

Speaking about heat, in 1999 my high school **Class of 1949** celebrated its Fiftieth Reunion at the Northwoods Supper Club in Marquette, attended by class members and spouses. It was a hot day. How hot was it? The bank thermometer a mile away registered 107 degrees. The air conditioning at the club malfunctioned and caused us to negotiate for reduced prices. It is arguably the hottest class reunion in the history of Eben/Superior Central. Our teacher-guests were Walfred Mickelson and Margaret Chartier-Nadeau. Elmer Aho from "our" class in Trenary provided the entertainment, star of the *Elmer Aho Show* each Saturday evening on Big Country Radio, WJPD Ishpeming.

Tanya Jennings and Dan Niemi.

In Havasu along with high school teammates Harold Kallio and Nestor Salminen we joined the Senior Slowpitch **Softball** League, and played for six years.

The Golden Years were also spiced by sadness and grief as one's heroes and peers died. I think, e.g., of David Halkola, Walter Kukkonen, Bernie Hillilä, Olaf Rankinen, Walter Werronen, Richard Rintala, George A. Bush, Ralph Jalkanen, and Ray Wargelin. They all spoke into my life.

Dan **divorced** Ann Brisson in 2004. Shortly he and **Tanya** (nee, Jennings) were married on June 21, 2005 on Waikiki Beach in Oahu. They purchased a house in South Marquette, from which Dan worked from home, and Tanya worked for Upper Peninsula Health Plan. Amanda, Dan's architect daughter in Washington, D.C., married Bill Mosher in 2009, where she helped design homes. Kristen was also a graduate of the University of Florida. Nicole Niemi-Lasak joined the staff at Munising High School, a grad of Northern Michigan.

There is an amusing story of when Tanya met Pearl. Pearl's test was a series of little questions and one big question: *Do you make pasties?* No. *Do you make donuts?* No. *Can you make bread?* No. (Things looked quite bleak to this point.) One more question, the big one: *Do you go to church?* Voila! She passed the exam.

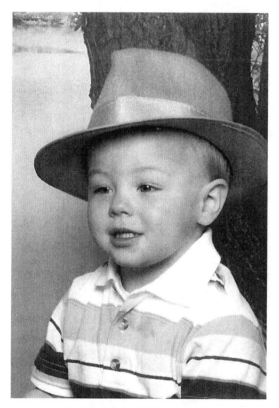
Jaydon Michael Alcorn-Niemi.

Meanwhile, at Kincheloe, grandson Nathan and Amber Alcorn of Brimley hooked up and the result was a new generation with the birth of **Jaydon** Michael Alcorn-Niemi on March 25, 2007. The youthful parents did not marry, and had joint custody. The little guy's clergy great-grandfather performed a magnificent baptism on the Fourth of July, 2007 at Lake Au Train. A loving God adopted the young man into his eternal family.

Friends who spoke into my life during these years were Mel Johnson, Ray Holmes, Nestor Salminen, Harold Kallio and Giles Ekola.

I need to declare that at the turn of the century, when George W. Bush miraculously became the nation's president just in time to cope seriously with the War on Terrorism, I joined the **Republican Party**. After twenty years of harassment Osama bin Laden's minions murdered almost three thousand citizens on September 11, 2001 with an attack on New York and Washington. President Bush rightly used force to rid the world of a "little Hitler" in Saddam Hussein. The bold move resulted in two more countries enjoying free elections in the Middle East, though it was not easy. The perpetrator was found and dispatched in West Pakistan in 2011.

I participated in three *Tea Party* rallies in 2009-2010, in Arizona and Nevada, and was pleased in the election landslide in November 2010 to take back our country from excessive government control (soft socialism) and a paralyzing national debt. The movement strove to restore the republic to the kind of grassroots energy envisioned by the founders and enjoyed in earlier years.

Marcia and I have enjoyed our retirements together. We vowed we would do some traveling, as depicted in the next chapter. St. Augustine once wrote: *The world is a book, and those who do not travel read only a page.* As a result we have visited twenty-two countries, and have been to fifty states in our great nation. During my lifetime the world population doubled.

Our top countries were Israel and Finland, with Canada, Germany, Italy, Greece and Turkey also high on the list. Everyone should try to go to the Holy Land, but then, of course, that could be my Christian bias.

Au Train Red Fox; Dan Niemi photo

CHAPTER THIRTEEN

Travel, Age 64-81, 1994-2012

Prior to retirement I had made several trips abroad beginning in 1972 to Finland with the entire family. The first one was a month's trip with the compliments of my grandfather, Manu Niemi, to introduce my sons to their heritage. As we were building the new church in Munising in 1972, I also wanted to check out Finnish architecture since Eino Kainlauri, a Finland native, was our architect. We met Finnish relatives for the first time. Jet travel was still seemingly only in its infancy. Finnish-Americans under the banner of *Sauna Society* had chartered our plane out of Duluth. In Finland we rented a Volkswagon mini-bus with which we did a grand circle tour of the country. We visited Mikkeli, Savonlinna, Ilomantsi, Joensuu, Koli, Suomussalmi, Rovaniemi, Haaparanta, Kemi, Oulu, Ylikiiminki, Kalajoki, Vaasa, Lapua, Seinäjoki, Juupajoki, Tampere, Mänttä, Lohja, Halli and Helsinki. Isn't it nice to have roots?

Coliseum in Rome.

The Danish Mermaid in Copenhagen

Our next trip in 1978 was a Catholic Pilgrimage to **Rome**; thirty-six Catholics and four Lutherans went together from the Munising area. We went to communion all over Rome, including at St. Peter's Cathedral. The all inclusive trip cost $ 575, and we visited the **Vatican**, the Coliseum, Forum, Trevi, major churches, catacombs, the Pope, Sorrento, Pompeii, Capri Island, Pisa, Florence, *David*, and Tuscany.

* * *

In 1983, soon after Marcia and I married, we took our mothers, my sister Betty and a few friends on a trip to **Nordic-country capitol cities**, Copenhagen, Oslo, Stockholm and Helsinki. Each country offered something special . . . Bergen, the fjords, a Viking museum, Tivoli, Turku Cathedral and Silja Line. For Marcia and me it was like another honeymoon. I had been in the employ of the college only several months.

It took another nine years, in 1992, that a work trip with Finlandia University took us back to **Finland** to attend a college reception in Helsinki and to make certain key cultivation visits. It was also the year of the *"Roots In Finland"* events whereupon expatriates were welcomed to visit the fatherland. Finns are quite emotional about preserving their roots. Although we Finno-Ugrians claim less than thirty million people in the world, we are one of only twelve distinct language groups on the planet, according to National Geographic Society. I am ashamed to disclose that Vladimir Lenin was primarily Finno-Ugrian. No wonder socialist Finnish halls in some communities had classes on Lenin.

The 1992 trip afforded Marcia to search for her roots in Övertoneá, Sweden. We found the site on the Tornio River from which her grandmother, **Albina Aili**, part **Sami**, emigrated to Ironwood. It was wonderful to meet some of her relatives.

Just prior to Marcia's retirement we took several spring-break trips to Cozumel and Playa del Carmen, **Mexico**, at all-inclusive Diamond Resorts. All-inclusive means you only cry once, when you pay upfront, and then the entire week's amenities seem like they are free. We enjoyed snorkeling on some of the finest coral reefs in the world.

legendary "Lost City" of Petra.

Petra's Treasury Building

* * *

With retirement we kicked it into high gear. Three months after I retired I joined a **Holy Land** tour with *Luther Seminary* to Israel and Jordan. It was awesome to be in Israel. So impressed was I that the following year I took a group of twenty-five on a similar trip. How amazing was Petra, the Holy Sepulcher, Gordon's Tomb, Via Dolorosa, Sea of Galilee, Capernaum, Gethsemane, Dome of the Rock, the Wailing Wall, Nazareth, Jericho, the Dead Sea, Masada, Bethlehem, and Qumran. The reading of the New Testament came alive after having visited the Holy Land. As group leader I needed to assert myself in Jericho to obtain a larger bus. They tried to do a number on us, but I was assertive. It was my version of "the battle of Jericho," and I won.

In 1995, and to ease the shock of retirement for Marcia, we took a nine-day *Circle Tour* of **Lake Superior** at the beginning of the school year. We did it with our just-purchased first Cadillac, the Fleetwood model. Devoid of motel reservations, this explains how long it took, not having a schedule; we dined at the famous *Hoito Café* in Thunder Bay, a "must" for every Finn.

Istanbul, Turkey

Istanbul's Blue Mosque

In 1996 we continued our New Testament studies with a tour of St. Paul's congregations in **Turkey and Greece**. Sixty percent of the New Testament books were written from Asia Minor. From this trip names such as Istanbul, Nicaea, Ephesus, Izmir, Pammukale, Bodrum, Troy, Pergamum, Philippi, Thessalonika, Delphi, Kalambaka, Athens and the Acropolis fill the mind with warm feelings. We purchased a Turkish carpet in Diezle. We were awed by the tremendous odds against which the gospel of Jesus prevailed in the infancy of the Jesus movement. Modern Turkey is a well-kept secret while Greece seemed also nice. I had the privilege of leading our 46-person group in devotions in Laodicea, mentioned in the Bible's last book.

* * *

Dr. Luther.

The following year our growth trip was to **Germany's** *Lutherland*. We landed in **Berlin** and we flew home from **Vienna**. We walked the *Unter den Linden* in Berlin, saw Leipzig's St. Thomas Church were Bach created great music, lingered in Wittenberg where a simple monk changed theology and the world, visited Eisleben where Martin Luther was born and died, gazed upon Gutenberg's first printing press in Mainz, and sailed the fastmoving Rhine River. I led the group in prayer in Worms, where Luther made his *"Here I Stand"* speech against the pope and emperor's inadequacies. We visited Mozart's Salzburg, visited Heidelberg, and marveled what a world class city Vienna was. Our Lutheran Reformation heritage came powerfully alive to us on this Peter Sethre-led tour by Luther Seminary of St. Paul.

In 1998 we went to **Italy** with a dozen of our friends. I had a chance to return the soup spoon which I stole twenty years earlier in Siena, and cleared my conscience. This trip included Assissi (as in St. Francis), the most famous square in the world, St. Mark's in Venice, a gondola ride, the leaning tower of Pisa, and yet again another view of the great *David* by the master Michelangelo. The time in **Florence** was never enough. In Sorrento I became more convinced I was not meant to be a dancer, as this gorgeous Italian girl dragged me onto the stage. We had a fresh look at **Pompeii**, the number one artifact of its kind. It was a treat to visit Monte Cassino Monastery, and drive near Cisterna (where Captain Mickelson my high school coach was severely wounded.) We drove through the Apennines (mountains) where uncle Lauri Sipilä was wounded and where Len Salminen won his Silver Star in 1944. San Marino was a new country for us, where the chief export was postage stamps.

We began the **new millennium** in the year 2000 with a trip to the Crucifixion of Jesus, an all-day live production in **Oberammergau**, Germany, on July 23. This event has been held since 1633 every ten years. The trip also included Munich (the heart of Hitlerism), Innsbruck, Switzerland, Paris, and London, all of them fun to see. I seldom drink beer but when I do I drink it at the Hofbrauhaus in Munich, where Adolf Hitler launched his notions of the Nazi *Third Reich*. In **Paris** we drank in the *Arch de Triumphe*, Notre Dame Cathedral and the Eiffel Tower. The country was infested with pickpockets. We experienced a fast train from Paris to London under the *Chunnel*. In **London** we saw where Lake Havasu's London Bridge came from, we toured Westminster Abbey, and attended the stage production *Phantom of the Opera*.

* * *

Finally, in 2002 we were old and tired enough to begin **cruising**. The first of three cruises was to **Alaska**. The other two were **Western Mediterranean** (2003) and **Hawaii** (2005). Cruising is easier for senior citizens as one can live on the boat, and venture out to ports of call only if one so desires.

On the inside passage venture, we embarked from Vancouver, Canada. We visited Ketchikan, Juneau, and Skagway. My confirmand, a Lutheran pastor in Whitehorse, Yukon, **David** and **Sharon Taeger**, visited us for a half day in Skagway. David's roots, like mine, were also in Tiistenjoki, Finland. The Indian culture of the area was outstanding. We saw the glaciers, but only a few whales.

The following year (2003) we took the Mediterranean cruise out of Lisbon, Portugal, touching in ports-of-call in Barcelona, Spanish Morocco, Majorca, France, Monte Carlo, Corsica, and Rome. Our cruise-mates again were Marlys and Lance Roberts and Darley and Rudy Kemppainen. We spent a day in Rome with Dr. Steve Raica, head of the American College in Rome, and a Munising native. On each cruise I gained a net of five pounds.

I made a surprise birthday party visit to Finland in July 2003 to attend a fiftieth-year birthday party of **Veli Sipilä**. That was the year when as I approached the Sawyer International Airport near home, four black bears in single file walked across the highway bringing our car to a halt. On this trip I sang *"Roots in Finland"* in Finnish to the group of four hundred, but also spoke at an *Awakened* movement evening service outdoors with two hundred present. I attended the notable Kaustinen Music Festival and visited Bishop Jorma and Marjatta Laulaja. I discovered my communist cousin's, Wäinö Sjögren, tombstone at Juupajoki, who had been executed in St. Petersburg in 1942. A fiftieth birthday is huge event in Finland. I participated in my first *savusauna* (smoke sauna) on this trip; the highest quality steam (löyly) is only possible in a sauna which has no smoke stack.

Waikiki Beach in Honolulu where I was exiled.

Our third cruise was in 2005 to **Hawaii** with a side trip to the Republic of Keribati with the same previous partners. Excitement began quickly as I left my passport in Lake Havasu. The boat left without me for Maui. I was exiled to the Radisson Hotel in Waikiki Beach for the weekend, at which time I made arrangements at church on Sunday for Dr. Nicholas Christoff to marry Dan and Tanya. Following a new passport obtained Monday morning I caught the cruise in Maui, flying from Honolulu to Maui. It was a $500 mishap. My U.S. Navy grandson, Brandon, based on Oahu, took us for a day's tour of the island. We were treated to a gigantic whale show off of Maui, and we did an exciting helicopter tour of the canyons of Kaui. At Maui we saw an abundance of whales.

*   *   *

St. Petersburg, Russia

St. Petersburg, Russia.

Having been appointed trustee for millionaire **Arvo Heino**, a Cold Spring farmer, I went to Finland again in 2007 in order to search for seventeen heirs in his prepared trust. I met wonderful people. I sought out more of Antti Piimänen's churches (my relative) and sang karaoke in Vantaa. It was a special treat to visit Piimänen churches, the Turku Cathedral and Naantali. Piimänen was in the family tree of my grandmother, Alma Niemi.

Attached to this trip I joined twenty-eight others in visiting nine congregations in **Russian Karelia** and the Theological Institute in Keltto, a St. Petersburg suburb. I helped to spearhead a fund drive which raised $ 95,000 to build a **new church** for the Läskelä congregation, which was dedicated on May 19, 2011. A third of this amount was given by the passengers of our Bus # 129. We had heard unbelievable stories of hardship suffered by the Ingrian Christians under the dictatorship of Josef Stalin, who succeeded Vladimir Lenin in the U.S.S.R. After seventy years communism collapsed in Russia in 1998 and there are now new congregations each year as deprived people are hungry for the Word of God. The **Ingrian Lutheran Church** is today the fastest growing Lutheran Church in Europe. On the way home I visited expensive Iceland for two days.

*   *   *

Our most recent trip, to date, was in June 2010 to **Cancun**, Mexico, to attend the wedding of my eldest grandchild, Amanda E. Niemi, to William Mosher, a native of New Hampshire. Unfortunately it rained a lot, disrupting the wedding. The wedded couple lives near Reston, VA, where they serve the common good as an architect and a teacher of "gifted pupils."

*   *   *

St. Augustine was right about travel being a very educational endeavor. I have been to thirty different countries.[70]

"Give thanks to the Lord, for he is good."[71]

3730 Northstar Dr., Lake Havasu City, AZ

CHAPTER FOURTEEN

The Future, Age 80ff, 2012ff

We are now coming to the close of these memories. This has been a lot of nostalgia, and nostalgia is important and therapeutic. The Chinese psychologist Ding-Guo Gao suggested that *"a person immersed in nostalgia can feel connected even when he or she is alone. Nostalgia works therapeutically because you are reliving your social connectedness."* Dana O'Briain of the UK suggested that *"nostalgia is heroin for old people."*

These memoirs are not to be confused to the "Me Essays," which have become so prevalent among children and youth in our age of narcissism. Some sermons, too, of late have degenerated to nothing more than "me essays," in other words merely talking about one's self. My seminary warned us about it. My story is not about me, as is apparent.

It is nostalgic to review the miraculous road that my Lord God set out for me. One is given a calling, and while mistakes were made, God not only forgave but participated in the struggle for wholeness. Although Christians sin, they do not cease to be Christians. While the death of a non-Christian is the end of their perceived life, to the Christian we've only just begun. Eternal life began the day we believed the One who said *"I am resurrection and I am life.*

How shall I **bequeath** to future generations? Perhaps the same way in which it was bequeathed to me. Someone told someone else. Martin Luther, in a sermon preached in 1534, reminded us that Christ singled out two organs as important: ear and tongue. *"These two organs alone make a difference between Christians and non-Christians: a Christian speaks and hears in a different manner and has a tongue that praises God's grace and preaches Christ, declaring that he alone can make us blessed. The world does not do that. It speaks of avarice and other vices, and preaches and praises its own pomp."*[72]

How will the Christian faith that I cherished be bequeathed to my sons, grandchildren and, e.g., to those three thousand four hundred and fifty-five souls for whom I was a spiritual leader as their shepherd? Who will articulate the treasure of the gospel to those in the future? Perhaps partially through the magnificent seven of my youth who became pastors. My legacy was obviously not silver or gold, for I gave that away to the needy along the way. St. Peter said on Pentecost, *"Silver and gold I do not have, but that which I have, I will give you. In the name of Jesus Christ of Nazareth, get up and walk."*[73] Unlike presidents of nations, and others, the intent of my legacy was not to make me look good, but to promote the finest of all products, Jesus Christ.

That is the greatest legacy imaginable, the scriptural *"pearl of great price,"* which runs counter to the seductive atheistic faulty premise of materialistic reductionism of our age of post-modernism. In a hostile spiritual climate, at what price were we willing to take the cross into that realm as we identified with our Lord and Savior? Perhaps we needed to become lawbreakers rather than betray our faith, as we chose to be intolerably intolerant. Syncretism was not the answer. Today's youth express it best with the curt, "Whatever…" perhaps having heard it from a syncetist parent.

Bernie HIllila, in his short book *The Finnish Line*, suggests that each of us is like the narrow "waist" of an hourglass, in that through me pass the generations of the past, and through me are channeled genes and values, the living Christian faith, for the future. The descendents are of greater importance than the forbearers.

Beside clear air and water, the more important is that they expect our values, our faith in Jesus. This ancestor and forbearer pressure is far more important than perceived present peer pressure. A lot of people are counting on you and me. I don't wish to let them down! This is our precious legacy, far more than silver and gold….or self.

* * *

There is good news. The future looks terrific because I have read the Book, the owner's manual, and we know how the story ends. The Jewish savior promised, *"Be faithful until death and I will give you the victor's wreath of life."*[74]

Many people spoke into my life. Many of them spoke words. The **word** came to me throughout my life and spoke life into my life. Saving faith has to do with words, beliefs, doctrines, and not merely deeds or activism. Doing came as a result of words. The **Word** was present defying an abortion, when I was baptized at Farm Luoma in Eben. The words of that hymn at age ten, just before God fished me out of the stone quarry. That was the Ebenezer word, my "stone of help." I *"drank from the spiritual Rock . . . and that Rock was Christ."*

Go, my children, with my blessing, never alone;
Waking, sleeping, I am with you; you are my own.
In My love's baptismal river I have made you mine forever.
Go, my children, with my blessing, you are my own.

It brings tears each time I sing it in church. But there's more. The Word came to me at age sixteen at Camp Nesbitt when I first took ownership of forgiveness and absolution, the gospel, because of my sin debt and burden that I had been carrying.

Go, my children, sins forgiven, at peace and pure.
Here you learned how much I love you, what I can cure.
Here you heard my dear Son's story; here you touched Him, saw His glory.
Go, my children, sins forgiven, at peace and pure.

Swiftly move to the word that came through the call of the prophet Isaiah when I was eighteen, who raised the question *Who will go for us,* and the answer is suggested, *Here am I, Send me.* Now we are looking at calling, career, and life mission.

Go, my children, fed and nourished, closer to me;
Grow in love and love by serving, joyful and free.
Here My Spirit's power filled you; here His tender comfort stilled you.
Go, my children, fed and nourished, joyful and free.

Then came the time to find a life partner. It came with the created order of things. I found two life partners, Betty and Marcia, but not at the same time. This hymn did not have this verse until 1983:

In this union I have joined you, husband and wife,
Now my children, live together, as heirs of life.
Each the other's gladness sharing, each the other's burdens bearing,
Now, my children, live together as heirs of life.

Then came old age, when once strong men are bent: he goes to his eternal home.75

I the Lord will bless and keep you and give you peace;
I the Lord will smile upon you and give you peace;
I the Lord will be your Father, Savior, Comforter, and Brother,
*Go, my children; I will keep you and give you peace.*76

The great hymn became **the story of my life** and my career. The Word of God spoke to me at important moments. By grace I have been saved and faith itself is not my own, but it is the gift of God to everyone and not the works that we have done. So we do not boast of this, because it is God's great gift. Amen.77

*   *   *

When you reduce it down, there are just two groups in the world, those who believe and those who don't. The first group loves the Holy Bible, seeking it out, can't get enough of it, but the second group is tickled by the notions and philosophies of **false prophets,** of which the following are just a few: Niccolo Machiavelli, Reno Descartes, Thomas Hobbes, Jean-Jacques Rousseau, John Locke, John Stuart Mill, Richard Simon, Johann Semler, Kant, Charles Darwin, Alfred Kinsey, Betty Friedan, Friedrich Nietzsche, Vladimir Ilyich Lenin, Margaret Sanger, Sidney Simon, Adolf Hitler, Sigmund Freud, and Margaret Mead, in the Western world.

The story was told from Gevas, Turkey, that while shepherds were taking their breakfast, one of their sheep jumped off a 45-foot cliff to its death. They were stunned as the balance of the 1,500 sheep mindlessly also jumped. The good news was that the last 1,000 sheep landed on the soft woolly bodies of the earlier ones, and lived. A total of 450 sheep died.

Who were the false shepherds and leaders in our church? By conscience we tried to avoid the mistakes of the sheep who blindly followed one another over the cliff, as the blind led the blind. We pray: *Savior, like a shepherd lead us, much we need Thy tender care; In Thy pleasant pastures feed us, For our use Thy folds prepare* (Thrupp). Christians boldly say: The Lord is my shepherd!

I alluded in my commencement address at age eighteen, that we are all on the train of life. I didn't realize the deep truth of the matter at the time. But on that train it doesn't matter how fast we are going if we are going in the wrong direction. Wasn't it Dietrich Bonhoeffer who said: *"If you board the wrong train it is no use running along the corridor in the opposite direction."* I wrote earlier how in 1964, returning from a church meeting, I was on the wrong plane on a dead end. But the correct plane was still behind me, landed, and rescued me. In my first ride as a teenager, the train went from Eben ("stone of help") to Munising (Eden Church), where I served for eighteen years as a pastor. There is some symbolism there. And so, God has been involved in my train ride of life. We needed to make certain we were on the right train.

*   *   *

Les leading Suomi Conference in 2001 in Pelkie.

Let's revisit Cold Springs. How were things in Cold Springs, sixty years after leaving it? By the new millennium most of the neighborhood now belonged to one of the churches in Chatham or Eben.

The Chatham/Eben area has produced the following **pastors and missionaries** since 1903: Samuel Krankkala, David Samanen, Albert Hautamäki, Florence Hautamäki-Mäki, Les Niemi, Patricia Lelvis, Harold Kallio, John Kallio, George Wieland, Ray Johnson, Paul Kelto, Rebecca Erickson, James Johnson, Erick Westlake, Leslie "Skip" Täkkinen and Roger Kangas. I may have missed some.

I celebrated my **Fifty-fifth anniversary** of my ordination on June 20, 2009 with a Finnish service in Ishpeming. By this time you may be asking what it was that kept my motor running, my engine of faith.

For the last two decades, especially since retirement, I have enjoyed special daily sessions with my Lord in which I immersed myself in the Word of God. Five and a half decades as a pastor taught me this and now I have more time for it in retirement.

Les and Marcia Niemi, 2011.

Although I wore out many Bibles in two languages, my latest favorite was the Beckian Bible, the only English version of Lutheran origin, ideal for devotional purposes. How enriching it was to enjoy personal devotions in two languages, of which, strangely, *Finnish* seemed more profound and basic than English. Some of my Finnish sources had been Martti Simojoki, Jorma Laulaja, *Tunnussana* (Daily Texts), and in English, Luther ("*Day by Day We Magnify Thee*" edited by Marshall Johnson), *Our Daily Bread* (Reformed Church), *Meditations* (Wisconsin Synod), *Magnificat* (Roman Catholic).

Interestingly, the Moravian Daily Text "watch words" (*Tunnussana*) have been used by a surprising number of great leaders since its first issue in 1731 by Count Nikolaus Ludwig von Zinzendorff in Herrnhut Germany, including the noted Dietrich Bonhoeffer until his martyrdom under Hitler in 1945. Singing of solos, except for our gala liturgy, didn't enter my life until after retirement. But my serving as congregational pastor/cantor had been a joy for my whole career. At the beginning of the new millennium when I could not afford to buy an original copy of Luther's 1546 *Small Catechism*, although I had an opportunity, I was successful in obtaining a copy of the contents, in German, worth more than mere leather covers. Striking was the irony of the initial seminary purchase of the New Testament in the Greek language in 1951 for one dollar and sixty cents . . . so cheap and yet such a treasure. Content always trumps the wrappings.

My daily reading of God's Word actually began at the age of seventeen in high school when I joined the then-popular *Pocket Testament League*. Hallesby's devotional books were helpful to me as a young Christian. All this spoke to my tradition of pietism. Often my sinful life was anything but pious.

* * *

In 2009, e.g., the Evangelical Lutheran Church in America, by boldfaced manipulation decided to forsake the **created order**, to forsake the 2000 years of church **tradition**, and worst of all, to forsake the **Word of God**, by approving of homosexual unions and the ordination of practicing homosexuals. Six hundred some-odd self-absorbed people in Minneapolis assumed they could re-define the ageless meaning of marriage and our sexual code in August 2009. Some things in life are not up for a vote, and the meaning of marriage is one of them. Does that strike you as a bit outrageous? Does the church have the right to re-write the holy Scriptures? Is that not the question? Any wonder that the cross was turned upside down by a tornado at a nearby Lutheran church the very day of infamy that debate on the issue was begun. It became the flashpoint indicative of a far deeper and more profound faith crisis in the ELCA, for the church of Christ has always been under pressure to compromise.

They paid no heed to the warning sign: *There is a way that seems right to a man, but its end is the way of death.* **(Proverbs 14:12)** To go against conscience is neither right nor safe, for it holds eternal ramifications. On this train of life the head engineer and the conductors seriously forgot to listen to the hymn writer who penned the simple but crucial words:

> *God's given us His holy Word*
> *To help and guide the way;*
> *And if we read and follow it,*
> *We will not go astray.*

The subsequent trials of the ELCA indicated that astray we went. Both the nation and our church qualify for the judgment of our God and to receive what we deserve. Someone mused that her main gifts were merely preparing social statements and keeping a clergy roster, but little else, basking in the abundance of cheap grace without the cross. It is not cheap grace "when God calls a man he bids him come and die," as the 1945 martyr Bonhoeffer wrote. Then, like now, an oath of loyalty was required. The repetition of history is uncanny. It pains me to draw attention to the ugliness of our dilemma, but Luther pointed out that if we are cowards to attack at the hottest point of the battle, we are not worthy of our calling. Who can stand up to be the heroes of our time? It is now our turn. We need to be only ordinary heroes, who know what they believe and why they believe it, and live out their convictions.

My church, likening it to the train, became uncoupled at the Summit, and the railway cars were parting, ever so slowly at first, but now heading in opposite directions and now picking up speed, ne'er to be connected again. As each of us must decide which side we are on we bid farewell to some former friends now coasting in a different direction.

On the subject of the culture of death, I agonized over the drastic shift in direction culture took during the past four decades. When I was a young pastor the community gathered at churches for milestone events such as baptisms, weddings, birthdays, anniversaries, and various other rites of passage. The church was bubbling with life and celebration. By the time I reached age eighty society was shifting to hold such events, of all things, at funeral homes. The room down the hall housed the display of caskets and urns. Didn't they notice that the facility was sometimes surrounded by a large cemetery filled with gravestones? Am I unreasonable to suggest that such a trend was another symbol of our times affirming that we indeed lived increasingly in a culture of death and extinction. My life began in the Great Depression and eighty years later the pundits told us that an even greater depression was lurking. Major economic crises and other catastrophes were predicted.

I found great significance in the accelerated incease of the intensity and frequency of natural disasters of recent years. Add to this our enormous economic dilemma and the impending possible reality of a sneak nucleur attack of any one of our major cities. Were these the judgment of God upon a nation that has forgotten Him?

The gift of discernment is one of the gifts of the Spirit. Has it concerned you as you perceive what has been going on all around you? What have been some of the telltale signs of the times? And where are you, or your church, in all this?

Shouldn't we be reporting to one another as we see the following: the enormity of the silent holocaust (abortions) of our time, the meaning of marriage (as highlighted by same sex unions, practicing homosexuality among clergy, and polygamy), weakening of the family unit, the erosion of morality, e.g., incited by pornography, incitement of student riots, school takeovers by faulty textbooks and non-discerning teachers, the parenting displaced by the state, elimination of prayer from the public square, the social gospel replacing the true revealed gospel of Jesus, the discrediting of our U.S. Constitution, the continued hatred of the Jews, creeping socialism under the guise of centralized control, and the impulse to crush the rights of conscience?

And this list was only for starters. What did it mean to be the true church today? Raise these issues in the family of faith, and speak of them with your children before it is too late. Adults know more than children. Let us be vigilant and at least as shrewd as the children of darkness, whose hearts are not ruled by the indwelling Jesus the Christ.

*   *   *

Nostalgia longs for the good ole days. Now to borrow a secular reference from the song *"Memories"* from the popular Broadway play, *"Cats:"*

> *"Daylight, I must wait for the sunrise*
> *I must think of a new life and I mustn't give in.*
> *When the dawn comes tonight will be a memory too*
> *And a new day will begin."*[78]

In real life, we sometimes swung between cynicism and optimism, the culture of death and the religion of hope, between the works of darkness and the Light of the world. The difference came when we entered by the "Door," and overcame the "unbelief gene" which was such a powerful propensity. Only Jesus can be that Door. St. Peter reminded us *"In great mercy he has birthed us to a new life and given us a living hope by raising Jesus.*[79] Sometimes this experience was accompanied by noticeable feelings and emotions, but always it was followed by a changed heart and loving service to fellow travelers.

My twofold ministry encompassed the best of times and the worst of times. At this point in time for me the times were of utmost clarity. In good times and in bad, it was a good time to be a Christian pastor. Faith is marvelously resilient.

If Jesus is only a good guy and that's all he is, a good guy who worked hard and died, but if he was who he said he was, the Lamb of God who took away the sin of the world, that's worth crowing about.

The Augsburg Confession of 1530 concurs: *"Through the Word and Sacraments, as through instruments, the Holy Spirit is given. He works faith, when and where it pleases God, in those who hear the good news that God justifies those who believe that they are received into grace for Christ's sake."* So when someone comes to faith (even me) it is not something I can control.

A great British churchman put it: *"Christ offers something for nothing: He even offers everything for nothing. In a sense, the whole Christian life consists in accepting that very remarkable offer."*[80]

"Amen. Come, Lord Jesus!"[81]

Gosh, the future looks exceptionally good, as a result! My story is primarily a witness to faith, expressed in my two-pronged ministry, the parish ministry and a ministry to accumulated resources, and all to the glory of God. My story is nothing more than a witness to the power of God's Word, which could be likened to what was spoken to Jeremiah the prophet:

"Before I formed you in the womb I knew you, before you were
Born I dedicated you, a prophet to the nations I appointed you. . . .
To whomever I send you, you shall go, whatever I commend you,
You shall speak. Have no fear before them, because I am with you. . ."

"Be my rock of refuge, a stronghold to give me safety,
For you are my rock (Eben-ezer) and my fortress. . .
For you are my hope, O Lord; my trust, O God, from my youth.
On you I depend from birth; from my mother's womb you are
My strength."

Psalm 71

* * *

I feel so badly for my family, and others, especially my grandchildren. I have written these memoirs out of love for you. I rejoice that my story may make an eternal difference in your life. For some it will be the planting of a seed. For others it will be a watering of an already growing faith. And for yet others, the harvest of everlasting life as you head for home. *"This is my story, this is my song, praising my Savior all the day long,"* as the song goes. I feel so badly that only eighteen percent of our, Marcia and me, grandchildren are where they ought to be in their Christian journey. And some of them would make such wonderful Christians.

If I have seemed overbearing about these priorities of life, it was because of the overbearing love of God to a sinner like me. I am pleased to push the point. I have something to crow about. *"More than that, our boast is only in God through our Lord Jesus Christ, who has now given us this changed relationship,"* wrote St. Paul in Romans 5:11. I once met a pastor on a tour bus in Italy who, offended by my overbearing devotional, said he never gave the answers until the person asked.

Nice thought, but when they are too slow to ask, one can legitimately dangle the carrot. I like my program better for we don't have time to play games, nor merely crack jokes at funerals because the matter is a life and death matter.

Being Finnish, this is not out of character for me. Finns say it like it is. I also get it from my mother who didn't mince words, but said it honestly. Finns are noted for directness. Its like the Finn who couldn't lie on his telephone answering service, saying: 'I'm not here now.' Instead he said directly, "Obviously, I am here now, but when you call I may be gone. If you are a telemarketer, or work for Suomi College, leave your phone number, and I will call you at dinner time."

(Other Finnish traits are: Shyness, sisu, stoicism, honesty, creativity. cleanliness, logicality, quirkiness, frugality, extremism and faith).

If you knew me long enough, there were times when I disappointed you, stemming from the fact that I was a sinner like others, at times much worse in fact. St. Paul wrote: *None is righteous, no, not one.* I let down folks we loved. And people whom we loved also let us down. People we trusted hurt us by things they did or said. Make no mistake, my life as a Christian and the life of the world was thrown into continuous conflict. It was hand-to-hand conflict between me as a Christian and me as part of the world in sharpest contrast. The battle raged. And by ourselves we have utterly no chance whatsoever, but with Christ we win.

But there is One who never lets us down. His name is God the Father, Son, and Holy Spirit. Our faithlessness did not cancel His faithfulness to us. Even though the world, which including us, turned against Him, He sent His Son to save us. If He was willing to give His life for us, surely He is faithful. Paul wrote further: *"What if some were unfaithful? Does their unfaithfulness nullify the faithfulness of God? Never."* (Romans 3:3)

One day we will be summoned in life to move beyond the curtain to share in the joy and elation of the glorious life to come with your Lord Jesus Christ, having been called by Him. Unfortunately there will be some who did not hear the call, or chose to ignore it. The church bulletin board warned: *"Eternity: Smoking or non-smoking."*

Dietrich Bonhoeffer reminded us that *"should one not rejoice at a full church, or that people are coming who had not come for years, and on the other hand, who dare analyze this pleasure, and be quite certain that it is free from the seeds of darkness?"*[82]

Closing prayer:

Forgive me for wanting to be used by You in a way that looks good to others. Help me to be a witness even through my weaknesses. Amen.

* * *

A SPIRITUAL AUTOBIOGRAPHY (Legacy)

My story is a story of a spiritual autobiography. You may disagree with my world-view, but you do so to your eternal peril. Martin Luther King, Jr., once said: "Our lives begin to end the day we become silent about the things that matter." This writer cannot imagine any matter larger than that of the welfare of one's soul. Man is not merely body and soul, rather he is a soul which happens to have a body.

The enormity of the one great act of God in Jesus Christ can be truly cherished only after we have agonized over the reality of our sin. Reason cannot comprehend it, which is why Martin Luther called reason "the devil's whore." Biologists, psychologists and moralists fail to find any evidence of sin. They scream: illusion, fiction. And if sin is merely an illusion, so will be the redemptive work of Christ on the cross.

The hereditary sin is so deep a corruption of nature that reason cannot reach it nor understand it. It must be believed and the revelation is in the Scriptures alone. If you don't believe the bible regarding your sinfulness, ask your neighbor.

The answer is the inner experience of Christ, without which we have nothing. It has been comforting that the Church of Finland and the Ingrian Church have taken a firm stand on the gospel of Jesus. The Suomi Conference in spirit is a spiritual extension of this goodly heritage in America. In unity we speak in behalf of the language of faith but not the language of doubt.

Sin demanded the need for blood which sounds far too primitive for the wheezy stomachs of those who think themselves far too enlightened and sophisticated for such. But I didn't make the rules. God used earthy concepts in our salvation history.

St. Paul from Tarsus used his low level style to talk to Greeks when he wrote: "*I did not come with excellence of speech or wisdom declaring to you the mystery of God..... none else but the crucified Christ.*" Similarly I used central Upper Peninsula "talk," not pompous speech, to reach U.P. audiences. This is why August Mäki said: "I haven't ever heard it told so clearly." Paul did not parade sophistication but the deep things of the soul like sin, grace, forgiveness, and faith. The life is in the blood, the blood of Jesus, and once and for all.

Again, two minutes after we die, we either will be supremely elated, or unbelievably terrified. If it, God forbid, be the latter, we would give anything and everything for one more minute on earth to be able to repent, have our load of sin forgiven and invite Christ within. When my brother died in 2009, why did he burst out crying just before the moment of his death, this sixty-six year old man? Why . . . ?

In each of my parishes, and beyond, I tried to be the coach on third base, waving the runner home. On close calls at home, it is music to hear the Umpire shout: Safe!

Life is not merely a few shining moments, however. It is usually what happens in the long run. Life is a long season, as opposed to a brief tournament.

When Itzhak Perlman in 1995 gave a concert at New York's Avery Fisher Hall and suddenly a string snapped on his violin, he did not stop and leave the stage, but kept on playing. He finished the concert to a large roar from the audience at the conclusion. When later interviewed he said: *"You know, sometimes it is the artist's task to find out how much music you can still make with what you have left."*[83]

Life is a long season. The race is not always to the swift or the battle to the strong. It may rather be, by God's sheer grace and gift, what we can do with what we have left, what we have been given. I'm talking faith, not good works. This is especially appropriate toward the end of the race. For me when reduced to bare simplicity it will always look something like this:

THE CROSS STANDS,
THE WORD ENDURES,
AND GRACE SUFFICES.

Les at Age Eighty.

I will give Martin Luther the final word when he preached on John 14 that "I can declare with unswerving faith and with an undaunted conscience, 'Even though I am a poor sinner, still Christ is holy with his baptism, Word, sacrament, and Holy Spirit.'[84]

That's my program. And that's my story, my life, and my ministry. I will pit my future on it because it is based on God's love and grace, made clear in His magnificent Word. My memoirs deal not only with the past but also the future. Now, what about you? What is your world view?

"I conclude with the words of St. Paul, paraphrased:

"If you confess with your mouth that Jesus is Lord, and believe in your heart that God has raised him from the dead, you will be saved. Faith of the heart brings justification, confession of the mouth brings salvation. Scripture tells us that not one who believes in him will be shamed. . . All have the same Lord and from him love suffices for all who call upon him for help. For it is written: Everyone who calls for help of the Lord will be saved. But how can they call for help having not believed? How can they believe that of which they have not heard? How can they hear if no one preaches? And how can anyone preach unless one is sent? It is written: How wonderful are the footsteps of the one who brings good news! But not all have opted to hear the gospel. Isaiah said: Lord, who has believed our words? Faith

is given birth by hearing but hearing is birthed by the word about Christ. I now ask you: Haven't they at least heard it? Of course they have: their voice has echoed to all and their words to the ends of the world." Romans 10:9-18.

In the very end, when all is said and done, and the computer has written, *If we confess our sins, He is faithful and just to forgive us our sins and to cleanse us from all unrighteousness,* reminded St. John in first letter. Someone coined this the "soupbar gospel". Thanks be to God! The future looks bright indeed.

ENDNOTES

1   Luther, Martin, *The Small Catechism, Lord's Prayer*, 1546.

2   Psalm 139:7.

3   Psalm 51:5.

4   1 Samuel 7:12.

5   Matthew 2:10.

6   Colossians 2:12.

7   Johnson, Marshall, *Day by Day We Magnify Thee*, Martin Luther, Sermon 1522, p. 38

8   A Porcelain Pioneer kitchen stove sold for $ 99 in 1929 and had warming closets and a warm water reservoir; ours was ivory and green; the glass footrests cost 57 cents each.

9   Mom hinted that abortions were available by merely taking a pill. When was my sibling aborted?

10   Romans 8:37.

11   John 10:7-10.

12   *Voice of the Spirit*, Newsletter, Bible Camp, 1947.

13   Romans 5:1.

14   Wargelin, Raymond, *Church Yearbook*, Suomi Synod, 1945, p. 112.

15   The miracle of new birth in Christ deserves yet an additional word. I was very fortunate to meet the Lord Jesus when I did in the 1940s. False gospels had appeared centuries earlier, especially with the so-called Age of Enlightenment, so youth are today in far greater danger. But the basic issues concerning salvation have not changed. Atheism would have you believe that the inner life is merely fantasy and thus not real. Just as we have one brain with two hemispheres, we are tempted today to worship rational science, but overlook the spiritual dimension which houses the biggest organ, one's conscience. Jesus warned: "Man shall not live by bread alone."

I sometimes wonder how God could speak to my conscience considering how limited my pre-knowledge was at age sixteen. But, thankfully, the secret of faith is not how much you know, but that you know. Luther said: "not by my own reason or effort..." And so prior to the Thursday, August 7, my knowledge was piqued by Pastor Koski's comments on Bible curiosities, Bill Puotinen's sharing of the meaning of justification by faith, the importance of God's Word, and the means of grace, Emil Paananen's explanation of Jesus' encounter with Nicodemus. This birth by baptism is by water and the Spirit, infused in baptism, or on separate occasions. Karl Wilkman taught what worship means, and Pastor Frank Berg invited us to recognize that now was the acceptable time to deal with life's greatest human problem, presenting a solution in the love of Jesus. Berg's morning presentations centered on the work of the Holy Spirit. The theme for the week was "By Thy Spirit." And Les Niemi was listening. Something always happens when God speaks, regardless how he speaks or whom he uses, for he is a living God.

I seemingly heard for the first time. I was merely open and I received it as a gift. It was powerfully tied to the forgiveness of every one of my sins, past, present and future. Martin Luther said in 1533: *Reason must bow and must confess her blindness in that she wants to climb to heaven... while she cannot see what lies before her eyes. Namely, the coming of Christ.* My awakening restored me to the status of my baptism when I was an infant. (That baptism was so important to me that for a quarter of a century I carried a copy of it in my wallet.) And it is such a privilege to share this moment with you in this memoir.

The Suomi Synod church camps meant business. It was far more than mere head knowledge, or only education. It went right down to the soul. It was not merely fun and games. It was Law and Gospel at its delicate best, like the expert surgeon operating on our precious souls. And we got it right because the Holy Spirit was guiding the hand of the operator. Suomi Synod pietism was experiential Christianity. And ultimately the only real game in town.

Yes, we know from Martin Luther that the kingdom of God comes even without our prayers. But we pray primarily that it may come to us, and our loved ones, our congregations which we served, and our nation. How I thank God for those *Kodak* moments in which I have been used by God to lead others to enter by the Door into the sheepfold, and when I could serve as the coach at third base waving the runner home. The Bible says; how beautiful are the feet of those who bring good news.

16   Psalm 84:10.

17   Romans 1:17.

18   Simojoki, Martti, *The Struggle for Wholeness*, p. 279.

19   Matthew 6:33.

20   Romans 10:17.

21   Matthew 6:33.

22   Lutheran Church Ministerial Handbook.

23   Romans 1:16.

24   Wargelin, Raymond, *Kirkollinen Kalenteri* (Church Yearbook), 1955.

25   Ruotsalainen, Paavo, *The Inward Knowledge of Christ*, p. 66.

26   1 Corinthians 1:18.

27   Cameron owned and ran the only bar in town; It was from this bar that twenty-eight year old George Nuutinen went home, where he lived with his widowed mother, took his gun, and committed suicide in the woodshed. I officiated at the funeral which was attended by Mr. Cameron and the barfly friends. They were unhappy with my funeral sermon.

28   Bogetto, Norma Jean, *Dust Off Your Brain*, 2009, p. 40.

29   Acts of the Apostles 16:9.

30   Mattila, Rachel, personal letter, 1960.

31   Tahtinen, Ellen, *The Ontonagon Herald*, January 1961.

32   Romans 12:3.

33   Psalm 121:1.

34   Genesis 2:15.

35   Genesis 2:19.

36   Joel 2:5.

37   Longfellow, Henry Wadsworth, *Hiawatha*.

38   1 Corinthians 12:4-7.

39   James 1:22.

40   This was the initial organization of *Alger-Marquette Community Action Board* (AMCAB).

41   This was an Alger-Marquette group which oversaw the construction of low-cost housing for low income people; Dick Dodge, a Native-American was the first CEO.

42   Now called *Pathways*, I was the first chairman of the merger of a number of mental health organizations. Community Mental Health provided low cost services for a cross section of society. Heavily funded by federal and state, we helped close Newberry State Hospital, which was both good and bad. My Au Train sauna was once involved in a scandal by the program in which two psychiatrists were fired, and rehired after a trial, over non-professional conduct in the sauna. I was Alger County commission appointed, 1968-75; Others from county were George Chudacoff, Dan Malone, and Gunnard Lindquist.

43 January 22, 1973 was a sad day in America when the Supreme Court legalized abortion in the *Roe vs. Wade* decision. Up until then and for five years, I did extensive problem pregnancy counseling with Michigan Clergy Council for Problem Pregnancies. Many came to me with abortion in mind and changed their minds, keeping the infant. I had hoped my compassion for their plight might have depicted the passion and love of Christ toward them. Some suicides were prevented.

44 I went to the local Draft Board in Munising to help plead the case of George Wieland, who was being drafted. Soon I was asked along with Fr. Frank Lenz to serve on the board ca 1967 during the Vietnam War. We soon merged with Marquette and Iron Counties. It was dissolved with the accord reached on January 23, 1973 under Richard Nixon. I served in the ninetieth to ninety-sixth years of the Independence of the United States, and received ribbons and certificates from Presidents Richard M. Nixon and Gerald Ford. I served to help contain the advance of Communism in the Cold War. On January 21, 1977 Jimmy Carter pardoned almost all Vietnam War draft dodgers, and so did I.

45 I served on this council when it was chaired by a recovering alcoholic, Doris Murk, who did a good job. She oversaw the *Alcoholic Anonymous* programs in Munising.

46 I was a charter member of the *Alger County Historical Society*, and a good friend of its founder, Fr. Emil J. Beyer. He began the group by collecting a series of 8x10 black and white photographs of historical items. Years later my dad was an active member, helping to remodel and maintain the first headquarters, the Lobb House, and other historic signs. Both of us were avid readers of history.

47 I joined the Rotary Club shortly upon arriving in Munising, having been sponsored by Bill Bowerman. It was an opportunity to become acquainted with men outside of my parish; I was president for two years, and treasurer for over a decade. One of my spearheaded projects was to sponsor a basketball team in the city league from *Camp Cusino*, a trustee penal camp in Shingleton.

48 Tillich, Paul, *Honestly and Consecration*, 1970.

49 Wagoner, Harold E., *Accent*, 1972.

50 Tocqueville, Alexis de, *"Democracy in America."*

"The political activity which pervades the United States must be seen in order to be understood... No sooner do you set foot upon the 'American soil than you are stunned by a kind of tumult. . . . Everything is in motion around you; here, the people of one quarter of a town are met to decide upon the building of a church; there, the election of a representative is going on; a little further the delegates of a district are posting to the town to consult upon some local improvements; or in another place the laborers of a village quit their plows to deliberate upon the prospect of a road or a public school. Meetings are called for the sole purpose of declaring their disapprobation of the line of conduct pursued by the government; while in other assemblies the citizens salute the authorities of the day as the fathers of their country. . . . The cares of political life engross a most prominent place in the occupation of a citizen of the United States. . . ."

51 Luther, Martin, *Thus Daniel's life is nothing but a fine, clear mirror. In it we see the conflict and victory of faith, which, by the grace of God, triumphs over all men and devils....*

52 Ezra 8:8.

53 2 Samuel 7:2.

54 Luke 9:62: *No one who grabs the plow and keeps looking back is appropriate for the Kingdom of God.*

55 Oswald, Roy, of Alban Institute of Washington, D.C.

56 Luke 4:24: *Truly, no one is a prophet in his own country.*

57 2 Timothy 4:7.

58 878 First Parish (TC 346, Ewen 285, Paynesville 203, North Bruce 44)
1,180 Second Parish (Republic 851, Champion 283, Michigamme 76)
1,297 Third Parish (Eden Munising 1,128, Presbyterian Munising 169)
100 Skandia student pastor role.

59 Isaiah 55:11.

60 1 Corinthians 3:6-7.

61 Metaxas, Eric, *"Bonhoeffer,"* 2010, p. 57.

Bonhoeffer was hanged by the National Socialists on April 8, 1945, two weeks before the allied forces freed the prison at Flossenberg, and a week after Easter.

62   1 Corinthians 1:31.

63   *Philanthropy* Magazine, 1989.

64   Briggs self-analysis test: You are "outgoing, easy going, accepting, friendly, enjoying everything and making things more fun for others by their enjoyment. Also warmly enthusiastic, high-spirited, ingenious, and imaginative. You are able to do almost anything that interests you. You are quick with solutions for any difficulty and ready to help anyone with a problem. You like sports and making things. You often rely on your ability to improvise instead of preparing in advance. You know what's going on and join in eagerly. You find remembering facts easier than mastering theories. You are best in situations that need sound common sense and practical ability with people as well as with things. You are responsive to praise and criticism. You can usually find competing reasons for whatever you want."

65   Luke 16:22a.

66   Schmidt, Soren, *Finlandia, Finlandia*, the new alma mater song at Finlandia University.

67   Johnson, Marshall, *"Day by Day We Magnify Thee,"* "Martin Luther," p. 58.

68   Ruotsalainen, Paavo, *The Inward Knowledge of Christ*, p. 36.

69   Spener, Phillip Jacob, *Pia Desideria*, 1675.

70   Finland, Canada, Italy, Mexico, Jordan, Israel, Turkey, Greece Germany, Austria, San Marino, Switzerland, Luxemburg, France, United Kingdom, Denmark, Norway, Sweden, Russia, Portugal, Spanish Morocco, Monaco, Keribati, Bahamas, Iceland, Ireland, Holland, and Spain.

71   Psalm 106:6.

72   Johnson, Marshall, *"Day by Day We Magnify Thee,"* "Martin Luther," p. 79, 1534.

73   Acts of the Apostles 3:6.

74   Revelation of John 2:10.

75   Vadja, Jaroslav, *Go My Children with My Blessing*, hymn 822, LSB, Welch 18th century.

76   Tikka, Kari, *The Luther Opera*.

77   1 Corinthians 1:23.

78   Musical: *Cats*.

79   1 Peter 1:3.

80   Lewis, C.S., *Mere Christianity*, p. 147.

81   Revelation of John 22:20.

82   Metaxas, Eric, "Bonhoeffer," 2010, p. 78.

83   Meilaender, Gilbert, *Playing the Long Season, First Things*, p. 19.

84   Johnson, Marshall, *Day by Day We Magnify Thee*, "Martin Luther," p. 277.

And what does the Holy Spirit have to do with me? Answer: 'He baptized me; he proclaimed the gospel of Christ to me; and he awakened my heart to believe. Baptism is not of my making; nor is the gospel; nor is faith. He gave these to me. For the fingers that baptized me are not those of a human being; they are the fingers of the Holy Spirit. And the preacher's mouth and the words that I heard are not his; they are the words and message of the Holy Spirit. By these outward means he works faith within me and thus he makes me holy.' (Sermons on John 14-15.)

APPENDIX 1

My Aunts, Uncles, and Cousins

My Aunts and Uncles - - - Dad's Family (all deceased)

Helmi Niemi Kaiser, husband Earl, 1 stepson

Arvo (Harvey) Niemi, wife Joyce (nee, Hase), no children
....
John Niemi, wife Beatrice (nee, Chartier), no children

My Aunts and Uncles - - - Mom's Family (all deceased)

Oiva Sipilä, died in infancy in Finland

Jalo Sipilä, unmarried, committed suicide

Eino Sipilä, unmarried

Werner Sipilä, wife Lydia (nee, Wiitanen), 1 child

Onni Sipilä, unmarried

Helen Sipilä Anderson, husband Carl, 3 children

Impi Sipilä, died as a toddler in Finland

Lauri Sipilä, unmarried

Elmer Sipilä, wife Hilma (nee, Koski), no children

Tyyne Sipilä-Erickson, husband Verne, 2 children

My Cousins - - - Mom's Side of Family

(Werner's Family)

James Sipilä, wife Carol (nee, Leppänen), 3 children

(Helen's Family)

Buddy Anderson, deceased in infancy

Joyce Anderson Joel, husband Lawrence, 3 children

Marvin Anderson, deceased, wives Rita (nee, Posant), Geraldine (nee, Mueller), 4 children

(Tyyne's Family)

Martin Erickson, wife Miriam (nee, Mattson), no children

Darlene Erickson LaChance, deceased, husband Peter, 4 children

* * *

Edward Niemi, wives, Pearl (nee, Sipilä), Lorraine (nee, Opitz); 4 children

Leslie Niemi, wives Betty (nee, Sjöstrand), Marcia (nee, Belmas); 3 sons

Betty Niemi Korpi Rämä McComb Marlow, husbands Jacob Korpi, Stanley Rämä, Robert McComb and Daniel Marlow; 1 child

William Niemi, deceased, wives Judith (nee, Vartti), Pamela (nee, Fitzgerald), Yvonne (nee, Price); 5 children

Edward P. Niemi, unmarried

Cousin Count

Total number of my cousins (above):   6

Total cousins, including me and my siblings: 10

Children of the cousins, the next generation: 10

Grand total, cousins and their children: 24

The Family Tree.

APPENDIX   2

My Grandparents and Great Grandparents

My Great Grandparents - - - Dad's Side of Family

Emanuel Isoniemi, my great grandfather
      Born in Pylkki Finland, 1852, Died in 1923. Married to:

Olga Emerentia, my great grandmother.
Born in 1852. Died in 1925.
Manu and Olga had 10 children. Three came to the U.S. and seven remained in Finland.

Anders Pylkki, my great grandfather.
      Born in 1807. Died in 1854. Married in 1844. 4 children.

Kristiina Paavola, my great grandmother.
      Born in 1813.

My Grandparents - - - Dad's Side of Family

Emanuel Niemi, my grandfather.
      Born in Juupajoki Finland in 1881. Came to U.S. in 1902. Changed name from Isoniemi to Niemi in 1912. Occupation: farmer in Chatham, Michigan. Died in 1970. Married in 1906 in Ironwood to:

Alma Sjögren-Järvi, my grandmother.
      Born in 1887 in Halli, Finland. Died in 1957. Emigrated in 1903.
      Manu and Alma had 4 children: Edward, Helmi, John and Harvey.

My Great Grandparents, Mom's Side of Family

Heikki Sipilä, my great grandfather.
      Born in 1861 in Tiistenjoki, Finland. Died unknown. Came to U.S. and disappeared. Married in 1879 to:

Maria Ulvinen, my great grandmother.
>   Born in 1859 in Tiistenjoki, Finland. Died in 1886. Had nine children: Elias, Heikki, Matti, Maria, Juho, Amalia, Hilma, Liisa, and Sofia.

Matti Saari, my great grandfather.
>   Born in 1851 in Hiipakka, Finland. Died in 1918. Five of his children came to America. A farmer in Tiistenjoki,. He was married to:

Maria Hiipakka, my great grandmother.
>   Born in 1850. Died in 1936.

Matti and Maria had 6 children: Susanna, Johan, Maria, Vihtori, Aukusti and only Sofia remained in Finland.

My Grandparents, Mom's Side of Family

Heikki Sipilä, my grandfather.
>   Born in 1879 in Tiistenjoki, Finland. Died in 1949, Eben, MI
>   Occupation: blacksmith and farmer, Eben, Michigan.
>   Came to U.S. in 1902. Married in 1899 to:

Maria Saari, my grandmother.
>   Born in Hiipakka, Finland in 1879. Died in 1965. Came to U.S. in 1902 to Cooks MI. Occupation: farm wife. Had eleven children: Oiva, Jalo, Werner, Eino, Onni, Helen, Pearl, Impi, Lauri, Elmer, and Tyyne.

INDEX

CPSIA information can be obtained at www.ICGtesting.com
Printed in the USA
LVOW030123160512

281918LV00002B/2/P